THE POLITICS
OF WESTERN DEFENSE

The Politics
of Western Defense

F. W. MULLEY

FREDERICK A. PRAEGER, Publisher
NEW YORK

BOOKS THAT MATTER
Published in the United States of America in 1962
by Frederick A. Praeger, Inc., Publisher
64 University Place, New York 3, N.Y.
Library of Congress Catalog Card Number 62–13491

© THAMES AND HUDSON 1962
PRINTED IN GREAT BRITAIN BY
THE CAMELOT PRESS, SOUTHAMPTON

CONTENTS

army formations—Nuclear weapons—Conflicting military requirements of conventional and nuclear warfare—
How can we enforce political control?—Dual purpose
weapons—Mobile 'fire-brigades'—A new protocol for
minimum force levels

The importance of nuclear submarines—The strategic
strike rôle—Protection of sea lanes—The Soviet submarine threat and its implications—Limited warfare and
coastal defence—Naval command structure—SACEUR,
Channel Command and SACLANT—NATO versus national
requirements—Weakness of present command structure
in the Baltic and North Seas, Channel and Mediterranean
—Alternative suggestions for command structure

Problems of nuclear interdiction—The conflict of military
and political requirements—Need to re-examine tasks and
command in the light of nuclear parity—Allied Tactical
Air Forces Central and Southern Europe—Air Defence—
Early warning systems—A NATO Transport Command?

Financial shortcomings—Formula for cost-sharing—
Authority of allied commanders in logistics field and
need to increase it—Lack of standardisation—The work
of WEU and NATO Armaments Committees—Special
logistics problem of ammunition—The level of stocks—
90 and 30 day levels—Mobility and flexibility—Plan
for the integration of the logistics system

PART FOUR—WHAT NEXT FOR NATO?

Disarmament can increase security—The definition of
Arms Control—The difficulties of inspection—The
chance of Soviet co-operation—An international Police

INTRODUCTION

Today it is impossible to separate military from political considerations or defence from foreign policy. In writing this book my purpose has been to try and furnish enough detail of military hardware to make military problems clear to non-military people like myself and to try at the same time to relate them to the key political issues as I see them. It is thus an attempt to assess both the political and military aspects of the NATO alliance, on which I believe our defence and prospects of any real progress towards disarmament must alike depend.

NATO has been a success. But, like all alliances, it is only as strong as the collective will of its members, which means ultimately the will of its peoples. Thus NATO's continued success will depend increasingly upon how far there is an informed public opinion about its purpose and problems. In a democratic society it is impossible to get the support and financial provision necessary for a defence policy unless its objectives are understood and approved by the majority of the people. This book is intended as a contribution to the public discussion required to achieve this end.

Its origins lie in four reports on the state of European security which I presented between 1958 and 1960 to the Assembly of Western European Union, which offers in its Defence Committee a unique opportunity to Members of Parliament to undertake a study of defence problems with their colleagues from the other Parliaments represented. During my period of membership I was able to visit most of the Allied Headquarters in Europe and to discuss these problems with the military commanders and with most of the Defence and Foreign Ministers of Western European Union. As *rapporteur* I also had the advantage of a visit to SACLANT and to the Strategic Air Command in the United States.

Since its beginning in 1956 the Assembly has been increasingly concerned with the need to reassess our defence policies in the light of the changed strategic situation resulting from nuclear parity and mutual deterrence. I was thus able to follow a path well charted by my predecessor as *rapporteur,* Colonel J. J. Fens. In particular my reports were directed to (i) the urgent need to augment our conventional strength and to achieve more effective defence through greater integration of the forces of the alliance, and (ii) the dangers of nuclear anarchy and the problems of working out a system of joint political control over both the strategic and the tactical use of nuclear weapons. It was from a consideration of these problems that I proposed in 1959 that there should be a European nuclear strike force.

These themes are further elaborated in the present book and I have also brought up to date as far as possible the factual material. However, I should stress that, as in the original reports, I alone am responsible for the views expressed. Indeed I doubt if many of my former WEU colleagues would go along with me in all my present conclusions.

I am indebted to the successive Chairmen (Marchese Lucifero d'Aprigliano and Colonel J. J. Fens) and members of the Defence Committee of the Assembly for their friendly guidance and for undertaking my military education which had ended prematurely when I was taken prisoner-of-war in 1940. I must also express my thanks to the many officers of allied and national forces, in Europe and the United States, who so generously gave their time to discuss these problems with me. My indebtedness to many writers on these subjects is apparent in the text, but in particular my thanks are due to Captain B. H. Liddell Hart, the Hon. Alastair Buchan (Director of the Institute for Strategic Studies) and Professor Henry Kissinger for their help and personal encouragement.

Dr. Per Fischer, the former Clerk to the Committee, helped me greatly with the reports and I have had the advantage of his valuable counsel in the preparation of the book. Mr. Stuart Whyte (of the Office of the Assembly) prepared and revised the technical appendices. I should like also to record my appreciation of the many helpful suggestions contributed by Group Captain Frank Gomersall, who kindly read the manuscript, and of the research and editorial assistance given by Mrs. Patricia Evans; without her co-operation the book would never have been completed.

All the factual information given is derived from public sources and it will be readily understood that the availability of such material is very uneven. As far as possible it has been brought up to date to the end of 1961.

F. W. MULLEY

House of Commons

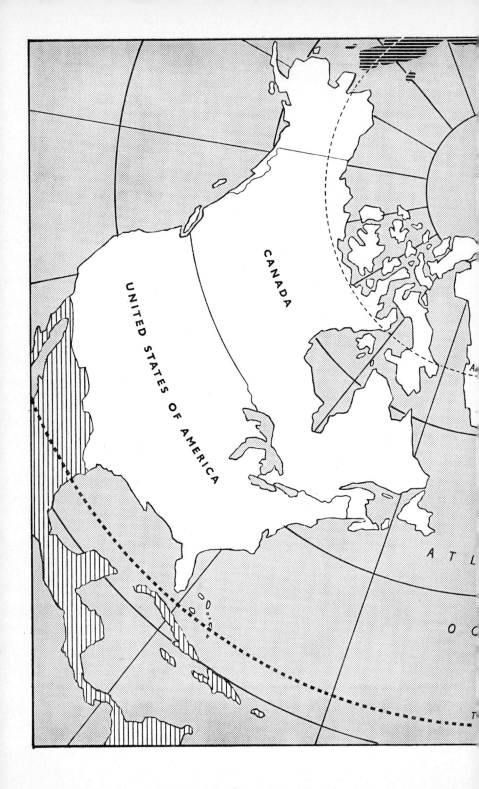

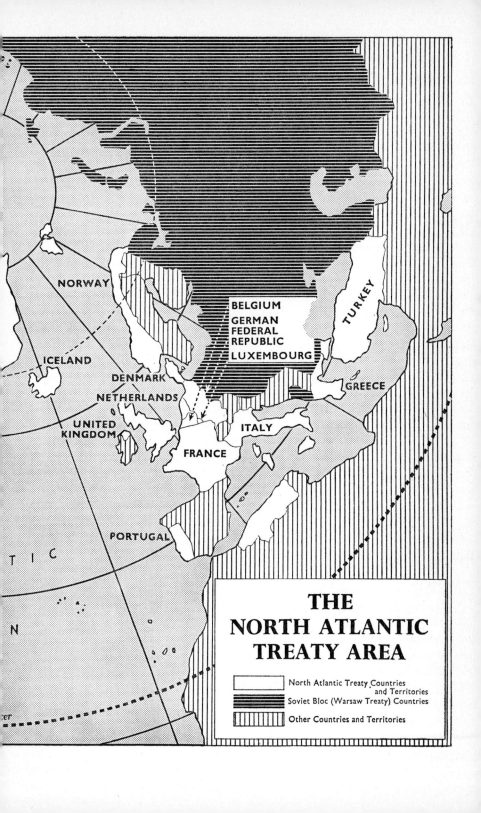

NORWAY

ICELAND

DENMARK

NETHERLANDS

UNITED
KINGDOM

FRANCE

PORTUGAL

BELGIUM
GERMAN
FEDERAL
REPUBLIC
LUXEMBOURG

ITALY

TURKEY

GREECE

**THE
NORTH ATLANTIC
TREATY AREA**

North Atlantic Treaty Countries
and Territories
Soviet Bloc (Warsaw Treaty) Countries
Other Countries and Territories

STATESMANSHIP, in the H-bomb age, must control not only the aims but the operations. It should direct military defence planning and the formulation of military doctrine. Hence statesmen and their diplomatic advisers must have a greater knowledge of military technique than they needed in the past. That is as important as for soldiers to submit to political direction. Even if we do not go so far as to merge the function of the Foreign Minister and the Defence Minister, they and their expert advisers must combine much more closely. It is a new version of Plato's dictum that the affairs of the world would not improve until either the philosophers became the rulers or the rulers the philosophers.

Captain B. H. Liddell Hart, *Deterrent or Defence*

POLITICAL PLANNING must be aware of military realities, and military plans in turn must be responsive to political considerations. . . . Our force goals, our military policy, our deployments and our war plans themselves must all reflect the purposes and spirit of our great community. Military and political problems are not separable, and military and political men must work ever more closely together.

President Kennedy, speech to NATO Military Committee, 10 April, 1961

PART ONE

Strategy and Politics

Chapter I

PRINCIPLES AND POLICY

Political policy must always be the master of military strategy. This is the first principle to be applied in a consideration of defence policy. The advent of nuclear weapons has pointed the grim truth of Clemenceau's dictum that war is too serious a matter for generals. Obviously, expert military advice must provide the basis for an intelligent defence policy. But unless the essential point is grasped that the purely military view is only one aspect of defence in its widest sense, then problems cannot be seen in their right perspective. The vastly accelerated pace of modern war means that decisions of vital consequence may have to be taken in a matter of minutes and it is imperative that the responsibility for these decisions rests squarely on political shoulders.

Defence and foreign policies are inextricably interwoven: the two can be considered separately but it is impossible to divorce the one from the other. It is a truism to say that the best defence policy a country can have is a good foreign policy, but the logical consequences of the truism are rarely appreciated. If it is impossible to provide adequate defence for one's country by independent effort, it is equally impossible to pursue an independent foreign policy. A unilateral foreign policy is a contradiction in terms and is no more tenable than a unilateral defence policy.

No country today can hope to provide adequate defence for its people in isolation. In 1957, with the Suez fiasco safely behind him, Mr. Macmillan made the point very neatly: 'The time has passed when countries, however strong, can follow independent policies.' This idea is expressed in the word 'interdependence' recently coined in international language.

The doctrine of interdependence was set out in the communique issued after the talks between President Eisenhower and the

British Prime Minister in October 1957, as the Russian Sputnik underlined the urgency of NATO unity:

> The arrangements which the nations of the free world have made for collective defence and mutual help are based on the recognition that the concept of national self-sufficiency is out of date. The countries of the free world are interdependent, and only in genuine partnership, by combining their resources and sharing tasks in many fields, can progress and safety be found. For our part, we have agreed that our two countries will henceforth act in accordance with this principle.

Although interdependence was the fundamental principle underlying NATO, for years little more than lip-service has been paid to it and it is only recently that the political implication has been faced at all. Even now the need for interdependence in international policy is still not generally accepted. The differing approaches of leading NATO powers towards negotiating with the Soviet Union, not to speak of their policies towards Africa, have tended to weaken the fabric of the alliance on which Western defence is based.

Obviously the implications of interdependence go much wider than defence arrangements and include the co-ordination of economic policies and programmes of aid to under-developed countries (which are beyond the scope of this book) no less than political co-ordination. Equally obviously the consequent reorientation in national thinking and habits will be a painful and difficult process. But translation of this principle into practice is an essential element in the working out of an effective Western system of defence.

It is easy to say, of course, that the best solution to the innumerable and complex problems presented by an alliance of sovereign states is for them to surrender their national sovereignty and form an Atlantic federation or to convert NATO into a supranational authority. There is no gainsaying the logic and tidiness of this argument but political realism suggests that such a solution raises even bigger problems than those it seeks to solve. In the same way one cannot, in the short run, advocate world government as the answer to the crises and tensions arising from a divided world and the failure to achieve disarmament. In the long run it can be argued that these ideals must be realised if we are to rid ourselves completely of the threat of war. But as the late Lord Keynes said, in another context, 'In the long run we are all dead.' We cannot escape our present problems by concentrating all our energies on counsels of perfection.

The next general premise is the most fundamental. It must be made clear beyond all doubt, not only to our own peoples but to the rest of the world also, that the whole basis and only purpose of Western defence is to prevent war. There is no disagreement on this in the NATO countries; arguments about defence policy are about the best means to achieve this end. Indeed the principle is embodied in the fashionable use of the word 'deterrent'. If war should break out, the deterrents will have failed. Mr. Macmillan expressed this view in his speech of welcome to General Norstad in 1957: 'Let us be under no illusion; military forces today are not designed to wage war; their purpose is to prevent it. There will be no campaigns like the old ones, with victory at the end of a long and balanced struggle; total war today can only mean total destruction.' In a more dramatic way, the point is made by the motto painted over the gates of the Headquarters of the American Strategic Air Command at Omaha, Nebraska: 'Peace is our Profession.'

Yet while peace has been maintained by a balance of terror—the capacity of each side to destroy the other—there can be no illusions as to how precarious a peace it is, sustained only by a war of nerves and by great and increasing expenditure of resources. The only satisfactory and permanent basis for peaceful co-existence is world-wide disarmament, both nuclear and conventional, coupled with such arrangements for control and inspection as will satisfy all parties to the agreement that its terms are being observed. Against the background of mutual suspicion and fear which divides the free world from the Soviet Union and her allies, it is idle to pretend that comprehensive disarmament agreements will be reached easily or soon. The arms race is bred of fear and mistrust, not vice versa. Indeed it can well be argued that once this mutual mistrust has been allayed sufficiently to make a disarmament agreement feasible, the machinery of inspection and control that is at present the *sine qua non* of an agreement will no longer be a stumbling block.

The history of disarmament negotiations since the war makes depressing reading. While the Soviet Union bears a heavy responsibility, we in the West are not entirely blameless. Too often we have allowed the Soviet Union to score easy propaganda successes by apparent reluctance to stick to our word when the Russians can plausibly present themselves as having accepted the major points in our proposals. Most of the problem of disarmament arises from the hard fact that those who want it most do not know how to get it and those who know how it could be achieved do not want it. That is to say, while pressure for disarmament comes primarily from public opinion, it can only be achieved as the result of action by governments. Unless governments, and the experts who advise them, sincerely accept disarmament as a major policy objective, negotiations will never make significant progress. And, just as effective defence can only be attained in the West by the collective effort and will of NATO members, disarmament can only become a practical possibility if they are united in their desire to obtain it and agreed on their approach to its problems.

But we must not let difficulties deter us from trying. Provided that the NATO forces are not weakened at any stage relative to those of the Soviet bloc, any agreement, however limited, would pay handsome dividends in terms of mutual confidence and by demonstrating that the fever of the arms race can be reduced without killing the patient. Like learning to walk, the first few steps are the most difficult. There was much optimism that a beginning could have been made by an agreement to ban nuclear tests after the United States, the Soviet Union and Britain agreed on a moratorium of such tests pending negotiations. However, these negotiations, begun on 31 October 1958, broke down after more than 300 meetings in June 1961 and with the resumption of testing we are all back where we began. Failure to get this treaty, before technical advances and the development of nuclear capacity by more and more countries undermine the effectiveness of its provisions, augurs ill for the progress of general disarmament negotiations.

Until disarmament agreements are concluded the West must seek to attain the most efficient collective defence system that is possible. Determination to provide adequate defences to meet all likely contingencies is in no way inconsistent with an equal determination to achieve disarmament. Indeed the first is a necessary condition for the second. The military and political leaders of the

Soviet Union are not lacking in realism and are unlikely to accept disarmament proposals based on theoretical strengths or to agree proposals which would result in parity between East and West at a time when the balance is greatly in their favour.

Defence and disarmament present special problems for democratic countries and particular difficulties for parties of the Left. This is well illustrated by arguments in recent years in the British Labour Party. Usually the Ministry of Defence is the graveyard of political reputations.

Except in times of crisis there is general reluctance to spend money on defence. The man in the street, as well as the politician, sees the money and resources spent on defence as standing between him and the new houses, new schools and new hospitals that seem so much more worth while. Reports of great expenditure on abortive or discontinued weapons and of designs which are obsolescent as soon as they leave the drawing-board undermine public confidence and pose political problems for Ministers.

There is also the problem of scientific manpower. Military superiority is more and more dependent upon the possession of the best fuels, the most resistant alloys and the most perfect electronic equipment. Competition in the field of physical science and mathematics has become as important as the quantity of armaments; scientists and technologists as important as soldiers. Thus while on the one hand a steadily increasing proportion of defence expenditure is devoted to purely scientific research, on the other a choice has often to be made between using the available scientific manpower and resources for military or civilian benefit. The prolonged and sharp controversy that took place recently over a British contribution to space research is a case in point.

Statistics of defence expenditure since 1955 disclose that in most NATO countries, despite the increasing complexity and cost of weapons and equipment, there has been a downward trend in the percentage of the Gross National Product devoted to defence (see Appendix C). In view of the shortcomings in the Western defence position, particularly in Western Europe, this is very disturbing.

It underlines the necessity of obtaining the maximum value in terms of collective defence for the money spent on defence by each individual country. This can only be achieved by integration and the planning of collective measures which offer greater security for a given sum than expenditure determined by solely national considerations would provide.

By contrast, totalitarian governments can give priority to defence projects and have a political flexibility impossible for democratic governments. It is easy for them to scrap out-of-date weapons and bury mistakes of design in the government archives. They can talk about disarmament and re-arm at the same time without any internal challenge of inconsistency. Also the fact that the details of defence policy and expenditure do not have to be explained to the people makes it very easy for the Soviet Union to maintain a level of military security that is not possible within NATO territories.

It is essential for a democratic government to have a body of well-informed public opinion behind its defence policy. There is rarely a serious likelihood of public opinion turning neutralist or denying the principles of adequate defence. But unless the objectives and broad outlines of policy are appreciated there is a real danger that the necessary men and money will not be forthcoming for the NATO alliance. Unhappily in many countries there has not been the public information and discussion required to give a firm basis for the NATO plans for efficient collective defence. While there must be restriction on the supply of military information to the public, security is often carried too far. Frequently matter which has appeared in American newspapers is still marked 'Top Secret' in Britain.

Governments and NATO authorities should consider how far and not how little they can take into their confidence Parliamentarians and responsible bodies and persons who interest themselves in defence questions. Otherwise those who have the responsibility of informing and leading public opinion are ill-equipped to do so.

This is not to say that there should be no limit to the amount and kind of information available. What is wanted is something between the almost automatic restriction of all military information in Britain and the view widely held in America that the press, acting on behalf of the people as they claim, should have access to almost every category of diplomatic and military intelligence.

There is much to be said in favour of President Kennedy's appeal for more restraint, although its timing just after the Cuba incident was unfortunate. An official censorship is inconsistent with a free society and the press cannot be expected to impose voluntary censorship upon themselves. Therefore it rests with the Government and Congress to cut off at source information which could be detrimental to security if published, although it is readily conceded that the established procedures of the American constitution make this a more difficult task than it is in Britain. However, it should be possible to strike a balance between providing sufficient material to enable public opinion to assess the real issues facing the alliance and avoiding publication of information which could damage our security.

With the horrors of nuclear weapons readily understood and in the absence of any defence in the orthodox sense against rockets, it will not be surprising if the feeling grows in the West that any attempts to provide adequate defence are fruitless. This sense of despair is genuine and comprehensible and cannot be overcome unless the NATO policy of deterrence and its relevance to the prevention of war and the hope of disarmament is understood and accepted. To spread this understanding is one of our most urgent tasks.

Chapter II

THE MEANING OF DETERRENCE

Is the theory of deterrence still valid? To what extent has NATO and national defence thinking been modified to meet the emergence of the rocket or guided missile as the major nuclear threat? What kind of war is the most likely outcome if our basic policy fails and the Cold War becomes a hot one? Can NATO forces deal with all likely contingencies? Together with the considerations of political supremacy and interdependence set out in the previous chapter, these questions provide the basis for an assessment of a NATO defence policy.

Before attempting any answer it is important to understand the questions themselves. For as in philosophy so in defence; sometimes if we fully understand a question we realise that either no answer is possible, or we know the answer already.

Obstacles to a clear discussion also spring from unavoidable emotional overtones which have become attached to words and phrases such as 'the deterrent', 'nuclear strategy', 'political control', so that they no longer mean the same thing to different people.

This confusion is particularly prevalent in relation to the theory of 'deterrence' on which NATO defence policy is built. It is sometimes suggested that this is an entirely new concept, acquired along with the atomic bomb, strengthened by the development of thermonuclear or hydrogen bombs and fortified further by the ballistic missile. Yet it is as old as man himself. It means no more and no less than the simple proposition that if I am able to hit back as hard or harder than the other chap can hit me, and he knows this, he will not attack me as it will not be worth his while to do so.

The principle was just as relevant in the days of bows and arrows and muzzle-loading muskets. It is only the phrase that is new. It became fashionable in the period immediately after the last war, when the Americans had first an atomic monopoly and then later such overwhelming atomic and thermonuclear superiority that one could speak of '*the* deterrent'.

This was the period of the Dulles doctrine of massive retaliation. Defence strategy was simple and seemingly effective— although there can never be positive proof of what caused peace to be maintained during this period. It was based on two main premises: first, that the full nuclear armoury would be used against any type of aggression, so that fear of such massive nuclear retaliation would be sufficient to deter a potential aggressor; secondly, that where the major powers were involved limited war was inconceivable, i.e. that any conflict would result immediately in a global nuclear war. As a consequence, military thinking was confined almost exclusively to terms of nuclear hostilities.

There was thus only one deterrent—the nuclear strike force of the United States: *the* deterrent was American H-bombs. When Britain developed her own independent strike force of first atomic and then thermonuclear bombs, this was described as 'the independent British deterrent'.

It had been known for some time that the Soviet Union had become a nuclear power and was developing her nuclear capacity. Nevertheless in the West there was still such confidence in American superiority that the policy of 'the deterrent' continued. It was not until October 1957, when the Sputnik demonstrated in a most dramatic way Russian technical advances in the field of rocketry, that second thoughts began to come. It did not require much technical knowledge to recognise that it would have been easier to land a rocket with a nuclear warhead on New York, London or Paris than to put the Sputnik into orbit.

Although this unmistakable revelation of Soviet nuclear capability had an immediate impact in the West and especially in the United States at the psychological and diplomatic levels, appreciation of the logical consequences in military terms was slow to develop. It took several years to eradicate the view that the only possible war was a global nuclear war; indeed this opinion still persists in some quarters. It is now increasingly accepted, however, that in the present state of nuclear parity a complete re-thinking of NATO military strategy is essential.

Nuclear parity, the existence of a situation whereby each side has the capacity to inflict crippling nuclear destruction on the other, has given rise to nuclear stalemate. Equality in nuclear potential is not essential for nuclear stalemate to apply. It is sufficient if the other side has the capacity to retaliate with nuclear weapons on the cities and civilian population of a country initiating nuclear war. No nation can now make strategic use of nuclear bombs without at the same time involving almost certain nuclear annihilation for millions of its own citizens. Thus a state of 'nuclear nullity', to borrow Captain Liddell Hart's phrase, arises in which the earlier doctrine of massive retaliation is neither realistic nor credible. No one can believe that the President of the United States or the British Prime Minister will authorise nuclear attacks on the Soviet Union in response to a frontier incident on the border of the Iron Curtain or a limited conventional attack. It is doubtful whether such a massive retaliation would in fact have taken place in the period of American atomic monopoly. Certainly no one can imagine such a decision in similar circumstances today, when it carries with it the automatic nuclear devastation a few hours later of New York and London.

In short nuclear stalemate means the end of '*the* deterrent'. Possession of a nuclear strategic strike force is no longer by itself a sufficient deterrent to an aggressor in all circumstances. Temptation to snatch any easy gains that present themselves still remains up to the limit that the aggressor believes he can safely go without invoking a nuclear war. The risks to the aggressor in any such action are very great and as long as uncertainty continues, as it must always do, as to the 'sticking-point' of the West, i.e. when it would be prepared to authorise a nuclear counterattack to deal with non-nuclear aggression, the risks may outweigh the advantages.

This is a highly dangerous situation. It is much better to replace the concept of *the deterrent* with that of *a series of deterrents*, a capacity to meet any type of attack or incident not involving nuclear weapons with sufficient conventional force to create a 'pause'. In such a pause there would be an opportunity for political action to clear up a mistake, and the decision to 'raise the stakes' or start a nuclear war would thus be forced upon the aggressor. Above all, the provision of adequate conventional NATO forces (which do not at present exist) would remove the temptation and risk of a sudden, swift pounce on an inadequately defended area of NATO territory, for example the Danish Islands, which the Soviet Union may one day believe it could get away with without invoking nuclear war.

The substitution of this 'balance of terror' for the previous American atomic monopoly has particular significance for the European members of NATO. Hitherto European countries could with good reason consider themselves covered by the United States nuclear umbrella, whether or not they made any defence efforts themselves. But now that both the United States and Soviet Russia possess sufficient strategic nuclear weapons to annihilate each other, it becomes unreasonable for any European country to expect the United States to expose herself to nuclear retaliation automatically in response to any and every attack in Europe.

This obvious consequence from the development of nuclear stalemate is reinforced by the advent of the intercontinental missiles which reduce the strategic value of European territory to American defence policy. America will soon no longer need to be defended from European soil alone, as she did when the bomber squadrons and missiles could only reach the Soviet mainland from European bases. Thus the certainty of American strategic nuclear retaliation recedes in the case of a limited attack on parts of Europe.

This is not to suggest that the United States will not honour her treaty obligations or that American policy in the foreseeable future will change so much as to mean a withdrawal of her forces from Europe. But it must be remembered that the North Atlantic Treaty does not require other members to give automatic military assistance to a member who is attacked; moreover there is no undertaking, and there cannot be, that nuclear retaliation is to be invoked under any circumstances. The American Strategic Air Command and the British Bomber Command are subject only to their respective national commands and do not come under NATO at all. Article 5 of the North Atlantic Treaty provides that an armed attack against one member shall be considered an attack against them all and that each member shall assist the member attacked 'by taking forthwith . . . such action as it deems necessary, including the use of armed force, to restore and maintain the security of the North Atlantic area'.

The chief danger of war breaking out arises from the possibility of a mistake or a miscalculation, not from a clear and unequivocal decision on the part of the Soviet Union or any other nation to begin a nuclear war. Frontier incidents in Europe, Berlin, another Hungary-type revolution or the involvement of great powers in a peripheral dispute in the Middle East, Africa or Asia seem more likely causes of friction than the global all-out aggression against which NATO strategy has for so long been directed. The possibility of American nuclear intervention in Indo-China in 1954 and the Soviet rocket threat during the Suez campaign in 1956 demonstrate the reality of the danger that any conflict involving NATO members, even outside NATO territory, may lead to the whole alliance becoming involved.

NATO should not only be prepared to deal with a localised or limited incident by conventional means; it should also have sufficient non-nuclear strength to meet any situation without immediate recourse to nuclear weapons in the hope that hostilities can be kept limited and the catastrophe of nuclear war averted. Indeed it is essential to have this conventional capacity to deny any prospect of easy gains, otherwise we run the risk of being forced by diplomatic blackmail into having to make the impossible choice of accepting as a *fait accompli* the occupation of some part of NATO territory or of starting a nuclear war.

The possibility of a surprise attack, a pre-emptive strike aimed at destroying the other side's nuclear arsenal to eliminate nuclear retaliation, cannot be ruled out, although it is the least likely contingency. It is quite unthinkable that the West would under any circumstances start a nuclear war by such a surprise attack. Indeed it is impossible for any democratic government and particularly for an alliance of democratic states. And while under a totalitarian régime it is a more practicable proposition, it is unlikely that the Soviet Union will take a cold-blooded decision to plunge the world into the immeasurable horrors of nuclear war.

Any surprise all-out nuclear attack would have to aim at nothing less than the total destruction of the other side's power of retaliation. On military grounds it is impossible to envisage that such an attack could destroy with certainty a sufficiently high proportion of the diverse means of launching a nuclear counter-attack to be worthwhile, in existing circumstances or in the foreseeable future. It is always just possible, however, that rash leadership, internal political considerations or sheer lunacy might be allowed to override rational political and military calculations, and we must be prepared for this contingency.

The best defence and guarantee against such an attack, since there is no means as yet of arresting missiles on their course, is to demonstrate beyond doubt our capacity to strike a 'second blow' of a crippling character after being subjected to an all-out surprise nuclear attack, no matter how thoroughly and efficiently planned and executed. This is the essence of the theory of nuclear deterrence now that nuclear stalemate has been reached. It demands (i) nuclear strike capability; (ii) the capacity to survive the surprise pre-emptive blow with sufficient means of counter-attack; and (iii) credibility—that any potential enemy should know of, and believe in, our capacity to strike the second blow. The consequences of this policy in terms of weapons and organisation are examined in later chapters.

The fact that our nuclear strategic strike policy is planned to survive a first attack and the emphasis on second-strike potential have another great advantage. If we can persuade the Soviet Union—and deeds are more eloquent than words—that we are concerned only with a second-strike, we may dispel the fear which is the real danger—fear that we are preparing to attack them and that they must strike a pre-emptive blow to forestall us. By improved methods of early warning, by concentrating on means of delivering our nuclear strike which could credibly survive attack, such as *Polaris*, and by eliminating those, as for example the *Thor* missile, which obviously could not, we fulfil two vital objectives. We prepare ourselves to counter a surprise attack: at the same time we demonstrate the defensive character of our preparations, thus reducing the fears and suspicions which are the most likely motivations for such an attack.

A deliberate and planned surprise attack by conventional forces, for example on the Central Front, seems even less likely than a surprise all-out nuclear aggression. The massing of the necessary divisions is hardly possible without alerting NATO and thus robbing the operation of the essential element of surprise. (A co-ordinated pressing of buttons for a strategic nuclear attack is obviously more likely to be accomplished in secrecy.) But the over-riding reason against a surprise all-out conventional attack, assuming that the West does not abandon its nuclear weapons, is the danger of starting a nuclear war. If the Soviet Union is prepared to run the risk of a nuclear war, it is hardly likely that she would surrender the great advantage of striking the first nuclear blow.

The only possibility of a deliberate surprise attack seems to be a limited attack on a small scale, for example in the Baltic where NATO defences are very vulnerable, in circumstances where the Soviet Union believed a nuclear counter-attack to be impossible because the speed of the operation would face NATO with a *fait accompli*. The way to prevent such a limited surprise attack is to strengthen the NATO Shield so that no temptation of easy small-scale gains exists. At the same time by providing an adequate NATO Shield of conventional forces, sufficient to hold for several days any conventional attack brought against it at any point, we greatly reduce and perhaps even eliminate the danger of a Soviet miscalculation—a miscalculation which could trigger off a nuclear war which they were as anxious as we to avoid.

In parenthesis, for reasons more fully discussed in later chapters, it should be said that forces equipped with tactical atomic weapons are not a substitute for non-nuclear ground forces with conventional capability. In present conditions a limited nuclear war is virtually impossible. Once nuclear explosives are used by ground forces, it will be extremely difficult to avert a global nuclear war.

Mistake remains as the most probable source of war, as inevitably it must in a world subject to the vagaries of human judgment and emotions. Mistakes which lead to limited clashes of conventional arms need not be cataclysmic if we in the West have sufficient conventional strength to contain an aggression resulting from a frontier incident or similar situation discussed above, for long enough to establish the mistake. The dangerous and immensely difficult decision in such circumstances is deciding when and how to 'raise the stakes' by the first use of nuclear weapons. This underlines the paramount importance of political supremacy and the retention of this decision in political hands. The outstanding problem for the NATO alliance today is to provide a means of joint political control over the initial use of nuclear weapons of all types. The problem is analysed and some suggestions are made for its solution in later chapters.

Effective political control is also essential to minimise the danger that someone may inadvertently set off a missile and thus start a nuclear conflagration as a result of an unclear signal or a misreading of a radar early-warning screen. This danger is very slight, but it can never be discounted completely. There cannot be a foolproof guarantee against human error. This worry doubtless preoccupies the Russian leaders as much as it does the West. But until both sides can agree to rid the world of weapons of mass destruction, all we can do is to reduce the risk as far as is humanly possible.

In essence NATO policy remains unchanged. The capacity of the West to strike a second nuclear blow is the deterrent against a surprise all-out nuclear attack. But the deterrent against anything less than a total global attack is the provision of equivalent means of counter-attack; tanks against tanks, and tactical atomic weapons against tactical atomic weapons. It does not require that we have equivalent strength in every field and at every point with the Soviet Union and her allies. It does demand that we have sufficient defences to prevent any easy spoils being offered and the ability to hold an attack for long enough to force the aggressor to raise the stakes.

The most pressing need is to furnish SACEUR with the thirty divisions regarded as an indispensible minimum to defend Central Europe. This is the special responsibility of the European members of NATO, including Great Britain. The paradox of this age of electronics and nuclear science is that as more and more complex and expensive means of delivering weapons of vast destruction are developed, the ordinary soldier becomes more important than ever. It is also a hard fact that the most costly item of a defence budget is the provision of adequate conventional forces. If we destroy the possibility of easy gains, then no aggression can be undertaken without the double risk of starting a nuclear war and of losing the nuclear initiative in so doing.

In the last analysis any policy based on deterrence is an act of faith. But would the atomic bomb have been dropped upon Japan if it had been thought that she could retaliate in similar measure? The stakes are higher than for any previous policy of deterrence or balance of power in history and this is perhaps our best guarantee. The terrible consequences to himself and the world are so great, that an aggressor is unlikely to take any risk of being wrong in his calculations. He will only strike if he is doubly certain that he can achieve his purpose without meeting full retaliation.

There is no alternative to this policy, short of capitulation, until multilateral disarmament makes it no longer necessary. The only alternative to the West's maintaining nuclear parity with the Soviet Union coupled with an adequate conventional capability would be to submit, under the duress of Soviet nuclear threats, to each and every demand the Soviet Union cared to make. There seems even less scope for passive resistance in the nuclear world than there was before, and it had no conspicuous successes even then.

Of course no policy can remain constant, and it is essential that we have flexibility to react to new circumstances. For example, the production of an anti-missile missile capable of shooting down ballistic missiles on their way to their targets would again radically transform our whole strategic thinking. The consequences for us of the Russians producing this first are obviously very serious since the basis of our second-strike capability would be undermined.

Both in the present and in the foreseeable future, Western security and also, paradoxically, any hope of effective disarmament, depend on the strength and adhesion of the NATO alliance. Only by collective effort can we provide the balanced forces that a policy of deterrence requires, and this will not be achieved unless the principle of political interdependence is accepted as well as common defence arrangements. National defence programmes and independent foreign policies are both anachronistic in the 1960s. The test of a NATO country's policies should be their contribution to the alliance.

Chapter III

THE EVOLUTION OF NATO

The North Atlantic Treaty was signed in Washington on 4 April 1949. While serious criticisms can be levelled at the present state of the North Atlantic Treaty Organisation (NATO) from both the political and military angles it is indisputable that in the twelve years of its existence much progress has been made towards the objectives set out in the Treaty. To realise how much has been achieved, one has only to compare the present unified defence system (despite its weaknesses) and the forces at General Norstad's disposal (despite their inadequacies) with the twelve divisions, most of them organised for occupation duties only, 400 aircraft and 400 ships at the disposal of General Eisenhower when he was appointed as the first Supreme Allied Commander in Europe (SACEUR) at the end of 1950.

NATO has succeeded in its main purpose of preserving peace. Of course it is impossible to furnish objective proof that the existence and development of a collective security system such as NATO has been a major factor in avoiding war. I believe, however that this may fairly be assumed and that a strong NATO is essential if peace is to be maintained in the future.

It is necessary to make this clear, since the emphasis in this book is on NATO's shortcomings in political and military organisation and strategic thinking rather than on its achievements. These achievements are solid and not to be underestimated. But we cannot rest content with the present state of the alliance. No organisation can stand still: it must move either forward or backward. Events have made the present time a turning point in NATO's history and the early 1960s will determine the direction it is to take. It is essential for NATO to move forward, and it is this that prompts me to point to the shortcomings and weaknesses in organisation and policy which must be put right if the alliance is to remain an important factor in keeping the peace.

c

When the Second World War ended in 1945 and our minds were on problems of demobilisation and the painful process of rebuilding our war-shattered economies, few people anticipated that within five years rearmament would again be a major issue. Most of us believed that the co-operation which had led to the overthrow of Hitler and Japan would continue for the mutual benefit of the whole world. There was great confidence that the new United Nations Organisation would succeed where the League of Nations had failed.

Events, however, soon dispelled our optimism and shattered the East-West alliance developed during the war. It gradually became clear that the creation of the United Nations did not mean an end of international tensions and the risks of war. After a brief spring of faith in the power of the United Nations we passed, without an intervening summer, to the bleak winter of the Cold War.

THE BACKGROUND

It is necessary to recall only a few items in the long list of examples of Soviet aggressive diplomacy and determination to provoke international tension to paint the backcloth against which the NATO Treaty was signed. Large Soviet forces were maintained in Eastern Europe and the 'satellite' forces were built up. Pressures were exerted in Persia and Turkey whilst guerilla war was encouraged in Greece. Communist control was effected throughout Eastern Europe and this was dramatically revealed by the seizure of power in Czechoslovakia in 1948. Russia and the other communist countries refused to co-operate in the Marshall Plan for the economic recovery of Europe. Peace treaties with former enemy countries were blocked and the Soviet veto in the United Nations was frequently invoked. Finally, and perhaps most significant, there was the blockade for a year of Berlin, after persistent breaches of the Potsdam Agreement.

Already before the NATO Treaty there had been a renewal of some old alliances. In March 1947 Britain and France signed the Dunkirk Treaty of Alliance and Mutual Assistance. A year later this had been extended to include Belgium, Luxembourg and the Netherlands as well by the Brussels Treaty of Economic, Social and Cultural Collaboration and Collective Self-Defence, signed on 17 March 1948. This grouping of the five nations later became known as Western Union. In many ways this Treaty provided a pattern for the North Atlantic Treaty. Three months later, on 11 June 1948, the United States Senate passed by a big majority a resolution sponsored by the late Senator Vandenberg, affirming American determination to exercise the right of individual or collective self-defence allowed by Article 51 of the United Nations Charter and recommending the 'association of the United States . . . with such other regional and collective arrangements as are based on continuous and effective self-help and mutual aid'. The way was being prepared for the transformation of the original Brussels Treaty, as the late Mr. Ernest Bevin, the then British Foreign Secretary, had hoped and planned, into the wider Atlantic Alliance.

In the meantime there had been a most significant development in economic co-operation. In June 1947 General Marshall, the United States Secretary of State, announced, in a speech at Harvard, a plan for the economic rehabilitation of Europe with generous assistance from the United States. Mr. Bevin responded with great vigour and imagination to this American initiative and together with M. Georges Bidault, the then French Foreign Minister, organised Europe to accept the Marshall Plan. This meant that not only was European economic recovery attained much faster than would otherwise have been the case, but that in the Organisation for European Economic Co-operation there was a machinery for inter-governmental co-operation which proved of tremendous value in all the complex economic problems involved in the years of post-war recovery. There was also an undeniable commitment of the United States to Europe which was further strengthened and given formal shape in the NATO Treaty.

THE NORTH ATLANTIC TREATY

The original signatories to the North Atlantic Treaty, signed on 4 April 1949, were Belgium, Canada, Denmark, France, Iceland, Italy, Luxembourg, the Netherlands, Norway, Portugal, the United Kingdom and the United States. Greece and Turkey acceded to it in 1952 and the Federal Republic of Germany in 1955. The Treaty itself was a model of clarity and brevity. Its purpose is well expressed in the Preamble:

> The Parties to this Treaty reaffirm their faith in the purpose and principles of the Charter of the United Nations and their desire to live in peace with all peoples and all Governments.

They are determined to safeguard the freedom, common heritage and civilization of their peoples, founded on the principles of democracy, individual liberty and the rule of law.

They seek to promote stability and well-being in the North Atlantic area.

They are resolved to unite their efforts for collective defence and for the preservation of peace and security.

In particular the Parties undertook to 'maintain and develop their individual and collective capacity to resist armed attack' and agreed 'that an armed attack against one or more of them in Europe or North America shall be considered an attack against them all'. NATO territory was defined as 'the territory of any of the Parties in Europe or North America, or the Algerian Departments of France, or the occupation forces of any Party in Europe, or the islands under the jurisdiction of any Party in the North Atlantic area north of the Tropic of Cancer or on the vessels or aircraft in this area of any of the Parties.'

The unique task of establishing an alliance between sovereign states for collective defence in time of peace without any direct surrender of national independence and thus without supranational institutions posed many problems. Gradually the political and military organisation, described below, was evolved, all agencies created by the alliance being subordinate to the North Atlantic Council, composed of the Foreign Ministers of the member countries. Parallel to the work of organisation, the Council was concerned to establish a common defence policy in the fields of armaments production and military strategy.

In April 1950 a four-year defence plan was approved. Shortly afterwards additional point was given to the need for the alliance by the communist attack upon South Korea on 25 June 1950. The following meeting of the Council was centred upon the problem of defending the NATO area against an aggression similar to that launched in Korea. A 'forward strategy' was adopted with the intention of resisting an aggression as far to the East as possible. But this required far greater resources than those available to NATO at the time. Accordingly it was necessary to build up military strength, revise defence plans and create 'an integrated force under a centralised command, adequate to deter aggression and to ensure the defence of Western Europe'.

The 'forward strategy' adopted by the Council necessitated the defence of Europe on German soil, which clearly meant that the military and political participation of the new Federal Republic of Germany was necessary. In addition, an assessment of the forces likely to be available to NATO led to the military conclusion that a substantial German contribution was essential if an adequate number of divisions was to be provided in Europe. The political problems of rearming Germany were, however, plain for all to see. There was controversy and reluctance in Germany itself and a bitter argument developed in the British Labour Party as plans to effect it were formulated. There were, understandably, also strong objections in France.

THE EUROPEAN DEFENCE COMMUNITY

At the Council of Europe Assembly in Strasbourg in August 1950, Sir (then Mr.) Winston Churchill had proposed 'the immediate creation of a European army under a united command in which we should all bear a worthy and honourable part' and which should be 'subject to proper European democratic control' and should act in co-operation with the United States and Canada. M. Robert Schuman had just published his plan which was to become the Coal and Steel Community. Thus it seemed both practicable and desirable that German rearmament should take place within a European framework, avoiding in this way the re-creation of German national forces. Such a solution would have served the dual objectives of strengthening the defences of Europe and at the same time moving nearer the goal of European federation.

On 25 October 1950 M. René Pleven, the French Prime Minister, presented an outline plan for a European Defence Community to the National Assembly and secured a vote in its favour of 343 to 225. He proposed 'the creation, for the purpose of common defence, of a European Army linked to the political institution of a united Europe' which would be 'a complete merger of men and equipment under a single European political and military authority'.

The British Labour Government in 1951 made it clear that Britain could not become a member of the Defence Community, although undertaking to be associated with it as closely as possible. When Sir Winston Churchill became Prime Minister after the General Election in October 1951, a change in British policy was widely anticipated, since, apart from Sir Winston's own commitments to the 'European idea', his Government was packed with members who had been enthusiastic supporters of British leadership in Europe and critics of the Labour Government's refusal to join the Coal and Steel Community.

Europe, however, was in for a bitter disappointment. The new Government followed the policy of the old. After protracted negotiations,[1] complicated by Governmental crises in France, the European Defence Community was finally strangled on 30 August 1954 by the French National Assembly who had given birth to the idea four years before. However, it must also be said that the British Government, whose Prime Minister had planted the seed from which EDC grew, must take a large measure of responsibility. Sir Anthony Eden, the British Foreign Secretary, had steadfastly refused to give the French the assurances of British commitment which they felt necessary for their own participation. Ironically it was soon to be revealed that Britain was to pay as big a price, in terms of a European commitment, for the less satisfactory framework of Western European Union in order to permit German rearmament as she would have needed to pay to secure the coming into operation of the European Defence Community. The failure of EDC also meant that Britain had irrevocably discarded the opportunity of playing a leading rôle in the political evolution of a united Europe.

Paradoxically, the failure of EDC prompted Sir Anthony Eden to take the initiative. With exceptional speed agreement was reached on an alternative plan to repair much of the damage to NATO strength which threatened to follow the rejection of the Defence Community and with it the provisions for German rearmament. In less than two months, on 23 October 1954, the Paris Agreements were signed. These provided for the following modifications in the Brussels Treaty of 1948:

(1) The termination of the occupation régime in Western Germany, the Federal Government agreeing to the maintenance on its territory of foreign forces at least equivalent in strength to those stationed there at the time of the signature of the Agreements.

(2) The accession of Italy and the Federal Republic of Germany to the Brussels Treaty, whose signatories were henceforth to constitute a 'Western European Union'.

(3) Within the framework of this Union, agreement on the maximum level of forces to be maintained by each member on the mainland of Europe, and the institution of a system of control over force levels and armaments.

(4) An undertaking by the United Kingdom to maintain on the continent forces equivalent to those assigned to the Supreme Allied Commander Europe (four divisions and the Second Tactical Air Force). The United Kingdom stipulated, however, that it would not be bound by this obligation in the event of a serious overseas emergency. It also reserved the right to ask the North Atlantic Council to review the financial arrangements for the maintenance of these forces if the drain on its foreign exchange proved too great.

(5) The accession of the Federal Republic of Germany to the North Atlantic Treaty.

(6) The establishment of a unified military formation by assigning to the Supreme Allied Commander Europe all forces of member countries stationed within the area of his command, with the exception of certain forces needed for the defence of overseas territories, for internal protection and for police duties.

On 6 May 1955, all the necessary ratifications having been deposited, the modified Brussels Treaty came into force and on 9 May the Federal Republic of Germany became the fifteenth member of NATO.

WESTERN EUROPEAN UNION

Western European Union as established under the modified Brussels Treaty consists of a Council of Ministers (with headquarters in London) and an Assembly (with headquarters in Paris). The Council consists of the Foreign Ministers of the seven countries and the Assembly of the Members of Parliament of those countries who are elected or appointed as their country's representatives to the Consultative Assembly of the Council of Europe. The Council of Europe was established in 1949 and now has sixteen member nations: Austria, Belgium, Cyprus, Denmark, France, Federal Germany, Greece, Iceland, Ireland, Italy, Luxembourg, Netherlands, Norway, Sweden, Turkey, United Kingdom. It consists of a Committee of Ministers and a Consultative Assembly of Parliamentarians. The Consultative

Assembly concerns itself with political, economic, social, cultural and legal matters but the military aspects of defence are not within its competence.

The modified Brussels Treaty provides a greater degree of commitment for its members and a greater guarantee of military aid is provided for a member attacked than that contained in the NATO Treaty. But following the precedent of the original Brussels Treaty Organisation which delegated all its defence and military functions to NATO shortly after the formation of NATO in 1949, the Council of Western European Union has likewise delegated these responsibilities to NATO. Similarly, although a Standing Armaments Committee exists to further the common production and standardisation of weapons in WEU, it is overshadowed by the work of NATO in the same field. The procedures established in WEU, however, serve as a pattern for the NATO work.

The main responsibility in defence matters exercised by the WEU Council is in respect of the work of its Agency for the Control of Armaments. Its duties are to inspect and report on the level of stocks on the mainland of Europe and to ensure that prohibited weapons are not being manufactured. It has also to determine the level of stocks of atomic weapons produced on the mainland of Europe that its members may maintain there. This has not so far been applied, but it will presumably have to be done once French production of nuclear weapons passes the experimental stage. In all these matters the Council acts by a simple majority, in contrast to NATO unanimity.

The Council is also required to see that the maximum levels of forces laid down in the Treaty are not exceeded. This has not been any problem, nor does it appear likely to become one. On the contrary, the difficulty has been to persuade members to maintain their forces at the promised levels, although these are well below the permitted maxima. Only in the case of the United Kingdom is there an undertaking to keep a minimum number of forces in Europe and the Council's consent, by majority vote, is required to permit the withdrawal of forces below the four divisions and the Second Tactical Air Force committed in the Treaty, except in the event of an acute overseas emergency. On two occasions withdrawals of British troops from Germany have been authorized.

In general, the WEU Council has been loath to take any decisions in defence matters, or to take any initiatives in this field within the North Atlantic Council, for fear of creating the impression in NATO that the seven members are acting in consort or forming a Western European Union pressure group. However, because WEU is the only body consisting of the six countries forming the European Economic Community plus the United Kingdom, it has been of great value as a framework for political consultation between 'the Six' and the United Kingdom and for negotiations towards a solution of the problems posed by 'the Six' and 'the Seven'.

The WEU Assembly owes its existence to the fact that the provisions of the European Defence Community for a parliamentary body were taken over in the Paris agreements. Unlike the European Parliamentary Assembly, it has no executive powers but only consultative status. It has power in certain circumstances, however, formally to disagree with decisions of the WEU Council. It also has control over its own budget.

In the defence field, through its Committee on Defence Questions and Armaments, it has devised procedures and opportunities to provide valuable information and experience for its members. In this way it can play a big part in assisting to develop an informed parliamentary and public opinion on the work and policies of the alliance. In particular the Assembly has stressed consistently the obligation to re-think the strategy of NATO in the light of nuclear parity, the importance of providing more conventional forces and the need to establish joint political control within the alliance over the use of nuclear weapons. In this way it has perhaps exerted an influence towards the change of emphasis in NATO policy. It has certainly provided a unique official forum for discussion of these matters. The Assembly has also been concerned to suggest and to discuss ways of solving the deadlock between 'the Six' and 'the Seven'.

Western European Union had important responsibilities for the administration of the Saar, but these ended when the Saar was incorporated into the Federal Republic of Germany in 1957. It also had important responsibilities, inherited from the original Brussels Treaty Organisation, to develop co-operation in the social and cultural fields. After lengthy discussion and negotiation, and in the face of considerable opposition from the Assembly, the Council transferred its social and cultural activities to the Council of Europe in 1960. This, incidently, has been the only tangible achievement of the many efforts made to produce a measure of 'rationalisation' of the various European institutions.

In 1962 the future of Western European Union is uncertain. While it would be most unwise to drop the arms control function contained in the modified Brussels Treaty, the desire of the Six for closer political consultations among themselves on the lines of the Fouchet plan (put forward in October 1961) and the British application to join the Community have together diminished the rôle of the WEU Council. The Council meeting arranged for December 1961 was cancelled as the Six had not reached agreement among themselves on amendments to the Fouchet plan.

THE PRESENT STRUCTURE OF NATO

The North Atlantic Council is the highest authority in NATO and all its decisions require unanimity. It meets at the level both of Ministers and of Permanent Representatives. While the members are usually represented at ministerial meetings by their Foreign Ministers, it is possible for other Ministers to attend if the agenda makes this desirable. In December 1957 the Council met for the first time at the level of Heads of Government.

The Secretary-General, Dr. Dirk Stikker (Netherlands), who is also Chairman of the Council, is responsible to it for organising its work and directing the Secretariat. There is a Deputy Secretary-General and four Assistant Secretaries-General, directing the Divisions of Political Affairs, Economics and Finance, Production and Logistics and the office of the Science Adviser. An Executive Secretary acts as Secretary to the Council.

The highest military organisation consists of the Military Committee, the Standing Group, the Commands and a Regional Planning Group.

The Military Committee, meeting in Washington, is composed of Chiefs of Staff of the member countries. At this level it meets at least twice a year. Between these meetings, Permanent Military Representatives are appointed to enable the Committee to function in permanent session.

The Standing Group, also in Washington, is the executive agent of the Military Committee and is composed of representatives of the Chiefs of Staff of France, the United Kingdom and the

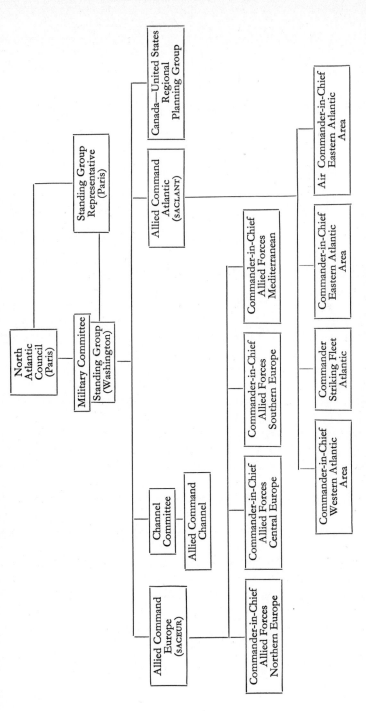

OUTLINE OF NATO MILITARY ORGANISATION

United States. It is the body to which the NATO Commanders are responsible and has the task of co-ordinating defence plans originating in the Commands and of making recommendations to the Military Committee and the Council. The Standing Group is also responsible for the NATO Defence College in Paris and for a number of specialised military agencies.

The NATO area is divided into three Commands (Europe, Atlantic Ocean and Channel) and a Regional Planning Group (Canada-United States).

Europe Command covers the land area extending from the North Cape to North Africa and from the Atlantic to the eastern border of Turkey but excludes the United Kingdom, Portugal and Algeria which are national responsibilities. It is under the Supreme Allied Commander Europe (SACEUR) and its headquarters, Supreme Headquarters Allied Powers Europe (SHAPE) is located near Paris.

SACEUR is responsible, under the general direction of the Standing Group, for the defence of the Allied countries situated within the area of his Command against any attack. In peacetime he is responsible for the organisation, training and equipment of the forces assigned to him, for the preparation of plans and for making such recommendations on military matters as he thinks fit. He has direct access to Chiefs of Staff, Defence Ministers and Heads of Government of member countries.

He has a Deputy Supreme Commander as well as a Naval Deputy and an Air Deputy. There are four subordinate Commands directly responsible to him: (i) Northern Europe at Kolsaas (Oslo) in Norway (ii) Central Europe at Fontainebleau in France (iii) Southern Europe at Naples in Italy and (iv) Mediterranean at Malta.

Atlantic Ocean Command extends from the North Pole to the Tropic of Cancer and from the coastal waters of North America to those of Europe and Africa, including Portugal, except for the Channel and the British Isles. It also has responsibility for islands in this area, such as Iceland and the Azores.

The Supreme Allied Commander Atlantic (SACLANT) has his headquarters at Norfolk, Virginia, in the United States. Unlike SACEUR, SACLANT has no forces permanently assigned to his Command, although the forces earmarked to be assigned to him in war are available for exercises. SACLANT's responsibilities are thus almost entirely operational. He has a Deputy Supreme Commander.

There are three Commands directly responsible to SACLANT: (i) The Western Atlantic Area with headquarters at Norfolk, U.S.A., (ii) the Eastern Atlantic Area with headquarters at Northwood, England, and (iii) the Striking Fleet Atlantic Command with headquarters at Norfolk, U.S.A.

Channel Command covers the English Channel and the southern part of the North Sea. It is controlled by the Channel Committee, with headquarters in London, which consists of the Naval Chiefs of Staff (or their representatives) of Belgium, France, the Netherlands and the United Kingdom. Directly under the Channel Committee is the Allied Command Channel. The Allied Commander-in-Chief Channel is a British Admiral with headquarters at Portsmouth, and there is a Maritime Air Advisor (a British Air Marshal with headquarters at Northwood, England) to the Allied Commander-in-Chief in this area.

Canada-United States Regional Planning Group, which covers the North American area, develops and recommends to the Military Committee, through the Standing Group, plans for the defence of the Canada-United States region. It meets alternately in Washington and Ottawa.

A general view of the basic organisation of NATO is given in the chart on page 29.

Chapter IV

SOVIET STRATEGY AND FORCES

' "I have spent all my life in trying to guess what was on the other side of the hill." That was one of Wellington's best-known sayings. It aptly defined the primary requirement in generalship, and in statesmanship—to guess what is going on behind the opposing front, and in the opponent's mind. Imagination is as important as information, and all the more where the latter is unreliable. To look at the situation—especially *your* situation—from *his* point of view is the best way of trying to get into his mind.'[2] This passage by Captain Liddell Hart squarely puts the basis and the grounds for an assessment of Soviet strategy.

Sir Winston Churchill supplies an equally apt quotation to illustrate the difficulties of trying to do so. In a broadcast in October 1939 he said: 'I cannot forecast to you the action of Russia. It is a riddle wrapped in a mystery inside an enigma.'[3] This comment is just as true today.

Part of our difficulty arises from the tremendous military and diplomatic advantages which accrue to the Soviet Union from her system of government, chief among them being the 'intelligence gap'. She is able to preserve secrecy about her military installations and policies, whereas in an open society one can read of new nuclear bases in all the newspapers, if only as the venues of protest marches. She has no problem of having to persuade public opinion to vote the money necessary for defence expenditure; and if a change of policy means the waste of vast outlays of money and effort, she has no awkward questions to face. The absence of any organised opposition permits a degree of flexibility and opportunism in diplomacy which can never be attained in a democratic society where leaders must explain why their actions today are inconsistent with their speeches of yesterday. These factors give the Soviet leaders a great power of initiative as well as the freedom to retreat rapidly and easily from any position should the need arise. Also—and in this respect the West would do well to emulate Russia's example—there is a marriage between foreign policy and defence policy, both being made to serve the same ends.

In fact the Russian leadership controls the international temperature almost as easily as the American President regulates his bath water. This is not to say that society in the Soviet Union or in the communist bloc is completely monolithic in structure. Mr. Khrushchev no doubt has to carry the hierarchy with him in the Soviet Union and this may cause him from time to time to *reculer pour mieux sauter*. Difficulties do arise in relations with the satellites and there is the influence of China looming larger every year. But for the most part fence-mending exercises can be conducted in reasonable privacy. On the other hand there is the overriding restriction of Marx-Leninist philosophy, the ideological straight-jacket within which communist policy must move.

It would be wrong to imagine that Soviet society is likely to evolve from communism to democracy in the course of time. Such an assumption ignores the basic fact of the communist system—the Communist Party. Mr. Khrushchev won and holds his position through his control of the party machinery. If Soviet society were to change, the power and right to exist of the Communist Party would disappear and Mr. Khrushchev would go with it. The rôle of the Communist Party explains why there can be no half-way house between communism and democracy, as is aptly illustrated by the recent history of Yugoslavia.

The fact that there are relaxations in the rigours of Soviet society and a rising standard of living, coupled with the confidence that comes from the belief that they have the edge in the world balance of power, must surely mean that the communist régime in Russia is more and not less secure. This does not mean that they want war. On the contrary: they are confident that they can achieve their purpose without it. They find confirmation for their confidence in the disarray of NATO and the divisions within its ranks; from the other side of the hill, it may well seem that they have only to wait for world domination to come within their grasp as one does for a ripe fruit to drop from a tree. The main danger of war lies in the risk that their confidence may prompt miscalculation; and in the rigidity of their basic communist doctrines in contrast to the day-to-day flexibility available from the wide range of military and political options open to them. Mr. Khrushchev's military and political strength give him an immense freedom of manœuvre in the world; nevertheless, he remains a prisoner, even if a willing one, of the communist ideology.

Thus while the Soviet Union has vastly greater power than the West for manœuvre in day-to-day diplomatic tactics, she has no corresponding flexibility in terms of long-range strategy. In short, while it is possible to deduce the *ends* of communist policy, the *means* frequently defy prediction. Undoubtedly this combination of great tactical flexibility and long-term ideological rigidity creates frustration and difficulties for the West in any attempt to evaluate probable Soviet reactions to any situation or to forestall possible Soviet moves against our weak points. But we must accept it as one of the facts of international life.

As has been indicated in the previous chapter in describing the events which led to the formation of NATO, Soviet policy in the immediate post-war years was to enlarge her sphere of influence by aggressive diplomacy and by exploiting the advantage of her strategic position in Eastern Europe and anti-imperialist or revolutionary unrest anywhere in the world. Considerable Soviet expansion was achieved without the loss of a single Soviet soldier. Undoubtedly this is still the Soviet Union's basic aim. But, after Czechoslovakia and then Berlin brought these frictions from the periphery of the Western sphere of influence to its centre, the West was galvanised into taking collective measures to oppose further Soviet encroachments. The advent of NATO meant that such activities could be pursued only with considerable risks.

DEFENCE AND DISARMAMENT

Over the past fifteen years, Soviet strategic concepts have varied considerably, reflecting at every stage the relative strength of the Soviet bloc and the Western world and in particular Russia's evolution as a nuclear power. Much can be learned about Soviet policy shifts from a study of the various proposals she has submitted to the disarmament negotiations which have been pursued intermittently since 1946. Soviet disarmament proposals, designed to complement her defence policy, have always faithfully reflected her current military preoccupations and awareness of her strength or weakness relative to the West.

President Truman has reported that when told of the development of the American atom bomb in 1945, Stalin was not very interested. No doubt, in the light of subsequent espionage revelations, Stalin knew already and had decided that his policy was to minimise the effect of nuclear weapons in terms of political and military power. Certainly this was the public posture of the Soviet Union for the ten years following the war. Soviet propaganda pursued three themes during this period. First, that the decisive character of nuclear weapons was greatly overrated and that the overwhelming conventional power of the Soviet Union was more important; secondly, that nuclear weapons had a special character of horror and should be banned—this was the basis of the World Peace Movement which started in Stockholm in 1950; thirdly, that the only proper field for atomic energy was for peaceful uses and in this the Soviet Union would give the lead.

Yet at the same time she was making feverish and prodigious efforts to develop her own nuclear weapons and build up a long-range air force. The propaganda was a skilful cover for Soviet anxiety that the United States might exploit her nuclear strength and superior air power to attack Russia. The preponderance of American air power in the NATO forces combined with the paucity of ground forces in Europe pointed in this direction. In contrast with NATO policy, Soviet military thinking has consistently advocated the maintenance of balanced forces.

During this period Russia seemed to have the concept that any war would consist of a nuclear exchange followed by 'broken-back' warfare—a long drawn-out global struggle. In such a situation Russia would have an advantage over the West through her vast superiority in men under arms. This was undoubtedly a great asset and Russia was careful not to let it run down, despite the enormous cost in money and resources in developing nuclear capability. The Soviet army's weapons and equipment were modernised and the navy brought up to strength. Particular emphasis was placed on building up the submarine fleet so that it could fulfil a vital rôle in war by denying the use of the sea for supplies from America (then outside the range of Soviet attack) to Europe.

D

Looking back, 1953 probably marked the most favourable balance *vis-à-vis* Soviet strength in NATO's history, since from then onwards the staggering advances achieved by Russia in nuclear technology began to show results. She did not test her first atomic bomb until 1949, yet she exploded a workable H-bomb in August 1953, some months ahead of the first American workable H-bomb of March 1954. (The United States had successfully tested thermonuclear 'devices' in 1952.) After the death of Stalin in 1953, as part of the general ferment of ideas and policy rethinking that took place within the Soviet Union, there seems to have been an internal debate as to the consequences that flowed from the possession by both sides of nuclear weapons, in which some support was forthcoming for a policy of mutual deterrence. However, the prevailing view was in favour of continuing the global war strategy and there was no apparent shift of policy.

NUCLEAR PARITY

But as Russian nuclear capability developed and as the strategic implications were discussed in Soviet journals, Soviet military views were disclosed as being not unlike those of their military counterparts in the West. The importance of a surprise attack, hitherto officially rejected, and the possibility of a short war were accepted. Instead of minimising the rôle of nuclear weapons, Soviet strategy came to consider them as an essential part of defence. In 1955 there were already signs of a new defence posture based on the strategy that the Soviet Union must be prepared to survive a nuclear attack and still be able to retaliate, i.e. the 'second-strike' capacity which is now strongly advocated in the West. This demanded a great increase in air defences and a greater dispersal of Russian strike forces to avoid their total destruction.

Soviet writings often referred to the 'massive retaliation' doctrine of Mr. Dulles. Marx-Leninism did not allow account to be taken of the deterrent purpose of the American Strategic Air Command and the purely defensive character of the NATO alliance. To argue that the inevitable decline of capitalism would produce a last desperate aggression suited communist theories very much better.

As soon as Russian nuclear strength was self-evident, Soviet propaganda began to concentrate on her capacity to wreak destruction on her enemies and to threaten the overseas bases from which the United States could launch an attack. At the same time it has not freed itself from the previous ideological line of denouncing the use of nuclear weapons as immoral. The same inconsistency is revealed by the Soviet decision to resume nuclear tests. Thus we have had the confusing experience from the Suez crisis of 1956 to the Berlin crisis of 1961 of finding the two contradictory themes used simultaneously: a moral condemnation of nuclear strategy combined with references to Soviet nuclear strength and threats to use it in certain circumstances. These two themes have been the basis of the arguments used to try to exert pressure on the European members of the alliance to break up NATO—the clear political and military objective of Soviet policy. Threats have often been made that any country which allowed American or NATO nuclear bases on its territory was inviting its own destruction, the impression being given that this task would have priority in Soviet policy. No doubt the aim was to encourage the propaganda line that by their policy of maintaining foreign bases the Americans were wilfully exposing their European allies to danger while preserving their own skins and at the same time probably being neither able nor willing to intervene on their allies' behalf.

This propaganda offensive has continued despite the fact that the increase in the range of Soviet rocketry has brought the population of the United States into the front line and despite the obvious military point that to be effective, any surprise attack would have to deal simultaneously with the Strategic Air Command and missile bases both in America and Europe. Indeed this point is made by Marshal Yeremenko in an article 'Arguments against Foreign Bases':

> However, our military thought is founded on the indisputable proposition that the most effective way of finishing with an aggressor once and for all is to carry out retaliatory blows simultaneously both on his foreign bases and on his own economic and military strategic centres. This, by the way, is completely within the powers of the Soviet Armed Forces.[4]

This does not prevent him, however, summing up his article in these terms:

> Although in a strategic context the Western military bases in foreign countries are losing their former significance, the fact of their existence is a most serious threat to world peace. The fact of the

matter is that such bases are one of the most dangerous sources of military provocation by Imperialism such as might drive mankind into a fearful catastrophe. It is therefore quite clear how significant is the current struggle for the liquidation of military bases which is now being conducted by the socialist countries and all peace-loving humanity. Aggressive circles in the West attempt to prove that through this campaign the Soviet Union and socialist countries are attempting to secure for themselves a onesided military advantage. This invention is as absurd as it is ridiculous. The struggle against military bases on foreign territories is by no means a struggle for military ascendancy of one country or another but a struggle for preservation of peace.

SOVIET STRATEGIC RE-THINKING

The propaganda continues almost unchanged. But since 1959 there is evidence, particularly from the fundamental differences between the Soviet Union and China on the future of communist strategy, that there has been a good deal of re-thinking as to the consequences of nuclear parity. It seems reasonable to assume that from his side of the hill Mr. Khrushchev has drawn conclusions not unlike those increasingly held in the West as to the consequences of nuclear parity for us—(i) that global nuclear war is not essential, indeed is not credible, as an instrument of policy; (ii) that a limited nuclear war is not likely; and (iii) that war remains a possibility through accident or miscalculation and steps should be taken to ensure that if it happens the dangers of nuclear escalation are avoided. My guess is that Mr. Khrushchev is more worried today by the prospect of China becoming involved in hostilities with the United States and calling on him to honour their Treaty of 1950 with nuclear weapons than he is by any fears of NATO aggression. It is very doubtful if he would be willing to commit the Soviet people to suicide for wholly Chinese interests.

The evidence of more rational and realistic thinking on the part of the Soviet Union springs in part from the buoyant self-confidence engendered by her achievements in the nuclear field. The Russian leaders are still suspicious of Western intentions and quick and eager to exploit any weakness on our part. But the extreme defensiveness and fears of 'capitalist encirclement' that coloured her attitude and policy in the immediate postwar years have been greatly modified. Confidence that a military balance has been achieved has led to the renunciation of the doctrine that war between capitalism and 'socialism' is inevitable. Already in 1956 Mr. Khrushchev declared that war was 'not a fatalistic inevitability'.[5] By 1958–9 this view was being put even more definitely, reflecting the optimism engendered by rocket successes:

> The decisions of the 20th and 21st Congresses of the C.P.S.U., the declaration of Communist and Workers' Parties and the Peace Manifesto authoritatively explain that in modern conditions war is not inevitable, war can be prevented, peace can be defended and made permanent. This great idea has increased the efforts of the broad masses of the people in the struggle for peace many-fold and has armed them with a clear outlook.[6]

While Soviet recognition that war is not inevitable is growing, there is also evidence—in part perhaps because of the ideological dispute with China—of increasing awareness of the dangers of nuclear war. This is strikingly apparent among groups (economists and social scientists, for example) which, though influential, have not previously interested themselves greatly in foreign or defence policies. Certainly the dangers of nuclear warfare, supported by statistical data, have been stressed in official publications. For example, Major-General Talenski, in the article cited above, quotes from Western sources the figures of the estimated casualties—1,700,000 'killed' and three and a half million 'wounded', with no account of the radioactive effect of atomic bombs—which were involved in the 1955 NATO air exercise *Carte Blanche*. This exercise was designed to test the capabilities of tactical atomic bombing against enemy bases and lines of communication, and 3,000 planes were flown and 335 bombs 'dropped' during it.[7] He concludes, no doubt with one eye on his readers in Peking:

> The process of development of the technique for destroying people has led to such a situation that it is impossible to use weapons for deciding political questions as used to be for thousands of years. Nuclear rocket war is extremely dangerous, not only for the side which is attacked, but is suicidal for the aggressor himself.

Limited nuclear war has never been accepted by the Russians as a realistic doctrine, although their large army would have considerable advantages (because of its far greater reserves) over

NATO forces in a war in which nuclear weapons were confined to army atomic artillery. As many NATO experts do, Soviet military thinking denies the validity of distinguishing between the tactical and strategic uses of nuclear weapons and anticipates inevitable nuclear escalation if any nuclear weapons are used. The inherent dangers of the *nth* nuclear power problem have also not escaped Soviet notice, either in general terms or with particular reference to China.

If Russian assessment of the consequences and implications of nuclear parity is not unlike ours, what can this foretell for the future? How will she react to the further boost to her confidence and prestige which comes from the *cosmonaut*? It could mean a more energetic and genuine search for solutions to political questions and the path to arms control. But it could easily lead in the opposite direction, in the belief that nuclear stalemate means that resort to the aggressive diplomacy of the immediate postwar period could now safely be pursued since the West would be inhibited from using nuclear weapons. Certainly the supplying of arms to countries within the recognised sphere of influence of NATO members—as witness the active support and encouragement of the Castro régime in Cuba—could pay handsome dividends on the previous pattern without involving Soviet forces directly. Another possibility is a temporary relaxation of tension, although of course without any real surrender of military advantage, in the hope that internal pressures will blunt the effectiveness of NATO or even cause the alliance to fall apart. And in the meantime—just to keep the pot boiling, while Mr. Khrushchev decides which approach to try next—there is plenty of scope for activities in Africa, Asia and Latin America and for vigorous economic competition to prevent 'peaceful co-existence' from becoming too dull. It could be that Mr. Khrushchev is, as Lenin undoubtedly was, a keen student of Clausewitz and has reversed the latter's doctrine to read 'Politics is a continuation of war by other means'.

Alastair Buchan sums up Soviet strategy and puts its lesson for NATO thus:

An analysis of the strategic intentions of a power so secretive as Russia is at best only a very rough guess, and it is foolish to attempt to define them with any precision or to base Western calculations on any one speech or collection of writings. For all one can say with any certainty is that Russian policy is never dominated by any one single objective. As one eminent Russian expert put it at the Oxford Conference: 'Their idea is to set out three or four alternative policies and see what they can get.' By the same token, no policy is ever dropped if it proves unsuccessful—it is merely shelved for the time being. In consequence, the most important fact about the Soviet Union today that the NATO powers must confront is not Soviet missile prowess, or the efficiency of the Red Army, or steel production, or economic aid; but the great range of options that are now open to Mr. Khrushchev. If the international weather remains sunny he can press ahead with his policy of economic competition; if it darkens he has the full apparatus of military power with which to adopt, overnight, a far more menacing posture towards NATO than Stalin ever could. Consequently, it is the problem of achieving an equivalent flexibility which is the central task that he has imposed upon NATO in its second decade.[8]

There can be no doubt that in 1962 the diversity of her military power and her balanced forces give the Soviet Union military flexibility to match her range of options in the diplomatic field.

THE WARSAW PACT

The Warsaw Pact, concluded in 1955 as a counter to the decision to rearm Western Germany, in fact only gave formal effect to the network of mutual assistance treaties already existing within the Soviet alliance system. It embraces Albania, Bulgaria, Czechoslovakia, East Germany, Hungary, Poland, Rumania and the Soviet Union. Although not officially a member, China has pledged her full support. However, following the open breach between Albania and the Soviet Union after the CPSU Congress in October 1961, Albania's membership of the Warsaw Pact seems likely to be terminated and this may affect China's support.

The Warsaw Treaty Organisation is a far less complex organisation than NATO. This follows partly from the nature of the relationship between the Soviet Union and the other member countries, partly from military considerations—the Pact covers a compact area with no ocean between the most powerful member and her allies and difficult problems of supply, logistics and lines of communication do not have to be reckoned with as they do in NATO. A Soviet Marshal is the Supreme Commander of the Warsaw Pact forces, but there is no integrated command structure as exists in NATO. The forces allocated by member states remain under national command. It is virtually certain, however, that standardisation of weapons, equipment and procedures is almost complete.

It is estimated that the seven Soviet satellites in the Warsaw Pact can raise about seventy divisions, mainly of the conventional rifle type. These divisions represent about 900,000 men and in addition there about 400,000 men in paramilitary formations. Their equipment includes at least a proportion of the most modern weapons, including rockets. Their air forces number a total of about 3,000 aircraft, mainly jet fighters. It is safe to assume, however, that the strength of the Warsaw Pact depends almost wholly on the forces of the Soviet Union.

SOVIET FORCES

The Soviet forces[9] are divided into five arms, each with its Commander-in-Chief: (a) ground forces (b) air forces (c) navy (d) air defence and (e) missiles. In addition there is a well-organised system of civil defence, on a scale greatly in excess of that in NATO countries, complementing air defence which has been given priority in recent years.

Developments in rocket technology and nuclear weapons have caused the Soviet Union to follow the trend in the United States and Britain of putting more emphasis on firepower and less on manpower. But whereas in the West this was openly done on grounds of cost and the political difficulties of maintaining large conscript forces, the Soviet Union managed to score a propaganda success by presenting her manpower reductions as a contribution to international disarmament.

Despite the cuts which have been made, the Red Army is a most formidable fighting force, highly efficient and well equipped. The total strength of the armed forces for January 1960 was given as 3,623,000 as against 5,763,000 in 1955. On 15 January 1960 it was announced that the forces were to be reduced to 2,423,000 —a further cut of 1,200,000 men. Mr. Khrushchev has said, echoing Western Defence Ministers, that to offset these cuts the firepower of the Soviet Union has been greatly increased. He also claims that the increased firepower (missiles and nuclear warheads) is for defensive purposes: 'It takes troops to conquer a country, because you can destroy a country with hydrogen bombs and missiles but you cannot occupy it. This is why we are building up these means of defence'.

This policy was, however, reversed on 8 July 1961 when Mr. Khrushchev announced that because of the increasing war budgets of NATO nations, the Soviet Union had suspended demobilisation and had increased her defence budget by nearly one-third. While reiterating the strength of Soviet nuclear weapons and the efficiency of her rockets, Mr. Khrushchev laid renewed emphasis, in contrast to his speech eighteen months earlier in stating the policy now reversed, on the importance of conventional forces. Only time will tell whether this is only a temporary move to meet the external pressure directed against Berlin and the internal pressures of officers threatened with the axe, or whether it is a considered change of emphasis resulting from a reassessment of strategy. However, the Defence Budget announced for 1962 confirms the policy of July as does the estimate of 3,800,000 as the strength of Soviet forces at the end of 1961.

(i) *Air and missile power*

The Soviet Union was reported as having thirty-five Inter-Continental Ballistic Missiles operational at the end of 1960 and a capacity to produce 200 by the beginning of 1962. These are to be dispersed throughout the Soviet Union. Mr. Khrushchev is quoted by Marshal Yeremenko as having said on 14 January 1960:

> We are taking into account the fact that foreign military bases are located around our country. Therefore we are so distributing our rocket equipment as to ensure double and triple coverage. The territory of our country is vast, we have the possibility of dispersing our rocket equipment and of camouflaging it well. We are building a system such that if some means designated for carrying out a retaliatory blow are put out of action it will always be possible to bring duplicate resources into action and destroy the targets from reserve positions.[10]

The principal operational ICBM is propelled by a three-stage liquid fuel engine and has a range of 8,000 miles. There are two operational Medium Range Ballistic Missiles, both liquid fuelled, with ranges of 1,800 miles and 1,000 miles and up to 500 are believed to be operational. It seems likely, however, that the Soviet policy of having 200 ICBMs operational by 1962 has not been carried out: her estimated ICBM strength at the end of 1961 was between fifty and seventy-five. Competing demands of the space programme and the difficulty of concealing so large a missile probably account for her decision to concentrate on a smaller, second generation ICBM under development.

The Strategic Bomber Force consists mainly of the following aircraft:

(a) Sixty to seventy Tupolev 95 4-engine turbo-prop heavy bombers, NATO code name *Bears*. The maximum speed is 560 m.p.h. (900 km.) and the range is 7,000 miles with a bomb load of 20 tons.

(b) One hundred to 120 Myasishchev 4, 4-jet heavy bombers, *Bisons*, with a maximum speed of 600 m.p.h. (960 km.). The range is over 6,000 miles, the operational ceiling 45,000 feet and the bomb load 10 tons.

(c) One thousand Tupolev 16 twin-jet medium bombers, *Badgers*, speed 600 m.p.h., range 3,500 miles, the operational ceiling 40,000 feet and the bomb load 4-5 tons.

(d) Delta-wing 4-jet *Bounders*, with supersonic speed and a range of 1,650 miles. Numbers and status uncertain.

Bisons and *Badgers* have also been adapted for in-flight refuelling. Most of these aircraft are based in western and south-west Russia.

The air display in July 1961, the first big demonstration since 1956, indicated that manned aircraft have not been neglected during the period of rocket development. Two new types of supersonic bomber were displayed and these, and the *Bears*, carried air-to-ground missiles. It would seem that the Russians have a stand-off bomb similar to the United States *Hound Dog* and the British *Blue Steel*.

It seems very likely that the Soviet Union also has a space project for military purposes. Satellites clearly have excellent potential as reconnaissance vehicles, and it is possible to envisage a satellite being equipped with a missile capable of being fired by remote control from earth.

The Tactical Air Force consists of about 4,000 aircraft, including the supersonic twin-jet *Blowlamp* and the slightly faster twin-jet *Backfin*. These planes and missiles are replacing the older IL 28 turbo-jet *Beagle*, hitherto the mainstay of the tactical bombing force.

Air Defence has received considerable priority in its allocation of resources. It consists of increasing numbers of ground-to-air guided missiles and about 10,000 fighter planes of all kinds. (The *MIG 15* and *17* and the *Yak 25* have speeds of 685 m.p.h.) The latest supersonic fighters are equipped with air-to-air missiles. An extensive radar early warning system is in operation.

The Air Transport Fleet is highly developed and consists of about 2,000 aircraft. A *Convertiplane,* a type of vertical-take-off aircraft, was shown at the air display in July 1961 carrying troops and cargo. Claimed to be the biggest and most powerful of its type in the world, it was estimated as being able to carry over 100 passengers and to have a speed of over 200 m.p.h.

(ii) *Land power*

It is estimated that there are about 160 active divisions (not all at full strength), and a total manpower of 2,500,000. It is believed that at war strength an infantry division comprises 12,000 men and an armoured division 10,500 men. The airborne forces total approximately 100,000 men in nine divisions, and two divisions could be air-dropped in any single operation.

Outside the Soviet Union there are twenty armoured or mechanised divisions (comprising 6,000 tanks) in East Germany, and six divisions in Hungary and Poland. It is estimated that 125 divisions could be put into the field in Europe in thirty days and that the Soviet Union has a mobilisation potential of 7,000,000 men.

Over the last few years the Soviet Army has undergone a major reorganisation to meet the conditions of atomic warfare. Its old equipment has been almost entirely replaced and its firepower vastly increased. There are new-type tanks and the Soviet Army is also very strong in artillery, both conventional and atomic. An improved version of the German V2 ballistic rocket (with a range of 450 miles) is the standard equipment of the tactical missile units; there are also solid fuel ballistic missiles with a range of 50 miles and smaller versions, carried on self-propelled launchers, with ranges from 10 to 15 miles.

(iii) *Sea power*

According to *The Times* report of 17 July 1961, the Soviet Navy has increased in total tonnage from 600,000 tons in 1940 to 1,600,000 tons in 1960. This makes it the second largest fleet in the world after the United States (4,000,000 tons). The British Navy with 750,000 tons ranks third. The Soviet Navy consists of four fleets:

(1) The Baltic fleet, divided into a northern group with its main base at Tallin and a southern group based on Baltiisk;

(2) the Northern or Arctic fleet in the White and Barents Seas;

(3) the Black Sea fleet; and

(4) the Pacific fleet.

The main strength of the Soviet Navy lies in the submarine fleet and the large naval air force. The submarine force is estimated at about 450 units, of which more than half are long range. About six atomic powered submarines are believed to be nearing completion and there is evidence that ballistic missile submarines are under construction.

The surface ships of the Soviet Navy consist of twenty-five cruisers, 130 destroyers and 2,500 other vessels. Seventeen of the cruisers (Sverdlov type) have been launched since 1951. The greater part of the destroyers have been constructed since 1950 also. There are no aircraft carriers in the Soviet Navy, but there is a land-based Fleet Air Arm of about 3,000 aircraft, mainly *Beagles*, *Bisons* and *Badgers*.

Komet I, a sea-to-ground ballistic missile for use from surface ships (range 100 miles), is already in service and *Golem*, a missile designed for use by submarines, is under development. It is believed, however, that these missiles can only be fired from the surface and that there is as yet no Soviet equivalent of *Polaris*.

PART TWO

Nuclear Weapons

Chapter V

NUCLEAR CAPABILITY

The Western Alliance must retain the capacity to use nuclear weapons of all types so long as there is no effective disarmament agreement for mutual East-West renunciation. Thus while the Soviet Union has nuclear weapons it is necessary for them to be available to NATO in order to maintain the nuclear stalemate.

There is no doubt that NATO has been, and still is, unduly dependent upon nuclear weapons. There is urgent need for a reconsideration of priorities. Indeed the nuclear deterrent can only retain its credibility, and thus its effectiveness in preventing war, if it is supported by adequate non-nuclear forces. These points are argued in detail in later chapters.

The fact remains, however, that nuclear forces are an essential and major element of Western defence. They provide our deterrent against surprise attack and prevent our being subjected to Soviet nuclear blackmail, since without our own nuclear capability we should be defenceless against threats of Soviet nuclear power. It would be a case of Dullesian massive retaliation in reverse and there is no reason to suppose that the Soviet Union would respect the *status quo* in such circumstances.

It is now generally assumed that the United States and the Soviet Union both possess more than enough nuclear explosives to obliterate the world. But there is a great difference between parity in nuclear capability in which either side can obliterate the other and parity in which both sides can do so no matter who strikes first. Effective mutual deterrence is only achieved in this second case when neither side by striking first can destroy the other's ability to strike back. If this certainty of power of retaliation does not exist, both sides have a strong incentive to initiate an attack or at least to strike first in a critical situation in order to forestall a pre-emptive strike by the enemy which may seem imminent. And since this is a matter of military appreciation, the equilibrium is highly unstable.

'SURVIVABILITY'

The essence of a policy of nuclear deterrence is, therefore, the 'survivability' of retaliatory forces. Some authorities argue that in a few years' time, as the number and accuracy of missiles increase, it will become impossible to ensure that the retaliatory forces survive a surprise attack, so that such an attack would in any circumstances succeed. It is impossible to disprove this. At the same time it is essential to take all possible measures to demonstrate to a potential aggressor the risks inherent in such an assumption. For this purpose the retaliatory forces must be made as invulnerable, and as efficient, as human ingenuity can devise.

Early-warning stations are essential for this purpose. They are also essential to underline the defensive character of our strategic strike capability—our concern to be able to strike the *second* rather than the *first* blow. It is highly important to make the existing deterrent, consisting of manned-bomber forces and fixed-site missiles, credible as a means of retaliation as opposed to an offensive force; otherwise the suspicion may well be held by the Soviet Union that, despite our assurances to the contrary, we have provided such weapons for the purpose of making a surprise attack on them.

Since in an open political society there is no prospect of keeping secret the location of fixed-site missile bases, mobility must be the keynote of the policy to maintain a retaliatory force which could survive the most thoroughly planned surprise attack. Mr. Watkinson, British Minister of Defence, has said that this requires 'a wide dispersal of fixed sites, the use of railway trains or barges, of surface vessels, air-launching platforms and undersea launching platforms.'[11] The same considerations apply to manned aircraft as to missile sites, and both Strategic Air Command and British Bomber Command attach the greatest importance to dispersing and rotating their planes so as to minimise the risk of their being destroyed on the ground.

President Kennedy has stated the problem and the way to tackle it with great clarity in his review of Captain Liddell Hart's book *Deterrent or Defence*:

Hart—like many Europeans—under-estimates the American task of maintaining the security and effectiveness of the American nuclear deterrent. We face a real problem over the next several years in guaranteeing that our deterrent is safe from sudden attack and capable of effective penetration of Soviet defenses. We have no right to tempt Soviet planners and political leaders with the possibility of catching our aircraft and unprotected missiles on the ground, in a gigantic Pearl Harbor. This is our first defense problem. Second, we must bring into being as fast as our resources permit the new generation of mobile missiles, notably Polaris and Minuteman. We need these missiles not merely to provide an untargetable Free World deterrent, but also for a more constructive reason. The relative security from attack which the new mobile missiles allow should diminish the need for hair-trigger decisions and should give the United States, and the world as a whole, a greater degree of stability.[12]

TYPES OF WEAPONS

Before examining the strategic nuclear striking power of NATO member countries, it is necessary to stress that these forces are not within the NATO joint command but, as yet at least, subject to the control of their respective national Governments. NATO has no strategic nuclear forces as such, although much confusion occurs because there is no clear distinction between strategic and tactical weapons. There cannot be: it is the *use* which is strategic or tactical and not the weapon itself, although a common shorthand nomenclature has been developed which speaks of 'strategic nuclear weapons' and 'tactical nuclear weapons'.

Some weapons with a very limited range, for example Army support weapons like *Honest John* and *Corporal*, clearly can only be used in a tactical role. At the other end of the scale, it would be extremely wasteful to use megaton bombs for tactical targets. But, broadly speaking, nuclear weapons can be used on either strategic or tactical targets. An aeroplane armed with a nuclear bomb, for example, can be directed to bomb a city or a rocket base (clearly strategic targets), or a railway junction immediately to the rear of the enemy lines.

The determining factor in the case of missiles is the range of the vehicle rather than the power of the warhead. The nuclear fission bombs of 'Hiroshima' and larger size and the fusion bombs, used

E

either for purposes of mass destruction (the 'counter-city' strike) or aimed at nuclear bases and installations to destroy the opponent's own strategic retaliatory capacity (the 'counter-force' strike) are, however, commonly taken to be 'strategic' warheads.

The 'Hiroshima' bomb had an explosive power of 20 kilotons (i.e. equivalent to 20,000 tons of conventional TNT). The fusion bomb usually has a yield of 10 megatons (equal to 10,000 kilotons) or five hundred times the power of the 'Hiroshima' bomb. Theoretically there is no upper limit to the explosive power of a fusion bomb. I have used the term *nuclear weapon* to denote any weapon employing nuclear fission or fusion as a source of explosive power. A *fission* weapon denotes specifically an 'atomic' weapon in the kiloton range and a *fusion* weapon a 'hydrogen' or 'thermonuclear' weapon in the megaton range.

While the invention of nuclear weapons twenty years ago made enormous explosive power available, the development of missiles in the last ten years allows the nuclear explosive to be transported over inter-continental distances within a period of minutes and marks a revolution as big as the advent of nuclear fission itself. It is therefore essential to distinguish between the nuclear warhead and the means of delivering it.

No-one mistakes an aeroplane for a nuclear weapon, although it may have the capability of delivering such weapons. Yet various rockets are commonly referred to as if they are themselves nuclear weapons, and the question of the warhead is ignored. Obviously the warheads are useless unless they have effective delivery vehicles; but equally rockets are not nuclear weapons unless fitted with appropriate nuclear warheads. The possession by a country of rockets designed for use with nuclear warheads does not make that country a nuclear power unless it also has possession or control of suitable nuclear warheads. This is all very simple; but in discussions on arming NATO troops with atomic weapons and on whether or not Western Germany should be allowed to have nuclear weapons this important distinction is often blurred.

Taking the alliance as a whole, there is no problem of supply of nuclear bombs and strategic warheads. If production ceased forthwith there are ample stocks to maintain a credible deterrent. Dr. Ralph E. Lapp, a pioneer in the development of the atomic bomb, has said that the United States now has about 1,000 hydrogen bombs, each capable of destroying a city. He said it also had a stock of chain reacting materials large enough to produce an additional half a million hydrogen bombs, and these estimates did not take account of smaller bombs or of tactical weapons such as atomic cannon.[13] It is also true that the United Kingdom has by now produced sufficient nuclear explosives to be able alone to inflict on the Soviet Union such crippling losses as to make any Soviet attack unprofitable. In February 1961, the Defence Minister, Mr Watkinson, said, 'as it stands ready at this moment Bomber Command is capable, by itself, of crippling the industrial power of any aggressor nation', a claim repeated by the Secretary of State for Air the following November. France is in process of acquiring a nuclear capability and many other countries could do so if they wished.

The real problem is to maintain means of delivery which will satisfy the two tests, (a) that a sufficiently high percentage of the bombs would reach their targets despite enemy defence arrangements, and (b) that sufficient means of delivery would survive an enemy surprise attack. The West must always be able and ready to strike 'the second blow'. If this capacity is beyond question, it should never be put to the test. By definition, if a nuclear deterrent has to be used it has failed in its main purpose—to deter the enemy.

STRATEGIC RETALIATORY FORCES

Whatever may be decided about nuclear weapons within the alliance, there is no doubt that the responsibility for maintaining a credible strategic nuclear deterrent will rest in the foreseeable future with the United States, and particularly the Strategic Air Command (SAC).

(i) *The American retaliatory forces*

It is expected that the American retaliatory capability that will be operational during the early 1960s will consist of about 200 *Atlas* and *Titan* Inter-Continental Ballistic Missiles on hardened fixed sites in the United States, 550 B 52 inter-continental bombers and 1,000 B 47 medium bombers stationed in America and overseas, some 100 Medium Range Ballistic Missiles in Europe (under dual control, the missile controlled by the user country and the warhead held in American custody), the American fighter bombers

in the allied tactical air forces in Europe and in the Sixth and
Seventh Fleets in the Mediterranean and Pacific, together with
the nucleus of the fleet of *Polaris* equipped nuclear-propelled
submarines. The solid-fuelled *Minuteman* ICBMS are expected to
be ready ahead of the original schedule and the first of them is
likely to be operational in 1963.

The major part of this capacity is represented by the Strategic
Air Command which is a very efficient force. There are about
sixty bases in the United States and twenty overseas with a
fleet of about 3,000 aircraft. In December 1961 265,000 men
were assigned to the Command. From his underground command
centre, the Commander-in-Chief has complete control of
SAC's widespread operations and is able to order his striking force
of bombers and missiles into action within seconds. Various
teletype connections as well as a long-distance telephone system
link the command post with each of the bases, both in America
and overseas, and a powerful radio service completes this communications network. The Strategic Alerting System allows the
Commander to alert by telephone within thirty seconds each of
the Command's main air force headquarters, as well as the
subordinate command posts controlling each base, which can
also be contacted directly by an alternative routing if these headquarters are destroyed. The task of the Command centre could be
taken over at any moment by one of the headquarters should the
underground centre be destroyed by a direct hit. Logical development of this system would result in an airborne command centre,
and by the end of 1961 one was in operation for training purposes.

The backbone of the forces assigned to SAC is made up of
about 1,000 medium range *B 47 Stratojet* (6-jet engine) bombers
with a speed of 600 miles (960 km.) per hour and an unrefuelled
range of over 3,000 miles (4,800 km.). These are organised into
nineteen wings averaging 45 planes each and some of them
are always on temporary assignment overseas. There are about
550 *B 52 Stratofortress* (8-jet engine) heavy bombers, with a speed
of 650 miles per hour (1,040 km.) at an altitude of up to 50,000
feet (15,000 metres) and an unrefuelled range of over 6,000 miles
(9,600 km.). The most up-to-date aircraft, designed to replace
the *B 47*, is the medium range 4-jet, delta wing supersonic
bomber *B 58*, or *Hustler*, with a maximum speed of Mach 2 (over
1,300 miles per hour). It can carry a nuclear bomb, a battery of

cameras or electronic counter-measure equipment in a slim, disposable 'pod' mounted beneath the fuselage. Two wings of *B 58* bombers were introduced into service in 1961. The only other manned bomber—the *B 70 Valkyrie*, a supersonic inter-continental bomber with a speed of three times the speed of sound and capable of flying at an altitude of up to 100,000 feet (30,000 metres) is under development and its future is uncertain. Among bombers under design, the most important is the nuclear-powered *WS 125*. However, in March 1961 it was decided to reduce expenditure by limiting the *B 70* programme to research in the problems of high-speed flying and with the objective of preserving the option of development at a later date if such a bomber weapon system were required. At the same time the project of producing a nuclear-powered aircraft was taken out of the Defence Budget and transferred to the Atomic Energy Commission as a non-defence research item.

For use with manned bombers, SAC disposes of two main air-to-ground missiles: the *Hound Dog*, which can be used as a stand-off bomb or to destroy enemy defences barring the paths to the primary target area; and the *Quail*, a diversionary and decoy missile. The *Hound Dog*, designed for use with the *B 52s*, carries a nuclear warhead and has a range of 500 miles and a supersonic speed.

The *Skybolt* air-to-ground ballistic missile with a range of about 1,000 miles is under development by the Douglas Aircraft Corporation and is scheduled to be ready for service by 1964. Like *Hound Dog* (and the British *Blue Steel* stand-off bomb), *Skybolt* is designed to prolong the life of manned bombers and to fit the *B 52s* and the British *Vulcan* bombers. After abandoning work on its own intermediate range missile, the British Government announced in April 1960 that it had agreed to acquire *Skybolt* from the United States if and when it becomes available. In his special message to Congress on the Defence Budget on 28 March 1961 President Kennedy recommended the allocation of an additional $50 m. to the *Skybolt* programme.

The range and mobility of SAC's aircraft have been greatly increased by the introduction of the *KC 135* long-range jet strato-tanker, which is a military version of the civilian *Boeing 707* and is designed for air-refuelling. This new tanker, replacing the *KC 97* which is still operative on overseas bases, can refuel the

B 52 near the altitude and speed at which the latter aircraft normally flies.

SAC is in process of changing from a pure manned bomber force to a mixed missile-bomber force and is expected by the late 1960s to dispose of more missiles than bombers. SAC wants to maintain a proportion of manned bombers in the foreseeable future, however.

Missiles have a number of drawbacks *vis-à-vis* manned aircraft. A missile cannot be recalled once launched at a target; it cannot be directed from the original target to another; it is incapable of dealing with unexpected developments while in flight; it cannot relay intelligence back to its launching site concerning damage inflicted in the target area.

However, the new Administration is clearly putting increased emphasis on missiles. For example, no funds were included in the January 1961 Budget for the future procurement of *B 52* or *B 58* bombers, and President Kennedy has made it plain that he does not intend to change this decision. It must be recognised that the declared policy of the Kennedy Administration never to strike the first blow in any attack reduces the drawbacks of relying on missiles for defence. At the same time it underlines the importance of developing missiles (such as *Polaris* and *Minuteman*) which will be less vulnerable than manned bombers to a pre-emptive attack.

The first operational missile was the *Snark*, which has been described as an unmanned bomber. It is a turbo-jet powered air-breathing missile of near sonic speed and with a range of more than 5,000 miles (8,000 km.). It is now considered obsolete, however, and in March 1961 it was decided in view of the progress made with ICBMs to abandon the *Snark* programme.

The MRBM *Thor* bases already established in Great Britain have been built by SAC, but in accordance with the Anglo-American agreement control of these weapons is exercised jointly by both Governments. There are about sixty missiles operational in the United Kingdom. The only other MRBM bases operational in Europe are the *Jupiter* bases in Italy established under an agreement between Italy and the United States. Further bases are under construction in Turkey on a similar bilateral arrangement. These *Jupiter* missiles will be under the operational control of Supreme Allied Commander Europe (General Norstad).

However, SAC's plans are based on the fact that Inter-Continental Ballistic Missiles from the United States will constitute the main missile deterrent. At the beginning of 1962 three 'soft' and two 'semi-hard' *Atlas* bases, with a total of fifty-four missiles, and one 'hard' *Titan* base with nine missiles, were operational in the United States. The *Atlas* is a liquid-fuelled missile with a range of over 6,000 miles (9,600 km.). SAC's second ICBM is the two-stage liquid-fuelled *Titan*, larger than *Atlas*, but lighter, and with the same range and speed. It is also suitable for underground launching sites to provide maximum protection against attack. Eventually it is planned to have a total of thirteen squadrons of *Atlas* missiles and twelve squadrons of *Titans* (a total of 264 missiles), including six *Atlas* squadrons with twelve missiles permanently on launchers.

These missiles are to be followed by the *Minuteman* ICBM which is a three-stage solid-fuelled missile. Because of its solid fuel, *Minuteman* has three main advantages over its predecessors. Since solid fuel can be stored ready within the missile, it can be launched in a fraction of the time needed to prepare liquid-fuelled missiles for firing; simplicity of storage and maintenance makes it easy to 'harden' so that it can be protected underground to withstand all explosive attack short of a direct hit; most important of all, the solid fuel development also makes it mobile. Indeed it was planned to have a proportion of *Minuteman* missiles always on the move round the United States mounted on railway wagons while others will be positioned in small hardened sites. In December 1961, however, the plan for mobile *Minutemen* was abandoned on grounds of cost and it is envisaged as a consequence that the number of stationary missiles will be increased from 600 to 900 on completion of the programme. The development of this missile has been particularly swift and it is anticipated that the first *Minuteman* missiles will be operational by the end of 1963, one year ahead of the original schedule. Together with *Polaris, Minuteman* is clearly regarded as the chief weapon in the United States missile armoury. Production capacity is to be doubled and additional funds are being made available for research and development so that improved versions of the missile can come into service earlier than anticipated.[14]

The United States Air Force is also considering plans for operating in outer space. A manned hypersonic research aircraft, *X 15*, is being developed to obtain data particularly with regard to heating, stability control and the problems of re-entry into the atmosphere. The objective is to attain a speed of Mach 7 (over 4,500 miles per hour) and heights of up to 100 miles. *X 15* is reported as having reached a speed of 4,093 miles per hour on 9 November 1961 after leaving its carrier, a *B 52*. Contracts have been awarded to two competitive companies to produce design studies for a piloted rocket-boosted glider to be known as the *Dyna Soar* (dynamic soaring), destined to soar around the earth for very great distances at near satellite speed. Used as a reconnaissance vehicle, *Dyna Soar* might make surprise attacks impossible. Its development as a strategic bomber has also been envisaged. Considerable progress has already been achieved with the development of the satellite-borne *Midas* (Missile Defence Alarm System) which is designed to detect missiles immediately after launching, and the Administration is giving every encouragement to this project. By October 1961 four *Midas* satellites had been launched. When *Midas* is operational a network of the satellites will relay information to ground 'readout' stations, complementing the information provided by the ballistic missile early warning system. The British Government announced on 19 July 1961 that one of these stations would be established at Kirkbride, Cumberland, in the United Kingdom.[15]

The Administration is taking this aspect of defence very seriously and in 1961 allocated additional funds for the development of a number of space research programmes, including *Dyna Soar*, *Advent*, *Defender* and *Discoverer*. Further projects include the construction of vehicles which may be used as weapons-platforms in space, the establishment of lunar bases and, finally, the launching of permanent space stations. On 5 May 1961 the Americans succeeded in their first attempt at manned space flight when Commander Alan Shepard made a 15 minute flight in a *Mercury* capsule fired from a *Redstone* rocket. President Kennedy subsequently requested, in a Special Message to Congress on 25 May 1961, a further acceleration in America's space efforts with the primary aim of landing a man on the moon, and bringing him back to earth, by 1970.

SAC's ability to launch a second blow after a surprise attack is determined by the amount of warning and the speed of reaction of the forces under its command. It does not expect more than fifteen minutes' warning of a missile attack. Its ability to retaliate is ensured by the following measures: the maintenance of a constant alert force; the dispersal of aircraft; the so-called 'reflex programme'; the 'hardening' of missile bases.

A certain number of aircraft on each base is on a 24-hour-a-day alert and the ultimate goal is to have one-third of the bomber force on runway alert. On 18 January 1961 General Power announced that SAC has a number of *B 52* bombers continuously in the air on a round-the-clock basis so as to reduce to a minimum the time required to respond to any hostile action by an aggressor. In his special Defence Budget message on 28 March 1961 President Kennedy stated that he was seeking to be in a position to place one-eighth of the entire heavy bomber force on airborne alert at any time, and proposed that about half of the total force should be maintained on ground alert.

Because of the limits imposed by runway space and flight control, a dispersal programme is now underway which aims at establishing only one *B 47* wing and one *B 52* wing per base. This permits a greater number of aircraft to be airborne and ready to retaliate within the expected fifteen minutes' warning period; it also has the advantage, since there are more bases with fewer planes on each, of increasing the number of targets which would have to be knocked out in a surprise enemy missile attack.

The Reflex Programme ensures a rotation of *B 47* wings between the United States and overseas bases. The squadrons are sent to the overseas bases for a short period only, during which time they remain on actual alert, and the constant flying to and fro provides excellent training for the crews.

According to SAC's concept, while aircraft should be airborne before the actual blow occurs, missiles should survive the surprise attack. In order to ensure their effectiveness for a retaliatory blow they are being 'hardened' by placing them in underground concrete and steel silos, which have now been developed. These silos will contain all the necessary equipment; the roof will be opened after the attack and the missile will be launched from the underground ramp. They will also be more widely dispersed than originally envisaged. The concept of grouping missiles has been given up in favour of individual missile silos controlled from a central control post, at distances sufficient to ensure that a nuclear weapon could never destroy two at a time.

Target identification is done with the help of the various sources of information available to SAC. Crews are trained on targets selected according to the framework of SAC's emergency war plan, which is continually being adapted in the light of fresh information. The crews know the predetermined targets and the mission routes they must follow to reach them. The Positive Control Procedure guarantees that the aircraft, should they be launched on an actual alert, will not spark-off war as a result of a false alarm. They will fly to certain points well off the Soviet borders and will then return unless they receive special instructions to proceed.

The Commander-in-Chief of SAC asked that the *Polaris* MRBM missile-launching submarines of the United States Navy be also placed under his command, on the grounds that such an integration would eliminate duplication and increase the effectiveness of a nuclear counter-blow. But the Navy strongly and successfully contested this claim.

Subsequently, a central agency was set up to direct strategic target planning for an integrated missile-bomber force; this was preferred to the concept of a separate force comprising all land- and sea-based strategic nuclear weapons independently of the Service commands. It is, however, significant that General Power, while remaining Commander-in-Chief of the Strategic Air Command, is the planning agent for the Joint Chiefs of Staff. In announcing the creation of this new central agency in August 1960, Mr. Gates, the then Secretary of Defence, said: 'Although we foresee a continuing requirement for manned bombers for as far into the future as we can now see, with the passage of time an increasingly greater portion of the retaliatory force will be in ballistic missiles—both land and sea based.[16]

The Navy's claim to keep part of the strategic deterrent in its own control has been strengthened by the speed with which *Polaris* and the nuclear submarines to carry it have been produced for service—almost three years ahead of the original timetable. This nuclear-powered submarine fleet will make a most important contribution to the retaliatory force. By the end of 1960, two *Polaris* submarines were operational, three more had been launched and four were under construction, out of a total of fourteen authorised by the Eisenhower Administration.[17] President Kennedy increased the construction programme for 1961 from five submarines to ten, and has since recommended the construction of a further twenty-two, plus one additional tender, making a total force of forty-one submarines. The delivery schedule has also been speeded up so that from June 1963 the submarines should be delivered at the rate of one a month.[18] Each submarine will have a complement of sixteen *Polaris* missiles. By the end of 1961, six submarines with a total of ninety-six missiles were at sea.

By agreement with the British Government, facilities for a submarine depot ship and a floating dock are provided in Holy Loch in Scotland. This does not appear to give Great Britain a say in the use of the *Polaris* missiles on submarines operating from Holy Loch as do the agreements concerning bomber bases and *Thor* MRBM sites in the United Kingdom. Indeed, the *Polaris* submarines using the Holy Loch base will remain under the independent control of the United States Government and will not be assigned to SACEUR for his NATO tasks either.[19] However, in making the announcement of the *Polaris* agreement the British Prime Minister said:

> The deployment and use in periods of emergency of the submarine depot ship and associated facilities in the United Kingdom will be a matter of joint consultation between the two Governments. . . . Wherever these submarines may be, I am perfectly satisfied that no decision to use these missiles will ever be taken without the fullest possible previous consultation, and, of course, it is worth recalling that these mechanisms have a greater degree of flexibility than perhaps some of the present methods of launching the deterrent.[20]

The *Polaris* is the first American solid-fuel strategic ballistic missile. The problems of storage, launching at sea and rapid preparation demanded a ready-charged missile in preference to one using liquid propellants. Solid fuels are also more reliable and safer. *Polaris* is a two-stage rocket and three versions are projected. A1, the present operational version, has a range of over 1,250 miles; A2, which is expected to be operational in 1962, will have a range of over 1,500 miles; and A3, expected to be ready for service in 1964 (a year earlier than originally planned), has a proposed range of over 2,500 miles. The explosive power of the nuclear warhead has not been disclosed but it is probably of the order of one megaton, or fifty times as powerful as the Hiroshima bomb.[21] The missile submarine is the functional complement of the missile itself and is specially adapted to its purpose. Conventionally-powered submarines are not considered suitable for carrying *Polaris* as they are too easily detected—they have to surface from time to time, and also need to take in air in order to charge their electric batteries and expel exhaust. Nuclear submarines can spend several weeks submerged and need to return to port only every few months to change crews and take on supplies. It is thought to be possible, however, for *Polaris* missiles to be put on merchant-type surface vessels. It is also considered that *Polaris* missiles may be adaptable for use as land-based weapons and be carried on railway wagons and barges. A simpler and smaller version than the submarine type would probably be required for this purpose. Plans have been made to develop an MRBM small enough to be carried, together with the necessary launching equipment, on a lorry.

In addition to the *Polaris* submarines, the United States Navy has a nuclear strike capacity in the United States First, Second, Sixth and Seventh Fleets, each comprising about fifty ships and having aircraft carriers as a nucleus. The Second Fleet, which operates from the east coast of the United States, is also designated as the NATO Striking Fleet Atlantic.

(ii) *The British retaliatory forces*

Bomber Command, responsible for the delivery of British nuclear fission and fusion bombs, consists of four separate forces: the medium-bomber force consisting of squadrons of the three different V-bombers, and subject to national control only; the reconnaissance force; the newly-established missile force, consisting of sixty *Thor* missiles subject to joint United States-United Kingdom control; and finally the force put at the disposal of SACEUR to take part in his atomic strike plan and in reconnaissance, consisting of medium-bombers of the *Valiant* type and light-bombers of the *Canberra* type, subject to SACEUR's control.

The main element is the V-bomber force composed of Vickers *Valiants*, Avro *Vulcans* and Handley Page *Victors*, all capable of carrying nuclear or conventional weapons. Their performance compares favourably, as regards speed and altitude, with that of the bomber aircraft in the Soviet and United States Air Forces. They can be refuelled in flight from *Valiant* jet tankers. Progress has been made in the development of a guided stand-off bomb, *Blue Steel*, with a range of up to 300 miles. *Blue Steel* was expected to become operational in 1962 but in fact is not likely to be ready until much later. As the Mark 2 versions of the *Vulcan* and *Victor* come into squadron service, the *Valiants*, which in the past have formed a large element of the nuclear deterrent forces, will be withdrawn from the strategic role. A number have been assigned to SACEUR for tactical use in place of and supplementing the *Canberras* at present assigned; and they will give SACEUR's atomic strike forces a greater night and all-weather capability.

The Mark 2 V-bombers will have a longer range and higher ceiling and will also carry the powered stand-off bomb, *Blue Steel*. To arm these bombers there are growing stocks of British nuclear weapons, of both megaton and kiloton range.

The medium-bomber force has a range of some 3,000 miles which will be considerably increased as the Mark 2 versions come into service and will cover almost one hundred per cent of the principal Soviet cities and industrial installations. It is equipped with high-definition radar enabling it to bomb by night or through cloud from 50,000 feet. For defence, these bombers rely on elaborate electronic counter-measures equipment capable of jamming enemy radar and anti-aircraft missiles. Reconnaissance is effected by visual means or by radar, which has an outstanding capability: the entire North Atlantic can be covered in four sorties of a reconnaissance plane. *Thor* missiles have a range of 600–1,500 nautical miles if fired by the normal method, but can be fired at lower ranges by the 'lofted' method. The accuracy is said to be a circle of probable error of two miles at maximum range.

Like the Strategic Air Command, Bomber Command has concentrated on the problem of immediate reaction to an alert. While it is assumed that adequate strategic warning would be available through political and intelligence channels, the tactical warning would be short, in particular in the case of a missile attack. In a period of tension the aircraft would be directed to dispersal fields which are five times more numerous than those in normal use; this plan and the training of the aircrews to take off within three minutes after the tactical alert assure a very rapid reaction.

The existing NATO and North American radar installations will not provide warning of attack by ballistic missile, but will give the United Kingdom adequate warning of an airborne attack. The American-British ballistic missile early-warning system with stations in Alaska and Greenland and a third under construction in Great Britain, will give about fifteen minutes' warning of a missile attack from sites within the Soviet Union. This should suffice to get a great part of both SAC and RAF bombers off the ground. From missiles sited on the Iron Curtain, the system would give only four to five minutes' warning to the United Kingdom. This would be sufficient, however, to see a substantial proportion of the V-bomber force in the air.

Satisfactory arrangements for continuous target co-ordination exist between the Royal Air Force and the United States Strategic Air Command and SACEUR. This is particularly important as in case of an attack, for the present at least, the first retaliatory blows would have to be struck by British Bomber Command and the American bombers in Great Britain, Spain and North Africa, since SAC's main bomber fleet from America would still be crossing the Atlantic and the North Pole.

British Bomber Command is confident that the Soviet air defence can at present be penetrated and that the missions can be successfully carried out, although some losses have to be expected. The V-bombers are to be equipped with *Blue Steel*, the stand-off bomb, which can be launched some distance from the target, avoiding the close defences. The *Thor* missile at present in use may be expected to remain operational until about the middle of the 1960s. It has, of course, the great disadvantage of being a liquid-fuelled static missile. It needs a count-down of at least a quarter of an hour for fuelling, although it may be held at shorter periods of readiness if required. The decision originally taken by the British Government in favour of the *Blue Streak* long-range ballistic missile, a liquid-fuelled and fixed-site missile, was rescinded in 1960[22] and it seems to be no longer the intention of the British Government to develop an independent British missile.

Undoubtedly one of the factors in the decision to abandon the development of *Blue Streak* was the need to provide for mobility in the future planning of nuclear weapons. Long before this decision was taken, it was clear that liquid-fuelled fixed-site missiles would be obsolescent before 1965, and the 1960 British White Paper on Defence stated that 'the possibilities of mobile launchers, whether aircraft or submarines, for long-range delivery of nuclear warheads are being investigated.'

In the summer of 1960 it was announced that the British Government proposed to buy *Skybolt* for the Royal Air Force if and when it was developed for use by the American Air Force[23]. British representatives have been engaged in the work on *Skybolt* from the beginning in conjunction with the United States Air Force and the Douglas Aircraft Corporation. *Skybolt* is scheduled to be ready for service in 1964.

It has been suggested alternatively that Britain should produce her own air-to-ground rocket, either by developing a longer-range version of *Blue Steel* or by developing a low-level missile that could fly below an enemy radar screen. This would seem possible as a result of work done in the development of a general-purpose aircraft, the *TSR 2*. This is designed to have a supersonic, low-flying, all-weather capability and in its strike and recon-naissance role to be a suitable replacement for the *Canberra*. The British Navy's *Buccaneer* (NA 39), a low-level, long-range strike aircraft, is expected in service in 1962.

The 1961 White Paper on Defence made it clear that the British Government intends to remain an independent nuclear power, even if it must become dependent upon the United States for the supply of missiles to carry the British-made warheads. The Government reaffirmed its declared intention, announced when the *Blue Streak* missile project was abandoned, to acquire from America air-launched *Skybolt* missiles to be used in con-junction with the V-bomber force. On grounds of cost, and perhaps also of American reluctance to make other missiles available, it is not intended to acquire *Polaris*.

> Subject to the successful completion of its development programme, we plan to introduce *Skybolt*, the air launched ballistic missile being developed in the United States, in the mid-1960s. Production weapons will be bought outright and will be carried by *Vulcan 2*. They will be fitted with British warheads. . . . The speed of reaction of the Mark 2 V-bombers and their equipment, first with *Blue Steel* and later with *Skybolt*, ensures that the V-force will continue to provide an effective deterrent under our independent control during the next decade.[24]

The consequences of this decision, both for Britain and in

terms of the British defence contribution to NATO, are discussed in the next chapter.

(iii) *Future French retaliatory forces*

After being twice rejected by the Senate and after long and stormy Parliamentary debate, the French National Assembly finally enacted on 6 December 1960 the Government's five-year military programme, of which the most significant feature was the creation of an independent nuclear striking force.

The law provides for an expenditure of nearly 11,800 m. N.F. (£850 m.), about a third of the total military expenditure proposed for 1960–4, and includes an allocation of about 7,500 m. N.F. (£525 m.) to the nuclear striking force. More than 5,000 m. N.F. (£350 m.) is allocated for research on and construction of nuclear weapons; about 850 m. N.F. (£60 m.) for the programme for fifty strategic bombers (*Mirage IV*) and about 1,250 m. N.F. (£90 m.) for research on ballistic missiles. The Assembly's Defence Committee has estimated that a further 14,200 m. N.F. (£1,025 m.) will be required for the period 1965–9, viz. nuclear warheads 4,000 m. N.F., strategic missiles 7,200 m. N.F. and 3,000 m. N.F. for three nuclear-powered submarines with missiles.

The delivery of atomic or fission bombs for the *Mirage IV* should begin in 1963, be 'satisfactory' in 1964 and be completed by 1968. Hydrogen or fusion weapons are not expected to be ready until 1969.

The means of delivery adopted—fifty *Mirage IV* bombers—is claimed to be a stopgap only. Delivery dates for the *Mirage IV* (expected range 4,400 km. (2,750 miles) at a speed of Mach 0·9 and with a ceiling of 18,000 metres (58,000 feet) have not been given except that it has been stated that all would be in operation by 1965.

France carried out three successful test explosions of atomic weapons in the Sahara in 1960 and one test in 1961. The first is reported to have had an explosive power of 70 kilotons whereas the second, third and fourth are believed to have had a power of only a few kilotons. The purpose of the last three would appear to have been as a step towards producing tactical atomic weapons for use by ground forces or warheads for short-range rockets. A small atomic bomb of this type would also be required for use as a detonator of a hydrogen bomb, and these test explosions confirm that France is continuing her efforts to produce her own hydrogen bombs.

(iv) *NATO Forces*

In addition to the *Jupiter* missile bases in Italy and projected in Turkey, which will be under the operational control of SACEUR, the Tactical Air Forces assigned to NATO have a nuclear strike capacity. At present, however, SACEUR's nuclear weapons are designed for use in a tactical rôle and there is no NATO strategic nuclear force comparable to the Strategic Air Command or the British Bomber Command. The suggestion of the United States for a NATO multilateral MRBM force and their offer to make available five *Polaris* missiles and submarines by 1963 and to allow a further 100 missiles to be purchased thereafter was considered by the NATO Ministerial meeting in Paris in December 1960. The suggestion was still under study at the time of the December 1961 Council meeting and no decision seems likely in the immediate future.

THE MISSILE GAP

This survey of the nuclear capabilities within the alliance shows a diversity of means which should make it impossible for an aggressor to count on destroying them completely. The wide dispersal of Western strategic forces makes a simultaneous surprise attack on all of them impossible. Mr. Gilpatrick, the United States Deputy Secretary of Defense, stated on 21 October 1961:

> Our forces are so deployed and protected that a sneak attack could not effectively disarm us. The destructive power which the United States could bring to bear even after a Soviet surprise attack upon our forces would be as great as—perhaps greater than—the total un-damaged force which the enemy can threaten to launch against the United States in a first strike. In short, we have a second-strike capability which is at least as extensive as what the Soviets can deliver by striking first.

Most students of defence strategy, especially in America, feared that the early sixties would prove a period of extreme instability and weakness because the Soviet Union was expected to have a considerable lead in long- and medium-range missiles whilst the American deterrent would still depend upon manned

F

bombers and fixed-site missiles such as *Thor*, both vulnerable to nuclear surprise attack.

The 'missile gap' to Soviet advantage, allied to the 'intelligence gap' (due to the fact that it is impossible to conceal Western missile sites whereas the Russians are able to keep the details of theirs secret), could produce a situation, it was feared, where it would be at least rational for the Soviet Union to think they could destroy a very high percentage of American retaliatory power by surprise attack and thus make the risks worth while. Even if they did not take this step, at least the knowledge of their superiority in the missile field would encourage Russian aggressive diplomatic exploitation of every Western weakness and difficulty.

These fears were such that President Kennedy made the missile gap a prominent feature of his 1960 Election campaign. It was then estimated that by the end of 1961 the Soviet Union would have 500 to 1,000 ICBMs while the United States would only have seventy. In fact, while there is obvious difficulty in assessing Soviet missile strength, the estimate at the end of 1961 of Soviet ICBMs is between fifty and seventy-five while the United States has sixty-three ICBMs (*Atlas* and *Titan*) and ninety-six *Polaris* missiles operational, in addition to MRBMs in Europe and bomber wings. By 1965 it is predicted that the United States will have an 'invulnerable' solid-fuel missile force of about 1,500 *Minuteman* and *Polaris* missiles—in addition to first-generation liquid-fuel missiles and manned bombers. Thus the outcome for the early 1960s has proved very different from the forecast—although for Europe the growing Soviet force of operational MRBMs represents a considerable threat.

A wide gap between Soviet and American rocket development would carry very serious implications for the West. The shock which the launching of the first *Sputnik* some years ago caused to public opinion will still be remembered. The NATO Summit Conference of December 1957 was a direct consequence and the decision regarding interdependence was the Western reply to the Soviet challenge. Four years have gone by, and the Soviet Union has achieved further astonishing successes while interdependence is still little more than a word. The outstanding achievement of putting the first man into space on 12 April 1961 further underlined the Soviet lead. The first *cosmonaut*, Major Yuri Gagarin, made an impact on the Western world almost as great as the first *Sputnik*. Although it had been widely believed that the Russians would be the first to put a man into orbit, the fact of their doing so emphasised their immense advance in rocket technology, which must have great military significance. The precision with which these rockets can be launched indicates that the Soviet Union possesses guidance systems which should allow her to direct an ICBM onto a target as small as a single missile base.

It is widely recognised in the United States that the main reasons for this gap have been organisational confusion and inter-service rivalry. At the beginning of 1959 the National Aeronautics and Space Administration—NASA—was created for the purpose of organising and operating a national exploration and research programme. And more recently, following the success of *Lunik III*, responsibility for the research, development, testing and engineering of military space programmes has been vested in the United States Air Force. It is therefore to be hoped that the space programme will proceed more effectively and at less overall cost. President Kennedy's special message to Congress on 26 May 1961, with its frank recognition of America's lag in space developments and its avowed intention of devoting the necessary funds and resources to take a leading rôle, including landing a man on the moon by 1970, was a most encouraging sign in this direction.

However, it is not good enough just to rely on American efforts. The United States is at the same time continuing research and production of all other types of weapons and cannot be expected to devote unlimited funds to the space and missile programmes. There is the strongest case for a pooling of scientific abilities and a redistribution of efforts among all the NATO allies. A Soviet break-through to space vehicles for military uses or to an anti-missile missile would undoubtedly tilt the balance sharply in their favour. The Western allies will need to use all their talents, energies and resources to the full if we are not to be left hopelessly behind.

An immediate and urgent task for the West is to attain the highest possible degree of mobility for our deterrent forces. The 'hardening' of missile bases has minimised the danger of surprise attack, but this does not provide sufficient protection in view of the accuracy attained by Soviet missiles. Of our existing forces,

only the submarines are invulnerable to surprise attack. The
ICBMS and MRBMS, even if 'hardened' in underground silos, can be
destroyed if the accuracy of the missile is not less than the error
of $1\frac{1}{4}$ miles reported by the Soviet Union in the Pacific tests of
ICBMS early in 1960. The aircraft are invulnerable only if airborne.
The danger of a surprise attack was brought to light in a perhaps
over-dramatic form by General Power, Commander-in-Chief of
SAC when he said in 1960:

> The total number of installations and facilities from which we can
> launch nuclear-powered aircraft and missiles at this moment, is
> only about a hundred. All of these facilities present soft targets. It
> would take an average of three missiles in the current stage of
> development to give an aggressor a mathematical probability of
> 95 per cent that he can destroy one given soft target from 5,000
> miles away. This means that with only some 300 ballistic missiles,
> the Soviets could virtually wipe out our entire nuclear strike
> ability within a span of thirty minutes.[25]

The vulnerability thus disclosed will be reduced when the
solid-fuelled *Minuteman* ICBM and more *Polaris* MRBMS become
operational in the next few years. It should be possible to develop
mobile launching ramps for all our missiles. The fact that *Polaris*
has become operational several years ahead of schedule and that
the date for the deployment of *Minuteman* has been advanced by
two years is the reason for a more optimistic view of the missile
gap than was possible two or three years ago. American technology, in concentrating on solid-fuelled missiles and mobility,
may have provided the answer to the hitherto vast advantage of
the closed political system of the Soviet Union in the defence field.

On balance the organisation of Western strategic deterrent
forces has been maintained at a sufficient level to ensure effective
retaliation against serious challenge and to provide guarantees
against elimination by surprise attack. For the time being the
West has a lead in manned bombers. Thanks to the United States
bases in Europe, it also has an advantage in MRBMS, since the capacity to destroy Soviet sites is greater than the Soviet capacity to
destroy United States sites. The situation will become less favourable, however, as increasing reliance is placed by both sides on
ICBMS. Russian superiority in ICBMS is, in 1962, open to question,
and in any event counterbalanced by land, sea and air-launched

MRBMs. It is, therefore, not yet serious. But, as has already been made clear, the tremendous strides Russia has made in missile and space research and development carry a very grave warning for the West.

TACTICAL USE OF NUCLEAR WEAPONS

The introduction of nuclear weapons for tactical use in the NATO Shield forces in Europe was decided as early as 1954. At the Council meeting in December that year it was decided to abandon the goal, adopted at Lisbon in 1952, of ninety-six divisions to be ready within thirty days (of which there were to be twenty-five standing divisions on the Central sector). The revised goal was thirty standing divisions on the Central sector, including the twelve divisions to be supplied by Germany under the Paris Agreement of 1954, armed with 'modern' (i.e. atomic) weapons. The reasons for this change of plan were that it seemed on the one hand improbable that the Lisbon target would ever be attained, and, on the other, that reliance on nuclear firepower to offset the immense superiority in manpower of the Soviet Union was a highly attractive proposition. Since then NATO planning has officially been based on the principle that nuclear weapons would be used tactically in reply to almost any aggression.

This decision was one of the most unfortunate taken by the alliance, and with the retrospective wisdom of hindsight it is easy to say that it should not have been taken without a prior examination of all the consequences. But we must remember that in 1954 progress towards the Lisbon goal of ninety-six divisions of conventional forces was negligible. At the same time the American strategic deterrent was unchallenged; no *Sputniks* were on the horizon to blow away the doctrine of massive retaliation. There was thus little thought in the minds of NATO commanders or the Council that the so-called tactical weapons would or could be used in a limited war situation where there was not automatic and simultaneous resort to the strategic nuclear strike forces as well.

The central problem of today is whether any nuclear weapons can be used, and if so what weapons, to meet a limited conventional aggression without involving an extremely high risk of escalation into a global nuclear war. This problem was naturally not considered by the NATO Council in 1954 because according to the premises then held—that any war in Europe would auto-matically lead to global nuclear war—the circumstances which create the problem in the present situation of nuclear stalemate or mutual deterrence could never exist. The obvious advantage of using nuclear weapons to redress the balance of conventional forces was self-evident in the light of contemporary strategic doctrine, and the overriding drawback which poses the problem today was not then regarded as a relevant consideration.

It was also thought, when the decision was taken, that it would be many years before the Soviet Union could develop similar weapons and that the West would have a clear lead for a con-siderable time. This hope has not materialised: it is generally believed that both in equipping their troops with comparable atomic weapons and in training them to counter atomic weapons used against them, the Russians have at least kept pace with, and have probably even surpassed, us. These aspects of tactical weapons are more fully discussed in the later chapter on NATO ground forces.

If an attempt is to be made to limit hostilities to the tactical use of nuclear weapons, then a clear distinction has to be drawn between the strategic and the tactical use of nuclear weapons. Also, in my judgment, a clear distinction is essential between the use of even the smallest atomic weapon under development and conventional artillery. If we are to avoid an enemy's resort to strategic weapons as a result of mistaking our intentions, then it is necessary that any distinction must also be comprehensible to the enemy. Unhappily it is impossible to label a weapon 'tactical' thus making it clear that, for the moment at least, the level of nuclear exchange is not to be raised to strategic proportions. An agreement between NATO and the Warsaw Pact countries on what is a tactical weapon, or what is a tactical *use of* a nuclear weapon, would also seem impossible—or at least as difficult as, and less worth while than, an arms control agreement.

Even if we ignore the enemy's reactions, the problem bristles with difficulties. To add to the confusion, we meet two appar-ently contradictory arguments: on the one hand that it is impos-sible to distinguish between strategic and tactical weapons or even between the strategic and tactical use of such weapons; on the other that some of the smaller weapons, at least, are indis-tinguishable from conventional artillery and should be treated as such. Indeed when NATO decided to compensate for its numerical inferiority by introducing atomic weapons, it classified them as 'conventional'.[26]

THE PROBLEM OF DEFINITION

But although rarely admitted, this confusion is perhaps encouraged in order that one kind of weapon may be authorised or allowed in the guise of another, that is, weapons with a strategic capability may be authorised to fulfil tactical tasks. There are essentially two problems concealed in the arguments in the preceding paragraph, not one. There is first the problem posed by the Allied Tactical Air Forces in Europe which are composed of fighter-bombers equipped with American nuclear bombs, probably of the Hiroshima size, but are also capable of carrying fusion bombs of megaton size. It was the proposal by General Norstad that these planes should be replaced in due course by *Polaris* missiles that led to so much discussion in November and December 1960 and to the decision of the North Atlantic Council that the problem and the American offer to supply *Polaris* for SACEUR should be studied. Secondly there is the problem of the growing number and variety of ground-to-ground atomic missiles designed as Army support weapons. These problems require separate analysis and different conclusions.

In the event of war, the mission of the Tactical Air Forces would be in the first few days to participate in the nuclear strike plan, that is to say to engage in strategic bombing; in the second phase, they would be required to bomb tactical targets and give ground support. This illustrates the impossibility of classifying a great number of nuclear weapons as either 'strategic' or 'tactical'; it is the *use* which is strategic or tactical and not the weapon itself. Many weapons are capable of being used upon either strategic or tactical targets.

At this point it is usual to complicate matters further by showing how difficult it is to distinguish between strategic and tactical targets or tasks. However, their broad meaning is surely understood clearly enough. It is rather like being asked to define an elephant: we may have difficulty in finding the right words to describe the animal but we all recognise one when it comes along.

But strategic and tactical *use* cannot be defined by reference to the target alone. Such a distinction would permit an ICBM launched from America, with a megaton warhead, to a point on or near a battlefield to be classed as 'tactical'. This is just as unacceptable as calling one of the proposed ground-to-ground missiles with a range of 500 or 600 miles a tactical weapon. Where the explosive power of the smallest warheads varies from two to ten kilotons (or the equivalent of 2,000 to 10,000 tons of TNT) it is unreasonable to suppose that weapons of this magnitude (bearing in mind also the additional effects of radiation) could be used on any target without risking the spread of a limited war into an all-out global war. Clearly, therefore, no distinction is tenable which does not take account of the range and explosive power of the weapon as well as the target to which it is directed.

Thus the *Polaris* missile is just as much a strategic weapon in the hands of General Norstad as it is under the control of the United States Navy. It would in any case be extremely wasteful to use this weapon, and its megaton warhead, against traditional tactical targets. Even if *Polaris* is given to General Norstad he would also need some manned fighter-bombers to give close support to his ground forces with conventional bombs in the event of their being engaged in hostilities where it is desirable to seek to restrict them to non-nuclear weapons. This conclusion appears to have been broadly recognised in the discussions at the North Atlantic Council in December 1960 since there was reference to a nuclear strike force, which would seem to imply strategic rather than tactical tasks. The creation of such a force, and indeed the nuclear capacity of the existing Tactical Air Forces, poses the same political problems as do the strategic forces.

On the other hand, while any distinction drawn between nuclear weapons is an arbitrary one, it does seem possible to draw a distinction between weapons which have a strategic capacity and those which do not. I would suggest that to qualify for classification as a tactical weapon, a missile should have a range of not more than 150 miles (240 km.) and a warhead no bigger than 0·25 kiloton, i.e. equivalent to 250 tons of TNT or over twenty-five times as big as the largest type of conventional bomb used in the Second World War.

There will be objection to the above classification on the grounds that it is too narrow and that in specifying so small a warhead I have adopted an ideal rather than a practical standard. Details of the development of small warheads are classified as

secret, but it is doubtful whether any exist at present as small as
0·25 kiloton. However, it is likely that it will be possible to
produce these very small warheads for operational use in the
next two or three years. It is reported[27] that among the nuclear
weapons tested in Nevada in 1958 were seven with an explosive
yield of less than 100 tons, and that one had a yield of thirty-six
tons and another as low a yield as six tons—no more than that of
the biggest conventional bomb of the last war.

For purposes of political control and in order to try and restrict
hostilities to limited nuclear warfare, it may well be necessary to
have several classifications for the tactical use of atomic weapons,
based on targets, range and explosive yield. Thus there would be
not one decision to use tactical atomic weapons, but separate
decisions—to move from the first stage to the second, and so on.
It is, however, conceded that the variety of available weapons,
and the consequent even greater variety of range of firepower,
makes both limitation and control extremely difficult.

ATOMIC WEAPONS

Despite the enthusiasm which greeted the 1954 decision, and
the American undertaking in December 1957 to accelerate
deliveries of suitable weapons, atomic weapons for the use of
ground forces have in fact been very slow to make their appearance in the combat zone. The American troops were the first to
be equipped with them, and the British troops in Northern Germany followed; but the contingents of other nations in the Shield
forces were only during 1961 beginning to receive their first
nuclear weapons apart from the dual-purpose howitzers supplied
to some allies in 1959. In every case the Americans are supplying the weapons to other nations under a system of dual control.
The missile is controlled by the user country but the atomic
warheads remain under American custody. The weapon cannot
be used without the sanction of SACEUR in his dual role as the
Supreme NATO Commander and as the representative of the
United States Government.

The weapons mostly in use as surface-to-surface, Army support
weapons are the *Honest John*, *Corporal*, and the 280 mm. atomic
gun, with warheads ranging from one to twenty kilotons in
explosive power. *Honest John*[28] is an unguided missile with a
range of 15–20 miles (25–30 km.). A more compact version,

Little John, suitable for air transport, has reached an early production stage. The 280 mm. *atomic cannon* has a range of about fourteen miles but is extremely heavy and immobile, and it is likely soon to be taken out of service. The *Corporal*, the most modern of the missiles in service, has a range of about seventy miles and is the weapon of the two British missile regiments in North Germany. The *Sergeant* is designed as the successor to the *Corporal*. Although of similar range, *Sergeant* has the great advantage of a solid fuel propellant and an inertial guidance system. This means that it is a much more mobile and efficient missile. Successful test firings of the *Sergeant* have already taken place and it is expected to be operational in 1962. There is also the *Redstone*, an improved version of the German V2 of the Second World War and the largest guided missile outside the Soviet Union until 1959. It has a range of 200 miles. The *Pershing*, a two-stage, solid-fuelled improved version of *Redstone*, had successful test firings during 1960 and has a range of 300 miles.

In addition to the above missiles, which are all of American origin, the British Government is producing *Blue Water*. This is a solid-fuelled missile which will be highly mobile and transportable by air and will have a range of 100 miles. It was hoped that this would be adopted as the NATO standard Army support guided missile and it was reported that the West German Government was interested in it. However, it seems certain that the *Sergeant* will become the NATO weapon.

The most revolutionary weapon is the American *Davy Crockett* which is designed as a two-man weapon and which can be carried by hand or mounted on a small truck. It will give small units of troops firepower equivalent to that possessed by conventional heavy artillery. It will use the same atomic warhead as the United States Air Force *Falcon*, a short-range air-to-air missile, and while its explosive power has not been disclosed it is understood to be less than one kiloton. The *Davy Crockett* is due to go into production during 1962. Its introduction into service will mark a new era in atomic weapons, since it will not require a special unit or regiment but can be used by any infantry battalion in place of the conventional mortar. It may, indeed, become a company weapon.

In addition to the above Army support missiles there are the *Matador*, a jet-powered surface-to-surface 'flying-bomb' missile with a range of 500 miles, and the *Mace*, an improved version of *Matador* with a range of 700–1,200 miles, which are in service with the United States Air Force in Europe. They are designed to supplement the manned fighter-bombers in discharging the missions of the Tactical Air Forces. Because of the range and rôle of these missiles, their use should be subject to the same rules and considerations as are proposed for the Tactical Air Forces (already discussed above); they should be treated quite separately from the shorter range Army weapons.

All the Army support missiles can be used with conventional high explosive warheads as well as with atomic ones. It is, however, obvious that they are most unlikely to be used to this end since conventional firepower is more cheaply and efficiently provided by conventional artillery. Also, because of the great difference in explosive power between a conventional shell and the smallest atomic warhead, if the missiles are used in a conventional role they would need substantial support from conventional artillery to be effective.

The military limitations of these existing atomic weapons are greatly increased by the cumbrous equipment required and the time necessary to prepare for firing, due in large measure to the liquid fuel propellant. My own impression on seeing a test firing of a *Corporal* was to doubt whether such weapons could ever be really effective under conditions of active service. However, the emergence of a new generation of solid-fuelled and much more mobile weapons will to a great extent remove these difficulties. This fact, combined with the decision to distribute these weapons to virtually all the European NATO units by 1963, underlines the urgent need for the North Atlantic Council to assess their rôle and to decide how far it is possible to classify the various types. So far this important aspect has been neglected.

It is equally important to establish clearly at the highest level that in no circumstances can any atomic weapon be regarded as equivalent to conventional artillery or be subject to the same rules as to command and control. Whatever the problems of distinguishing between the various types of nuclear weapons and between their strategic and tactical uses, it is essential to draw a clear distinction between the use of any weapon employing nuclear explosives and those using conventional TNT shells.

Chapter VI

THE PROBLEMS OF POLITICAL CONTROL

While the major military problem confronting the West in the nuclear field is ensuring the capacity to retaliate immediately and effectively in the event of a surprise attack, the greatest political problem for the alliance is undoubtedly the political control of nuclear weapons.

Until the end of 1960, the question of the rôle of nuclear weapons and control over their use within the alliance had been deliberately evaded. However, talk of European deterrents and of NATO as a Fourth Power, together with the speeches and proposals of General Norstad, finally put this vital issue on the agenda of the North Atlantic Council meeting. No decisions were taken —except to study the problem in readiness for the next Council meeting in May 1961. The question was then further postponed since a re-examination of the needs of the alliance, both conventional and nuclear, had not been completed. It is probable that the issue would have been further shelved except for the fact that Herr Strauss urged at the December 1961 NATO Council that there should be a re-examination of the proposals for a NATO Nuclear deterrent force.

It is generally conceded that nuclear weapons, because of their special characteristics, must be subject to a degree of political control over and above that considered necessary hitherto for weapons of war. Awareness of the dire consequences for both sides of a war fought with nuclear weapons has revolutionised political and military thinking as much as the development of nuclear weapons has revolutionised war itself, and no-one would dispute the overriding need to keep responsibility for launching the nuclear retaliatory forces of the West firmly in the hands of our political leaders. The problem for the alliance is how to devise effective and credible machinery for joint control which will give all partners in the alliance a share in the vital decisions.

Since Hiroshima and Nagasaki there has been no question that the decision to use nuclear weapons in a *strategic* rôle must be a political one, taken at the highest level. But this decision has been, and still is, wholly national—the decision of the President of the United States or the Prime Minister of Great Britain. Until the era of Soviet thermonuclear capability dawned, there was no need for any other arrangement. But when the doctrine of massive retaliation had to go by the board because of changed circumstances, the whole balance of the relationship between America and the other members of the alliance was changed in consequence. At the moment of writing the principle of political control *exercised by the alliance as a whole* over the nuclear retaliatory forces has not been agreed, let alone the practical problems of 'who, how and when' involved in drawing up the machinery of such control.

When we come to consider the *tactical* use of nuclear weapons, we find that no clear procedure exists for political control over their initial use. As has been said already, so-called tactical use is envisaged of weapons with an explosive power equal to that of the atomic bomb dropped on Hiroshima. Present NATO plans are based on the deployment of such weapons on the Central Front, some of them being designed to support troops in the field. Thus apart from the special military considerations involved in their deployment there is the overriding problem of retaining political control over their initial use. The difficulties involved here are greater and more complex than in the case of the political control of the strategic nuclear forces and in a sense rather different considerations apply. I propose, therefore, to deal first with the more general problem of joint control over the retaliatory forces.

NUCLEAR ANARCHY

At present NATO is an alliance of free and democratic states in which there are two classes of members: those who dispose of nuclear weapons and those who do not. One may deplore the risks attendant upon a proliferation of nuclear powers but it is hardly surprising that France, for example, is seeking to join the nuclear club for reasons of prestige and in order to exert greater influence upon the affairs of the alliance. All the arguments which led

Britain to decide to develop her own independent nuclear weapons are equally valid from the French point of view for France herself, and there is no reason why other members of NATO should not decide to follow suit. The technical difficulties and the expense involved in the development of nuclear capability are formidable, but they are not insuperable (see Appendix B).

The dangers inherent in a situation of nuclear anarchy are grave and very real. The rarely-admitted basic reason for any Government's decision to embark on the development of nuclear weapons is the desire to be able to conduct an independent national foreign policy and to back it up if necessary with the threat of using nuclear weapons. This is a complete negation of the principle of interdependence within the alliance. Although strictly NATO's writ runs only within a defined area, there can be no doubt that the success of the alliance requires a co-ordination of its members' policies elsewhere. It is difficult to see how a NATO member could use nuclear weapons outside Europe without causing immediate repercussions within the NATO area.

From the military point of view a proliferation of national nuclear deterrents is wasteful. In the case of a general war (when one may assume that all of them would be used at the same time), operations against the Soviet Union would be duplicated, because any target co-ordination which takes place today between the United States Strategic Air Command and British Bomber Command, and which may be realised tomorrow between these two and the French Bomber Command, would probably not withstand the impact of an emergency situation in which new events called for completely different decisions. A satisfactory doctrine for the employment of a new weapon has to await the test of war to be proved.

It is also the case that the more a country spends of its defence budget on a nuclear armament programme, the less it will have available to spend on conventional weapons. Admittedly once the production stage has been reached nuclear weapons cost relatively less than conventional ones; but enormous sums are needed for research and development long before an atomic bomb small enough to transport in an aeroplane can be produced. The West has more than enough nuclear bombs and warheads. We are, however, seriously short of troops on the ground, and the capacity of our troops to fight for even a limited period with conventional weapons alone is far below what is needed.

But the fact must be faced that no matter how logical, wise and necessary it may be for the European members of NATO to concentrate on meeting their obligations by contributing their full share towards the collective 'Shield' forces with adequate conventional as well as nuclear capability, they will not be prepared to do this so long as they perceive that the only way to exert any real influence on vital issues affecting the alliance is to develop their own independent nuclear armoury. The Americans make it as difficult as possible for any nation to become a nuclear power by adhering rigidly to the policy laid down by Congress. In accordance with the 'declaration of interdependence' issued by President Eisenhower and Mr. Macmillan on 25 October 1957, the President submitted to Congress proposals for amending the Atomic Energy Act (the McMahon Act) to permit greater nuclear co-operation in the military field with America's allies. An amending Bill was passed on 2 July 1958 which permitted information about nuclear weapons to be disclosed to an allied country which had already made substantial progress in the development of such weapons. In the debates it was made clear that only Britain then fulfilled that condition. But the French have demonstrated that this merely buys time—engendering a lot of ill-will and imposing fresh strains on the alliance in the process; it does not solve the problem.

UNITED STATES POLICY

It really boils down to a question of confidence. Since 1957 two facts have become inescapable: that Europe is becoming less essential to the defence of the United States, and that the United States is vulnerable to attack from Soviet land- or submarine-based Inter-Continental missiles. So long as the deterrent consisted of atomic or thermonuclear bombs dropped from manned bombers, or even of Medium Range Ballistic Missiles, America needed European bases for her own defence, quite apart from her obligations under the North Atlantic Treaty. But as the bombers and short-range missiles are replaced by *Atlas*, *Titan* and *Minuteman*, and submarines carrying *Polaris*, the European bases, although useful, will no longer be essential to America. And with the great cities of America within comfortable range of Soviet missiles, will she really risk annihilation of millions of her people to save Paris or Brussels—or Berlin? The wheel has come full circle: a decade ago many European statesmen were worried lest American confidence in the power of massive retaliation and her own relative invulnerability might wreak nuclear havoc in Europe as the result of pushing the Russians over the brink; their fear now is whether America can be relied upon to commit suicide in the interests of Europe alone and may not prefer to accept some Soviet advance in Europe as a *fait accompli*.

This fear has been strengthened by a statement by Mr. Christian Herter, former United States Secretary of State, made before the Senate Foreign Relations Committee on 21 April 1959 when he was cross-examined prior to his appointment to succeed the late Mr. John Foster Dulles. Mr. Herter is reported as having said: 'I cannot conceive of any President involving us in an all-out nuclear war unless the facts showed clearly we are in danger of all-out devastation ourselves.' Taken by itself this statement is calculated to cause alarm in Europe; but if it is viewed in its context—one of several answers to questions about Berlin and the hypothetical shooting down of a single United States plane by a Soviet aircraft and the action then to be taken—it is clearly not a considered statement of American policy. Indeed few would quarrel with Mr. Herter's reply on the same occasion that he would not favour committing the United States to an *all-out* nuclear war in the initial stages of a conflict with the Soviet Union unless it appeared to be necessary for the protection of the United States.

President Kennedy reaffirmed unequivocally the United States' commitment to Europe in his Inaugural Address and in his message to the North Atlantic Council in February 1961, within three weeks of taking office:

Therefore I pledge the United States, and my own unremitting efforts, to the support of the principles which guide our effort, to the basic concept of unity which gives us strength, and to the institutions we have created to give working life to our common intent.

Effective collective defence is the first mission of our great alliance in NATO. Our task here is to convince any aggressor that an attack on the territory of NATO members would be met with swift and punishing resistance. While relying also on the growing strength of all, the United States will continue its full participation in the common defence effort. I am convinced that the maintenance of

United States military strength in Europe is essential to the security of the Atlantic Community and the free world as a whole. Strength in Europe, like strength here in the United States, is an essential condition of peace.

It is, however, pointless to reiterate the solemn pledges of America's leaders in order to demonstrate how ill-founded such fears are. This is not a matter of fact; it is a matter of faith. These fears can only be exorcised by an act of faith on America's part, i.e. by sharing with her European allies the responsibility of deciding to retaliate with nuclear weapons against Soviet aggression. No-one imagines that such a decision will be easy for America to take, or to work out. One cannot even be certain that it would by itself suffice to halt the proliferation of NATO nuclear powers. But it would be a very powerful factor indeed against the spread of nuclear anarchy; it would also go a long way towards achieving the ideal of interdependence. If we are to avoid a permanent crisis of confidence within the alliance we must make sure that there are no second-class members. The obligations, the responsibilities and the rights must be shared by all.

To a certain extent the question of political control also affects the credibility of the deterrent. It has already been emphasised that credibility is as important as capability in creating an effective deterrent. If European members of the alliance harbour doubts as to whether America will in the last resort risk fearful sacrifices to come to their aid, if the Americans do not feel they can trust other members of the alliance to have the courage of their convictions and exercise their share in the responsibility of using nuclear weapons if need be, how can we expect the Russians to take the deterrent seriously? Manifest doubt and disunity weaken the alliance just as much as shortcomings in military preparedness.

ALTERNATIVE SOLUTIONS

This crisis of confidence has been increasingly recognised in NATO military and political thinking as one of the most serious problems facing the alliance and many suggestions have been made for dealing with it. As well as (i) the ideal solution of comprehensive and controlled multilateral disarmament, there have been proposals for (ii) a non-nuclear club; (iii) a joint European Strategic Force within the framework of WEU; and (iv) NATO as the fourth nuclear power. These ideas will be examined separately before what seems to me a practical approach towards a solution of the problem is outlined.

(i) *The ideal solution—disarmament*

The ideal would be an agreement to abandon nuclear weapons coupled with conventional disarmament, both being subject to satisfactory control and inspection arrangements. This seems further off than ever with the failure of the Geneva nuclear test negotiations and the resumption of tests. At the beginning of the negotiations the United States and Britain gave up their former claim that a test agreement should be part of a package deal including the ending of nuclear weapon production and parallel reductions in conventional weapons and forces. However, after three years of negotiation, and when it appeared that an agreement was in sight, the Soviet Union in June 1961 adopted the view they had persuaded Britain and the United States to give up in 1958. This *volte face* and Soviet insistence upon the 'troika' idea which would give Russia a veto on all kinds of control machinery brought the talks to a standstill and ended hopes of a test agreement.

The fact must be faced, too, that any test agreement which might be reached would not bind the non-participating nations. France has quite rightly argued that a cessation of nuclear tests alone would by no means prevent the three governments concerned from producing in any quantities they wish the nuclear weapons which they have already tested. The only result would be that the gap between nuclear and non-nuclear powers would increase to the latter's disadvantage. Unless the production of nuclear weapons is also stopped by common agreement, France is not willing to forgo her right to become a full nuclear power.

As an agreement on the cessation of production would also have to cover conventional disarmament (the Soviet conventional superiority would otherwise regain its full weight), the French request and the Soviet attitude would bring disarmament negotiations back to the point at which they started years ago when, instead of the piecemeal approach, an all-round global approach was first attempted. The prospects of finding a solution to the danger of the spread of nuclear weapons through a disarmament agreement should not be over-estimated. However, at the beginning of 1962, with the promise of eighteen-power negotiations following the joint statement of agreed principles submitted by the United States and the Soviet Union to the United Nations, the prospect is more encouraging than at any time since Mr. Zorin walked out of the previous Geneva negotiations in June 1960. Disarmament is more fully discussed in Chapter XII.

(ii) *A non-nuclear club*

Another solution is the proposal that every nation with the exception of the United States and the Soviet Union should sign an agreement, preferably under the auspices of the United Nations, pledging itself not to test, manufacture or possess nuclear weapons. The agreement would be subject to full and effective international control. If such an agreement could be successfully negotiated, Great Britain would not only have to stop the manufacture of nuclear weapons but would also have to give up those in her possession. This proposal, which is quite different from unilateral nuclear disarmament, would leave Russia and America as the sole nuclear powers. This was of course the principal merit of the proposal and was considered to outweigh the admitted consequence that Europe would again have to rely on the American nuclear umbrella.

The idea of the non-nuclear club was strongly advocated by the British Labour Party in 1959[29] and formed the basis for the Party's defence and disarmament policy for the General Election in that year. But as the British Government, the only nuclear power apart from Russia and the United States, was not willing to take the diplomatic initiative by offering to surrender her status as a nuclear power if other countries would agree not to seek to attain it, such opportunity as there might have been for restricting the proliferation of nuclear powers by this means was lost.

It must also be stressed that this proposal was made before the first successful French atomic test early in 1960. The advent of France as a nuclear power and her attitude to this question, together with doubts as to whether all countries, for example, China, would agree, make the concept of the 'non-nuclear club' an idealistic solution rather than a practical proposition.

(iii) *A joint European strategic nuclear force within WEU*

In an attempt to overcome some of the obvious dangers of nuclear anarchy and at the same time to meet the growing fears in Europe, I proposed at the WEU Assembly in December 1959 that a 'Joint European Strategic Nuclear Force' should be created within the framework of Western European Union. The idea was supported by a majority[30] of the Parliamentarians of all parties represented from the seven WEU countries (Belgium, France, Germany, Holland, Italy, Luxembourg and the United Kingdom).

It was clearly not the function of a Parliamentary assembly to work out a technical blueprint for a plan of this character; indeed if the principle had been accepted by the Governments, many details would have had to be settled by negotiation. Put simply, what I had in mind was that within the framework of Western European Union, the seven countries should set up a political machinery to control all the nuclear bombs produced in the several countries. In other words, British bombs—and French, when available—could not be used except with the sanction and authority of the WEU Council of Ministers. In practical terms it would have meant that the British Bomber Command would be placed under European and not solely national control—rather similar to the decision taken in December 1960, for different reasons, to put Fighter Command under SACEUR's control.

At a later stage it might have been possible to devise some European machinery to undertake the research and development of nuclear weapons jointly for all countries. But this was not an essential or even necessary element in the scheme, which was designed primarily to permit joint political control. Its objectives were twofold: to enable all member countries to participate in the vital decision to use nuclear weapons and to stop the dangers and wasteful duplication of effort involved in each country seeking to produce its own national nuclear capability. It would have dealt with the question of cost and provided a joint system of financing the weapons to be jointly controlled but it would not have involved joint production or the sharing of atomic secrets. (Britain, the only WEU member who could have made these secrets available, was in any case prohibited from doing so under her agreements with the United States and Canada.) Nor would it have meant the sharing out of actual bombs or warheads: it would simply have transferred the control of those that existed from national to joint WEU control and direction.

Western European Union would have been particularly suitable as a basis for such a scheme because it has more far-reaching mutual defence obligations under Article V of the modified Brussels Treaty than exist under Article V of the North Atlantic Treaty. Article V of the modified Brussels Treaty states:

> If any of the High Contracting Parties should be the object of an armed attack in Europe, the other High Contracting Parties will, in accordance with the provisions of Article 51 of the Charter of the United Nations, afford the Party so attacked *all the military and other aid and assistance in their power.*

Article V of the North Atlantic Treaty states:

> The Parties agree that an armed attack against one or more of them in Europe or North America shall be considered an attack against them all and consequently they agree that, if such an armed attack occurs, each of them, in exercise of the right of individual or collective self-defence recognised by Article 51 of the Charter of the United Nations, will assist the Party or Parties so attacked by taking forthwith, individually and in concert with the other Parties, *such action as it deems necessary, including the use of armed force,* to restore and maintain the security of the North Atlantic area.
>
> Any such armed attack and all measures taken as a result thereof shall immediately be reported to the Security Council. Such measures shall be terminated when the Security Council has taken the measures necessary to restore and maintain international peace and security.

Also Western European Union already has in being a machinery for the control of the level of forces and arms production, together with a majority vote procedure for determining the level of stocks of nuclear weapons on the mainland of Europe. As well as the provision which prohibits the manufacture of atomic or nuclear weapons by Western Germany, Article III of the Third Protocol of the Treaty provides:

> When the development of atomic, biological and chemical weapons in the territory on the mainland of Europe of the High Contracting Parties who have not given up the right to produce them has passed the experimental stage and effective production of them has started there, the level of stocks that the High Contracting Parties concerned

will be allowed to hold on the mainland of Europe shall be decided by a majority vote of the Council of Western European Union.

Thus by *majority* vote the member countries must decide, for example, how many bombs France shall be allowed to have. Since the principle of control is already established, I believe that it should not have been difficult to build on this base—provided that the political will to do so had been present.

For Germany my proposal would have permitted equal participation in the decisions of the Council whether or not to use nuclear weapons. But it would not have involved any amendment of the Brussels Treaty under which Germany renounced the manufacture of nuclear weapons, since there would be no question of German production or possession of atomic or thermonuclear weapons.

For France it would have meant equal participation in European decisions and in the circumstances she might have felt that there was no case for continuing independent production. But if she had desired to go ahead with production of atomic weapons, the control over their use would have been in the hands of Western European Union and would not have been a matter for independent French decision.

Admittedly the consequences and the degree of national sovereignty surrendered would have been greatest for the United Kingdom, the only established West European nuclear power. Britain would have had to surrender national control of her weapons and to place British Bomber Command under the control of the WEU Council, in return for some financial contribution towards the cost of maintaining the strategic deterrent force.

In fact, behind the simplicity of the idea was a demand for a complete reorientation of British foreign policy. I made the proposal in the knowledge that its implementation would require an end of any British desire to pursue an independent defence policy as an independent nuclear power, although it would not have been inconsistent with British obligations to the Commonwealth or other commitments outside NATO. However, I can conceive of no circumstances in which a strategic nuclear force is necessary or would be helpful in discharging British responsibilities outside Europe.

Above all, for Britain this proposal would have involved the end of any claim to have a unique and special relationship with the United States. In short it demanded not only the surrender of British national sovereignty over her V-bombers but the surrender of Britain's pretence of being able to continue as a world power on the same footing as the United States and the Soviet Union. In reality the British Government has already moved from this position although she has been slow to admit the fact. But it must be recognised that the shadow of prestige and influence seems as real as the substance, and I did not underestimate how painful the necessary adjustment in thinking and behaviour would be. On the other hand there would have been the tangible commitment of Britain to Europe which would be more advantageous to both British and European long-term interests than the *status quo*.

Briefly the case for my proposal was that it offered an opportunity to move towards a solution of the *Nth* power problem (the spread of nuclear capability) and a chance to show that an effective system of joint control over the use of nuclear weapons was practicable. A successful operation of these principles could perhaps have led to their adoption later within the NATO alliance as a whole. Neither of these objectives could have been accomplished without the surrender of the independent national control over the British bomb, since the prestige as much as, if not more than, the military advantage of being a nuclear power prompts the desire of France today, and no doubt other nations tomorrow, to seek the status of a nuclear power. What is good for Britain, they argue, is surely good for us. Equally it would be impossible to have a European system of joint control without the nuclear weapons themselves, and these could only be supplied by Britain.

But the proposal, had it been adopted, would have had consequences wider than in the field of military arrangements alone. It could have been the beginning of a truly European approach to both foreign and defence policies, about which so much has been said in the last sixteen years and so little achieved. It would have assisted the solution of the problem of a divided Europe and produced the political and economic unity which is so essential if Europe is to play its proper role in the world. It would have given substance to the many speeches that British Ministers have made declaring that 'Europe includes the United Kingdom' and been a helpful prelude to our own application to join the Common Market. It would also have removed the suspicions of British intentions so widely held by our friends in Europe.

Although some technical difficulties might have arisen, they could have been overcome and a satisfactory machinery worked out to give effect to the proposal. Certainly the Council of Ministers of WEU did not rely upon technical objections in their reply to the recommendation of the Assembly.[31] They argued that the creation of a joint European strategic nuclear force under the control of WEU was contrary to the basic principle that NATO should be the organisation responsible for the collective defence in Europe of member countries of WEU. This was surprising, since the existing strategic forces have always been under independent national control and outside NATO. The merging of European forces under the joint control of WEU would surely have made NATO defence arrangements easier rather than more difficult. The Ministers also suggested that it would have a disruptive effect on NATO since it did not include all European members of the alliance. The alternative of inviting these countries to join WEU and thus participate in the plan does not seem to have occurred to them.

However, the idea of a joint European strategic nuclear force in the form I suggested was already dead by the time the Council replied. The opportunity was very strictly limited in time and events soon overtook it. The successful French test explosions and the subsequent decision of the French Government to develop independent nuclear capability put paid to the idea in France, where it had been given a mixed reception at the outset. But would the National Assembly, whose Defence Committee had carefully considered my proposal, have come to the same decision if the principle of a European force had been accepted by the other Governments concerned?

The crucial point of course was the attitude of the British Government, since without a British initiative the project could not possibly have succeeded, and the British Government was distinctly cool. And the decision in mid-1960 to abandon the production of *Blue Streak* and to acquire the *Skybolt* air-to-ground missile from the United States meant that the value of a British offer to provide the basis for a European force was very much less than appeared to be the case in 1959. The successful trials of

Polaris and *Minuteman*, each having the advantage of mobility, meant that European ideas about nuclear weapons turned from manned bombers to those missiles as 'delivery vehicles'.

The British Defence White Paper for 1961[32] made it clear that the British Government has still not refashioned its policy in the way my proposal demanded. The essential feature—that the joint force would take the place of independent national nuclear weapons—has still not been accepted by the other Governments of Western European Union either. Interdependence remains a very good theme for political addresses: it still has to attain the status of practical policy.

(iv) *NATO as the Fourth Nuclear Power*

After much confused speculation and discussion, the North Atlantic Council communiqué, issued after its meeting in Paris from 16 to 18 December 1960, reported that its permanent representatives were to study proposals made by the United States for a 'MRBM multilateral force'. The United States also offered to supply five *Polaris* submarines under NATO control by 1963, while inviting the other NATO powers to buy a further hundred *Polaris* missiles.

No clear idea emerged as to the purpose of this offer, which came as a climax to an unprecedented burst of energy by the Eisenhower Administration in its last months of office. At the NATO Ministerial meeting in Oslo at the beginning of May 1961 Mr. Dean Rusk confirmed the offer of five *Polaris* submarines on behalf of the Kennedy Administration, although no further mention seems to have been made of the suggestion that the NATO powers should buy an additional hundred *Polaris* missiles or of an MRBM multilateral force.

President Kennedy carried matters a stage further in his speech to the Canadian Parliament at Ottawa on 17 May 1961 when he made clear the willingness of the United States to establish a truly multilateral North Atlantic Treaty seaborne force. Emphasising the need for nuclear weapons available to the alliance to be 'at all times under close and flexible political control that meets the needs of all NATO countries', the President went on to say:

> To make clear our own intentions and commitments, United States will commit to the NATO command area five—and subsequently still more—*Polaris* atomic-missile submarines, subject to any agreed

NATO guidelines on their control and use, and responsive to the
needs of all members but still credible in any emergency.

Beyond this, we look to the possibility of eventually establishing
a NATO sea-borne force, which would be truly multilateral in owner-
ship and control, if this should be desired and found feasible by our
allies once NATO's non-nuclear goals have been achieved.

It may fairly be assumed that President Kennedy had two main
considerations in mind in making this proposal. First, it would
reassure European members of the alliance of the full commitment
of the United States to Europe at a time when the development of
Polaris, and soon *Minuteman*, promises to make the Americans
less dependent upon NATO bases. Secondly, it would go some way
towards dealing with the danger of the spread of independent
deterrents and the difficulty of restraining these ambitions while
the effective decisions are taken only by those members of the
alliance with nuclear capability, viz. the United States and, to a
lesser extent, the United Kingdom. There is substantial evidence
that some of the alliance's present difficulties stem from this
division into nuclear and non-nuclear members, and while one
cannot pretend that a proposal such as President Kennedy's
will by itself provide a solution, this evidence of a fresh approach
on the part of the United States is highly encouraging. Hard
thinking on the problems involved in sharing control of nuclear
weapons is long overdue and European members of the alliance
cannot now evade the issue by sheltering behind the Anglo-
Saxon monopoly. Members of an alliance cannot have it both
ways: if they wish to be treated as equals by the strongest partner
they must be prepared to shoulder their share of the responsibilities, moral and material.

It has been suggested that the original American proposal was
primarily designed to buy time, since it would take so long for the
Governments involved to work out a plan for joint political
control among themselves that the twin advantages of restraining
the proliferation of nuclear powers and solidifying the alliance
could be achieved by the United States without cost or relaxation
of her control of the alliance's nuclear armoury. Certainly the
divisions of opinion and the Governmental reactions to my
previous plan for a joint European strategic deterrent suggest that
if left to themselves the European members may well be content
with the shadow rather than the substance of nuclear weapons for

long beyond 1963. By making it clear that the provision of *Polaris* for NATO is conditional on the prior attainment of NATO's conventional force goals, Mr. Kennedy has indicated that it is not, in his view, an urgent matter.

But we must also take into account the onerous responsibilities of the Supreme Allied Commander, General Norstad. He has the obligation to prepare plans for the defence of Europe within the general directives given him by North Atlantic Council. His tactical airforces already have considerable nuclear strike capability and he must plan for the future when the missile replaces the manned bomber. He had actively canvassed for the provision of Medium Range missiles for some time before any proposal reached the North Atlantic Council. In particular he set out his views, in an address which attracted wide publicity, to the NATO Parliamentarians' Conference in Paris in November 1960. After referring to the meeting of the Heads of Government in 1957 which decided that Intermediate (Medium) Range Ballistic Missiles would have to be put at the disposal of the Supreme Allied Commander Europe, General Norstad said:

I believe there are three related but still separate and distinct areas for consideration. The first goes back directly to the Heads of Government Meeting and relates to the established requirement for my command for mid-range ballistic missiles. They are weapons on the 1,000–1,500 nautical mile range. This requirement springs from the functions of responsibilities which I now have and does not go beyond the scope of the presently-assigned tasks of my command. It should be looked upon as a modernisation programme because as we look forward to the period of 1963 to 1970 and thereafter it is clear that missiles will have to take over some of the rôles now performed by aircraft of the fighter-bomber or light bomber types. However, it is unlikely that even by the latter date the missile will entirely supplant the manned aircraft, particularly in NATO Europe and particularly because of the necessity and continued need for a conventional capability.

It is this idea of a modernisation programme which first gave rise to discussions of the *Polaris*, for instance, in relation to the NATO forces. This requirement continues to be of great importance and of increasing urgency. It is met, to a certain extent, by the *Jupiter* weapons, the Intermediate Range Ballistic Missiles, which are now coming into service under NATO, and we hope that, in the 1963–5 period, this capability will be improved by the introduction of extremely mobile units, some of which may operate at sea, and some of which may operate from land. This is the first of the three subjects, or areas of consideration; and this one springs from an existing NATO requirement which was originated by my Command and proposed and supported by me.

The second idea is that of a NATO strategic force. I emphasise the 'strategic' to indicate that it does not have the rôle to which I have just referred, that is, of taking over from the fighter-bombers and light bombers in their tasks of the direct defence of Europe. It would, in fact, be one of the heavy strategic retaliatory forces. This is an extremely interesting thought, but one which has not, to my knowledge, been proposed by or within the alliance. It has not been suggested by me, or my Headquarters.

The third subject is one which must be considered of the greatest overall importance. To explain this without using additional words, and thus running the risk of adding to the confusion, I would like to follow, this afternoon, the general lines of a statement that I made on an earlier occasion. A great and new question has arisen within the alliance; how do we meet a growing desire for a broader sharing in the control of nuclear weapons? How can the alliance, as a whole, be assured that such weapons will be available to it in all reasonable circumstances, for its defence, for the defence of Europe? These questions need to be carefully considered by the alliance. The forces which are assigned to the NATO mission require the support of nuclear weapons. The defence of Europe against a serious, large-scale attack, certainly depends on these weapons. A search for a fair solution to the problem of sharing and control is thus of the most vital concern to all of us. It is quite obvious that I, as a military man, am in no position to insist on a particular, specific solution to what is, overwhelmingly, a political problem. Further, I am well aware that there are several legal and technical problems which affect the distribution and the control of weapons in this category.

Many ideas have been advanced for dealing with these questions. It has been suggested, for instance, that the control of weapons might be passed to the alliance; that they might be committed to NATO for the life of the alliance in its present form.

When I speak of weapons, I am speaking not of the aircraft, or the missiles, or the guns which deliver the warheads; but I am speaking, in this sense, of the nuclear components which are now retained in the strictest custody. It cannot be assumed that the creation of a multilateral atomic authority, making NATO a fourth atomic power, as has been expressed, would necessarily influence the desire of some nations to pursue their own independent quest for an atomic weapons capability. However, such action might very well satisfy the desires and interests of others by meeting fully the military requirements, and by assuring an equal voice in the control of the particular pool of forces which could be established as essential to the direct defence of Europe.

There are several additional advantages or dividends to be gained by adding this responsibility to NATO. I will mention only one: for the alliance to have continuing life and meaning, it needs increasing authority; it needs power of some form. If politically feasible, action to pass to the alliance greater control over atomic weapons and to subject their use more directly to the collective will could be a great and dramatic new step. I realise that this is an important and a complex problem, and that progress may have to be made on a stage by stage basis. However, the general subject deserves—it demands—some early initiative.

In so far as General Norstad is requesting *Polaris* or other missiles as future replacements for his existing nuclear strike power contained in his Tactical Air Forces, there is no new principle raised in these proposals. Changing the means of delivering nuclear bombs of the same power of destruction on the same preselected targets does not change the *status quo* or justify suggestions of a new NATO nuclear force. The only change in the *status quo* would result from a change in the existing arrangements under which the control of the weapons and the custody of the bombs or warheads remain exclusively in American hands. But if, as has been suggested, the *Polaris* submarines to be assigned to SACEUR are to be manned by the United States Navy and attached to the United States 6th Fleet in the Mediterranean, there would be no change in the control *status quo* either.

The concept of a NATO strategic nuclear force is quite different. General Norstad makes it clear that it has not emanated from him or his Headquarters, although he does not seem unfavourably disposed towards it. In any case no such heavy strategic retaliatory force would be placed under SACEUR's command—it would require its own command, integrated with the Strategic Air Command and such other independent national strategic forces as exist within the alliance.

Incidentally the term 'fourth nuclear power' is a misnomer. A proposal which excluded national strategic nuclear deterrents within NATO, or within Europe, would make NATO the second or third nuclear power, not the fourth. And if the NATO nuclear force is to be additional to instead of superseding the national deterrents, then it would actually be the fifth nuclear force (assuming that France carries out her resolve to achieve nuclear capability).

Any such force which did not supersede the existing national strategic deterrents would be an unnecessary duplication and a wasteful use of resources: there is no shortage of nuclear weapons *within the alliance as a whole*. And besides being unjustified on military grounds, it would do nothing to solve the problem of political control. While the European members of the alliance would surely not object to the United States retaining part of its strategic force for non-NATO purposes, the continued existence of other national deterrents within the alliance would feed the ambition of the 'second-class' members to become nuclear powers too, and our existing difficulties in this connection would remain. Such a force would serve only to induce the European members of the alliance to neglect further their prime responsibility—to furnish SACEUR with the thirty divisions he needs so badly.

Inevitably the argument about what are tactical and what are strategic weapons or targets, already referred to in the previous chapter, arises to confuse the issue. We have got ourselves into difficulties because the Tactical Air Forces have already acquired the capacity of participating in the atomic strike plan and have been assigned to nuclear interdiction tasks well beyond the Iron Curtain without a proper political assessment being made of these plans and their probable consequences. The *Matador* and *Mace* missiles already in service in Europe pose the problem of how far we can go in classifying as 'tactical' weapons capable of long-range interdiction tasks. The issue of *Polaris* only underlines the problem. I hope the public discussion it has aroused will serve to produce the political consideration and decision the whole question demands.

It is quite wrong to blame General Norstad for formulating his requirements and bringing the matter into the political arena. Any criticism must be directed to the North Atlantic Council for evading the complicated questions posed by the emergence of nuclear weapons of strategic potential within SACEUR's command and for taking general decisions in 1954 and again in 1957 without recognising their full implications. There seems to be no doubt that tasks have been given to SACEUR, in plans approved by the Council, which demand nuclear capability similar to that of the strategic forces. It is no solution to leave SACEUR the tasks and to deny him the means of carrying them out.

According to the principles enunciated in the first chapter, if military requirements conflict with political policy the political will must prevail. But it is equally important that the political decisions be clearly expressed to avoid misunderstandings and that responsibility for them be borne on political shoulders, in this case by the North Atlantic Council. It must not be left to any military commander, no matter how distinguished, to take a decision to raise the level of a conflict from conventional to nuclear war. His discretion must be limited to responding to the use of nuclear weapons by the other side or other exceptional circumstances, clearly defined in advance by the political authority, where maximum speed of reaction is necessary. Apart from such exceptions the initial use of nuclear weapons of any kind, range or size must be reserved to the political authorities in the same way that the decision to declare war was so reserved in days when this was the accepted prelude to hostilities.

This problem arises because insufficient thought has been given to the implication of the change in NATO doctrine from the inevitability of global nuclear war to an acceptance, in the light of nuclear parity, of the concept of limited war. If the use of the strategic forces was to be automatic, the tactical use posed no problem since the decision to use the greater weapons obviously covered the lesser.

The serious military aspects of these difficulties are developed in Chapters VIII and X and the political problems arising from joint control of the tactical use of nuclear weapons are more fully discussed in the next chapter.

To sum up. I am opposed to the provision of *Polaris* or other missiles of like capability for SACEUR before the political problems of control are resolved and without a full re-examination of the tasks assigned to SACEUR in the light of the new strategy imposed upon us by the changed circumstances of nuclear parity. And there can be no merit in the idea of NATO as a fourth nuclear power if it would not fulfil its main political objectives of providing joint control and equal status within the alliance and might exacerbate the problem of procuring sufficient conventional ground forces —which rates the highest military priority.

Chapter VII

PATTERN FOR JOINT POLITICAL CONTROL

It is clear that the West must continue to have nuclear retaliatory forces and that the main burden for supplying them and keeping them invulnerable against a pre-emptive strike must rest with the United States. At the same time it is not reasonable to suppose that, since these nuclear forces form a key part of NATO strategy, the other allies will ever be content to allow all decisions as to their deployment and use to be left to the American President. NATO as a whole must be involved in these decisions, just as it is in the field of supplying conventional weapons. Unless some pattern of joint political control is evolved, the alliance will not achieve the political and psychological cohesion it needs. Equally there will be no enthusiasm to provide the conventional forces which are increasingly recognised to be the first priority of NATO military strategy and essential if the alliance is to be able to avoid reliance on nuclear weapons in each and every situation.

It is true to say that the working out of a joint system of control was virtually impossible during the period when NATO strategy demanded an immediate resort to the strategic use of nuclear weapons in the case of any aggression, regardless of its size or how it arose. It would hardly be feasible to expect fifteen nations to approve a formula in advance whereby the nuclear strategic forces of the West would be used first, or to agree to such use at short notice if a crisis arose.

However, while vestiges of the doctrine of massive retaliation still remain in NATO planning and strategic thinking, there is abundant evidence that, at both the political and military levels, NATO is moving towards the kind of strategy I have outlined. In his special message on the Defence Budget sent to Congress on 28 March 1961 President Kennedy said:

Our arms will never be used to strike the first blow in any attack. . . .
We are not creating forces for a first strike against any other
nation. . . . Any potential aggressor contemplating an attack on any
part of the free world with any kind of weapons, conventional or
nuclear, must know that our response will be suitable, selective,
swift and effective. We must be able to make deliberate choices in
weapons and strategy. . . . Our weapons systems must be usable in a
manner permitting deliberation and discrimination as to timing,
scope and targets in response to civilian authority.

This was a great step forward and was the more encouraging in
that the detailed proposals for defence expenditure and the
procurement of weapons and equipment were designed to
implement it. 'Suitable' and 'appropriate' tend increasingly to
replace 'massive' as the adjective applied to the retaliation to be
employed by NATO in the event of aggression.

CONTROL OVER STRATEGIC FORCES

The end of the doctrine of massive retaliation removes the most
powerful objection to joint political control in that there is no
longer the need for a joint political decision to be taken in an
impossibly short time. The bogey of 'fifteen fingers on the
trigger or fifteen thumbs on the safety-catch' of the Western
deterrent is no longer substantial. There are two sets of circumstances in which it might be necessary to authorise the use of
nuclear weapons: in response to a surprise all-out nuclear attack
from the Soviet Union, or as a result of the escalation of a limited
war situation. Time would not present a problem in either case.
In the first there would be no need for consultation since the
immediate response required would be authorised in accordance
with joint decisions previously reached to cover this contingency.
In the second there would be adequate time for the consultation
demanded by the developing situation. Thus the concept of joint
political control would not weaken the effectiveness of the deterrent or destroy its credibility.

There must, of course, be arrangements permanently in hand
to ensure that while, in President Kennedy's words, 'making
certain that our retaliatory power does not rest on decisions made
in ambiguous circumstances, or permit a catastrophic mistake',[33]
a surprise attack is met by immediate response from all the
strategic forces that survive the enemy blow. This is essential to

H

preserve the credibility of the deterrent. In the event of a surprise attack on the West, the loss of an hour may be as vital as the loss of a day. There must surely be secret directives, agreed in advance, whereby *in carefully defined circumstances which allow of no possibility of a mistake*, procedures are followed, subject to the final approval of the United States President or the British Prime Minister, to ensure an immediate response to a surprise attack. These arrangements must exist already under the present system of national political and civilian control, and there are no insuperable difficulties in the way of obtaining the approval of all members of the alliance to these provisions.

The problem has already been complicated much more by the advent of rockets (which, as yet, unlike the manned bombers, cannot be recalled) than it would be by changing from a system of national political control to a joint NATO political control. Just as national civilian control demands the working out of conditions and procedure for action in advance and, for example, probably requires in the United Kingdom the approval of a Cabinet of fifteen or more members, similarly under a joint control machinery the terms and conditions for dealing with a surprise attack would be worked out in advance and agreed by the fifteen members of the alliance. Indeed the decision to 'press the button' could well be delegated by the NATO Council to the man who, in fact, has the responsibility now: the American President. But there is a vast difference between his exercising it formally on behalf of the alliance as a delegated authority and his doing so on national authority only. It is common practice in many committees and organisations for the members to agree after discussion to delegate some executive functions to their chairmen or secretaries. The democratic nature of an organisation or the full rights and participation of its members are not impaired by such arrangements.

However, a surprise attack remains the least likely contingency. If the present military balance were seriously upset, if the United States should allow herself to lag so far behind Russian capability as to tempt a pre-emptive strike, then the danger would be very real. But it seems most improbable that the West, and particularly the United States, will allow such a situation to develop. The evolution of the almost invulnerable missile-armed nuclear submarine ensures that deterrence will remain mutual and makes the nuclear stalemate complete.

The real danger is the prospect of our finding ourselves at war through accident or miscalculation and not by anyone's deliberate choice. In these circumstances the decision whether to use nuclear weapons, and when and how, would be of vital consequence to the whole alliance; and, it must be recognised, far harder to take than in the simple, clear-cut case of the West having been attacked first with all the Soviet nuclear might.

Certainly it is not credible, no matter what existing NATO plans may prescribe, that the strategic retaliatory forces of the West would be invoked in the first stages of a conventional or even limited nuclear attack against us. Our whole strategy must be to 'seek to enforce a pause' and to place upon the aggressor the fearful responsibility of deciding whether or not to raise the stakes. But in the event of any kind of incident, the possibility of nuclear weapons being employed will have to be faced. In such a situation, can it really be accepted that the whole burden of decision should be borne by the President of the United States, perhaps after discussion with the Prime Minister of the United Kingdom?

Time would not be lacking for political and military consultation among the allies, since time would be required to assess the gravity of the position and to forecast the likely course of events. Full consultation within the alliance would surely take place in the event of a limited war situation, whether or not formal arrangements exist. One's mind goes back to the occasion when Earl Attlee, then the British Prime Minister, flew to see the American President, Mr. Truman, when consideration was being given to the use of atomic bombs in the Korean war. Limited and non-nuclear wars did take place, despite their conflicting with contemporary strategic philosophy, during the period when massive nuclear retaliation was the unchallenged NATO doctrine. It is surely all the more likely now, in the light of present strategy, that if the worst happens and we find ourselves faced with a limited aggression—which would almost certainly be a non-nuclear aggression—within NATO territory or indeed elsewhere, there would be joint consultation leading to a joint political decision.

If, then, some joint political decision is likely even under the pressure of actual or threatened aggression, why not produce the machinery now to facilitate and simplify consultation? And, even more important, why should the nuclear powers not now get the credit for sharing their responsibilities within the alliance, with the bonus of reducing the chance of war because of the additional strength and cohesion of NATO resulting from such an arrangement? The badly needed accretion of conventional strength is more likely to be forthcoming from the non-nuclear European powers if they participate in the policy-making on the eventual use of nuclear weapons than if the *status quo* continues. At the same time, the urge to acquire national deterrents will at least be blunted by such participation in joint decisions. The United States, Britain and France have nothing to lose and much to gain by the development of joint political control.

Given that the first requirement for a practicable system of joint political control is a strategy which does not involve an immediate use of strategic forces other than in reply to a surprise all-out nuclear attack, the second requirement is the assigning of control of these strategic forces to the alliance as a whole. Although the other nuclear powers must fall into line to make such a policy effective, the attitude of the United States is the key to the problem. In the foreseeable future the United States must and will provide the nuclear armoury of the West. The question is whether she will do so on the basis that all nuclear weapons remain, as now, under American national control, or whether control over some of them is assigned to the alliance as a whole.

It is recognised that to ask the United States to surrender sovereignty over a substantial part of her nuclear weapons is to ask a very great deal. But is there any alternative? There is no need, of course, for the physical transfer of any weapons to other NATO powers. The idea that control can be achieved without actual possession has already been achieved in respect of conventional forces. In assigning troops to SACEUR's command a nation assigns operational command in the event of hostilities, not physical possession. The concept of joint political control over nuclear weapons is no different in principle.

But although no transfer of bombs or warheads would be involved, legislation would almost certainly be required to enable the Americans to discuss questions concerning the operational use and planning of strategic nuclear weapons within the NATO council. In short, it would mean extending to the Council as a whole a good deal of the status accorded to Britain, as an established nuclear power, by the 1958 amendment to the Atomic

Energy Act. It is hard to believe, however, that any necessary amendment would be withheld if a strong President really desired it and could convince Congress that the MacMahon Act is operating in the opposite way to that intended when it was enacted. For instead of settling the *Nth* power problem it acts as a stimulant to nuclear ambition and provides a target for national nuclear achievement. What Britain did yesterday and France does today, other countries will want to do tomorrow. Only by extending the principle of joint control to the whole alliance is it possible to prick the bubble of exclusive privilege attached to nuclear capability.

The existing arrangements fail to achieve this end. Both the dual key system (the basis of the *Thor* missile agreement with the United Kingdom under which the warheads are under American control and the missiles are under British control, a joint decision being necessary before a missile can be fired) and the system for the *Jupiter* missiles in Italy (which are under the operational control of SACEUR in his dual capacity as a NATO and a United States commander) are unsatisfactory. Political expediency apart, it is doubtful if arrangements similar to the British agreement over *Thor* could be concluded with countries that are not established nuclear powers as defined by the MacMahon Act. In any case, it is certain that such agreements are neither sufficient to meet the political needs of the alliance nor relevant to its military requirements.

Nor is the idea of setting up NATO as the fourth (or more logically the fifth) nuclear power with a strategic strike force a substitute for a system of real political control of NATO's nuclear policy in which all its members participate. It would lead to a wasteful duplication of effort and achieve the worst of both worlds. What is required is joint political control over the existing nuclear weapons in Europe, not the giving of a few additional nuclear missiles to NATO. In other words, NATO should become the third nuclear power, since it is too much to ask the United States at this stage to place all her nuclear weapons, including those based in the United States, under joint NATO control.

What is suggested, then, is that all American nuclear weapons in Europe, including the Sixth Fleet and *Polaris* submarines operational from Europe and the elements of the Strategic Air Command assigned to Europe, be placed under NATO control.

In addition, of course, there would be the *Thor* and *Jupiter* nuclear missiles under SACEUR's operational control, together with the British and, when available, the French forces. There would be no need for the British to seek a replacement of the V-bomber force when it becomes obsolete, and equally there would be no case for the French seeking to have a nuclear force beyond the period of the manned bomber. In the meantime Britain and the United States could assist France, if she were to make this a condition of accepting the proposal, by the provision of technical information so that she could join in any test ban agreement that is reached with the Soviet Union. Also they could make bombers available now, while the *Mirage IV* is under development. This 'pooled' force would also take over such of SACEUR's long-range interdiction tasks as remained after the reassessment of his needs in the light of the changed strategic concept.

Thus the considerable surrender of sovereignty on the part of the United States would be matched by the handing over of control over their nuclear forces by Great Britain and France. Indeed it is not feasible to expect such a surrender from the United States except on these terms. There are signs that the British Government's attitude towards maintaining its independent deterrent are undergoing some modification, judging by the Prime Minister's speech at Boston in April 1961:

> We cannot want our allies to feel it essential to their honour or their safety to pour out their money in wasteful duplication. Probably the West does not need an increase in total nuclear power.
> Nevertheless this is a real problem. We cannot ignore it . . . but the health of our whole NATO alliance depends on finding a way of building a partnership in the nuclear as well as conventional field and to make it live. The prize of this would be great. It is a double one—the prevention of uncontrolled extension of nuclear manufacture and, secondly, the sense of real unity which would follow a new agreement with our own allies.

The likely attitude of France to these proposals, and indeed to the future of the NATO alliance, is by no means clear. President de Gaulle touched on this theme at his press conference in April 1961, when he is reported to have stated that it was the 'right and duty of the continental powers of Europe to have a national defence proper to them. It was intolerable to a great state that its destiny should be left to the decisions and actions of another power, however friendly. The danger of integration was that the integrated state was apt to become disinterested in its defence because it was without responsibility for it, and for this reason the whole alliance lost much of its resilience and force. What would happen in time of war?'[34] Yet he does not appear opposed to the idea behind this concept of joint political control, i.e. that there should be equal participation and full consultation on the formulation of NATO strategy as a whole, for he went on to say that 'the question of the use of nuclear armaments by the United States and Britain, as well as the use of their conventional weapons, must be completely clarified, for the continental powers, which were the most exposed, must know precisely with what arms and in what conditions their overseas allies would join them in the same battle'. However, it would be an error of optimism to expect France to surrender her nuclear ambition easily, even if her claims for full participation were met. In November 1961, de Gaulle reiterated his argument for French independent nuclear arms since 'a great nation not possessing them, while others do, cannot dispose of its destiny'.

The third requirement is to evolve a suitable machinery within NATO to provide a framework for control. While it is clearly impossible to formulate precise policies in advance because of the very nature of the problem which is most likely to arise, i.e. the possible escalation of weapons away from limited war—it is important to have the machinery for consultation working smoothly. It is not so much a question of saving precious time: in such a situation there will undoubtedly be sufficient time to weigh all the factors involved in a decision to use nuclear weapons. While the establishment of suitable machinery is desirable from the military point of view, from the political and psychological point of view it is essential if the European members of the alliance are to accept and believe wholeheartedly that they will participate in decisions over nuclear policy. Such machinery would also have the advantage of providing for better co-ordination of NATO policy in a wider context—for example, in arms control policies or the problem of Berlin.

The main reform needed in the existing NATO structure is in the work of the North Atlantic Council, which must take the responsibility for the present unsatisfactory state of affairs. The Council itself must undertake to lay down and supervise all the

major questions of NATO strategy. To do this the national representatives on the Council need to have the best military advice
available to them all the time, and this can best be achieved by
moving the military representatives' committee from Washington
to Paris. Also the Council as such needs an expert panel of
military advisers. The best means of meeting this need would be
to strengthen the Standing Group by ensuring that it is staffed
by very senior representatives of the United States, Britain and
France. These officers should be of a rank only one below that
of their respective Chiefs of Staff. There appears also to be a
strong case for having the Standing Group also in Paris with the
Council, rather than as at present in Washington.

Henry Kissinger has suggested that the Council should have an
executive or steering committee composed of the United States,
Britain, France, and Western Germany as permanent members
and three rotating members elected annually from among the
other eleven countries.[35] He suggests that the alliance should
accept decisions supported by a majority of five on this committee as binding. This idea is worth considering as a means of
providing a channel for quick decisions should necessity arise.
Alternatively, it may be possible to develop the existing Standing
Group in conjunction with the Secretary-General as the body to
interpret in an emergency policies determined so far as possible
in advance by the full Council.

The placing of all the strategic weapons of the alliance in
Europe under NATO control would undoubtedly necessitate the
appointment of another Supreme Commander, since it would
be neither appropriate nor reasonable to add this burden to the
already heavy load carried by SACEUR. The new Supreme Commander, Nuclear Weapons (no doubt to be called SACNUC in
NATO terminology) would probably have to be an American in
view of American predominance in this field, although it would be
an extremely reassuring gesture on the part of the United States
if she were able to suggest a European for the post. In this latter
case there would be an argument for having an American as
Secretary-General of NATO. The choice of an eminent American
with close links with the White House for this key post would
undoubtedly be of immense importance during this crucial period.
Also, if he were an American, it would no doubt be easier for
powers concerning nuclear policy in an emergency to be

delegated to the Secretary-General, as representing the civil and political authority to which the military power must always be subordinate. If either or both SACNUC and the Secretary-General were Americans, it would then seem desirable that non-Americans should be considered for future appointments as SACEUR.

There will no doubt be much controversy about the detailed arrangements for the exercise of joint political control, but this is the least of the problems which has to be solved. First of all—and this is absolutely essential—there must be acceptance in all aspects of policy, and not merely in political speeches, that the doctrine of massive retaliation is dead and has been replaced by mutual deterrence, which will soon become mutual invulnerability of strategic strike forces. Unless this is recognised, joint political control is clearly impracticable, and the arguments about the impossibility of taking decisions in thirty minutes or less with fifteen fingers on the trigger or fifteen thumbs on the safety-catch are valid.

The other vital ingredient is the readiness of the nuclear powers to place their weapons under joint control. President Kennedy's undertaking to consult closely with the United States' allies within the NATO Council on the precise form for use of the nuclear deterrent and his recognition that we have reached 'a turning point in the organisation's military planning',[36] together with Mr. Macmillan's Boston speech, give grounds for believing that this readiness may at last be forthcoming.

CONTROL OVER TACTICAL USE

It is not sufficient to have a credible and workable system of joint control over the strategic nuclear forces of the West. Unless there is a corresponding control over the initial *tactical* use of nuclear weapons, it seems probable that use of the smaller atomic weapons would, by a process of escalation, land us in a situation in which resort to the strategic weapons by one side or the other would be inevitable. While there is no difference of principle between strategic and tactical uses of nuclear weapons, the practical problems are particularly difficult in the case of the smaller tactical weapons.

For some years the Assembly of Western European Union has been concerned with this problem and has insisted upon the necessity of political control. In December 1958, on the basis of one of my reports, the Assembly passed a recommendation:

> That the existing arrangements whereby SACEUR alone can authorise within the framework of political decisions the initial tactical use of nuclear weapons within his command be confirmed; that the Governments of member countries take immediate steps to establish jointly political directives governing such *initial* use and covering, as far as is possible, all contingencies; and that authority for *subsequent* tactical use of nuclear weapons be vested in such military commanders as SACEUR may determine. . . .

The Council of Ministers in their reply gave the assurance:

> The Council has ascertained that the power to authorise the initial tactical use of nuclear weapons within the area of the European command rests with SACEUR, acting under political direction from the North Atlantic Council. It is not advisable to divulge the conditions under which this power would be used; to do so would assist a potential aggressor.[37]

While accepting as obvious that any conditions so formulated could not be published for security reasons, it is far from clear that any political directives have in fact been agreed. And if directives have been agreed it is extremely difficult to see how they could be effective, given the existing organisation of, and reliance upon, nuclear weapons within the allied forces in Europe. The above recommendation and reply were made at a time when nuclear capability was only slowly beginning to be introduced to the ground forces.

Also, and more important to note, the reply of the Ministers was made at a time when the whole strategy of NATO, and of the member Governments, was wedded to the doctrine of massive retaliation. The Assembly's concern was prompted by its rejection of that doctrine and its realisation of the new requirements and difficult problems forced upon us by the existence of nuclear stalemate.

When it was believed that any aggression would be met by strategic use of nuclear weapons, it was of little consequence how, where and when the smaller atomic forces were deployed. On the other hand if it is believed that conventional aggression is the most likely contingency and that it should be met if at all possible by conventional means, the decision on the initial use of nuclear weapons is of crucial importance. Obviously once political authorisation for the use of nuclear weapons has been given, the military commanders must have a say in the manner of their deployment and subsequent authority for their use. But control over the *initial* use of tactical weapons must be retained exclusively in civilian hands and be authorised only by joint political decision. Such authority would be given either directly after assessment of the actual circumstances or indirectly because the circumstances fell unmistakably within the category of a pre-determined political directive, e.g. in response to the use of similar weapons by the enemy. No new principle is involved since political directives on the choice of weapons and targets were issued in the Second World War.

It has been argued that it should be possible to classify nuclear weapons so that certain types of the smaller atomic explosives can be used by military decision in the same way that conventional artillery has hitherto been used. I have examined this idea in Chapter VI and suggested a possible basis for such a distinction. It is, however, extremely dangerous to suppose that any distinction will be clear to an aggressor; and unless he accepts that the use of nuclear weapons is not inconsistent with a desire to keep hostilities limited, the use of even the smallest atomic weapons may well begin the escalation leading to all-out nuclear war. Since it is hardly possible to pin on each warhead or shell a label for the enemy to read, our only hope of getting the Russians to accept that our use of small atomic weapons would not necessarily indicate the desire or the intention to resort to large ones, is by achieving their prior agreement to a set of 'ground rules' for this type of warfare. Does anyone believe that this is feasible?

Quite apart from the difficulties of reaching any such agreement with the Russians, it would be very hard for the West itself to come to a satisfactory definition of terms. Wide differences exist between military experts and between the services as to what is understood by the idea of a 'limited nuclear war', and the variety of missions for which the service chiefs may require nuclear weapons (e.g. tactical targets well inside enemy territory and port installations as well as all kinds of targets within the theatre of operations) is an additional complicating factor. The conclusion is inescapable that while distinction within the spectrum of nuclear weapons may be theoretically possible and convenient to ourselves for rough agreement on degrees of escalation, for practical purposes in the event of hostilities it is only the clear and readily appreciated distinction between nuclear weapons of all kinds on the one hand and all non-nuclear weapons on the other that really makes sense.

It follows therefore that it must be clearly established that an aggression short of an all-out nuclear attack will be met by conventional means and that no nuclear weapons will be used except on political authority. It is equally important to establish that if it is decided to authorise the use of nuclear weapons in particular circumstances, or to lay down a general directive authorising their use in certain clearly-defined contingencies (e.g. in response to the use of nuclear weapons against our troops), this decision would not be a blanket authority covering the whole spectrum of nuclear weapons for tactical use. Each level of escalation would need a separate and distinct political authority. For example, a decision to use the short-range Army support atomic weapons would not permit the Tactical Air Forces to use their nuclear bombs; a decision to authorise nuclear interdiction could well impose restrictions on the size of the bombs or warheads to be used and the range of the targets from the battlefield.

Thus it seems possible to recognise distinctions between targets and between the explosive power and range of nuclear weapons for our own purposes, provided such distinctions are not allowed to blur the fundamental distinction between nuclear and conventional weapons: and, of course, provided it is fully appreciated that the use of *any* nuclear weapons may set us on an escalator up which we shall be dragged inevitably to the full horror of global nuclear war.

It is perhaps this problem that President Kennedy had in mind when he told the NATO Military Committee in April 1961:

In our studies we have found a serious need for a sensitive and flexible control of all arms, and especially over nuclear weapons. We propose to see to it, for our part, that our military forces operate at all times under continuous, responsible command and control from the highest authorities all the way downward—and we mean to see that this control is exercised before, during and after any initiation of hostilities against our forces, and at any level of escalation. We believe in maintaining effective deterrent strength, but we believe also in making it do what we wish, neither more nor less.

But while at the highest levels it has always been agreed in principle that the tactical use of nuclear weapons would be a political decision, the admittedly very difficult problem of translating this principle into practice has not been tackled. The problem was indeed posed in the communique on the North Atlantic Council in December 1954 when the decision to equip the Allied Forces on the Central Front with tactical nuclear weapons was taken. It announced that SHAPE was given authority to plan defensive strategy 'taking into account modern developments in weapons and techniques', but that the decisions on the use of these weapons would be left in civilian hands.

The intention is still to equip all the NATO forces in Europe with tactical nuclear weapons by the end of 1963. The problem is therefore urgent. It is also very difficult. For American success in the scaling down or 'miniaturisation' of weapons designed for use by infantry battalions—for example the development of the two-man *Davy Crockett* atomic mortar—while increasing the military value of these weapons makes the practical problem of their control correspondingly more difficult. This is the very nub of the problem: how can political control be effective over weapons which may eventually be issued to every infantry company? Already the *Honest John* and *Corporal* weapons are an integral part of our ground forces, the missile regiments being under the same operational control as those using conventional artillery. One suspects too that our air forces work on the assumption that nuclear bombs will be used in almost every contingency. Indeed there is very real doubt as to whether our forces in Europe could resist any kind of conventional attack without immediate resort to the strategy and pattern of firepower imposed upon them by their atomic armoury.

It is credible to suppose that effective political operational control as to the choices of weapons to be used can be obtained over the air forces and navies. It is argued that atomic warheads on rockets used for anti-aircraft defences and atomic depth charges and torpedoes should be treated as conventional weapons, since their use would not begin the nuclear escalation which it must be NATO policy to avoid. These weapons constitute special cases where the military commanders could be given discretion as to their use once political authority had been given for the conduct of hostilities. The problem is essentially concerned with the atomic weapons for use by the ground forces and it is these which are usually meant when the generic term 'tactical nuclear weapons' is employed. It is these weapons which have too often been described as 'really an improved form of artillery'.[38]

Because of their proximity to the enemy and their consequent immediate involvement in any aggression that may occur, it is neither credible nor reasonable to expect that in an emergency the troops and their commanders will not use any and every weapon at their disposal to prevent their own defeat or their positions being overrun. They would be in no position to judge the situation on the front as a whole; and a failure in communications might well deprive them of accurate information as to the nature and size of the attack taking place. If, in addition, as seems to be the case, the whole of their training and all their exercises had been conducted on the basis that nuclear weapons would be used from an early stage in any engagement, it would be surprising if any system of political control could in those circumstances survive the test of events.

The advantages of tactical nuclear weapons envisaged when the original decision was taken in 1954 have not fully materialised since the Soviet troops now appear to be as well as if not better equipped with such weapons than our own forces. However, the fact that the Soviet forces have these weapons means that we must have them too. Just as the nuclear stalemate in strategic weapons depends upon each side having the power to retaliate in kind, so must we have tactical nuclear weapons to maintain a tactical nuclear stalemate. In other words, the tactical weapons must be considered less as weapons to be fired in the event of hostilities and more as weapons forming part of the series of deterrents we must maintain to prevent war or, if some aggression occurs, to limit its scope. Like the strategic deterrent, they will have failed in their primary purpose if they have to be used. And while the danger of escalation is the source of our anxiety about the employment of any tactical nuclear weapons, it is the danger of escalation which enhances their deterrent value.

If tactical nuclear weapons are to be retained and developed in NATO forces, as clearly they must be, they must be subject to as effective political control as the strategic deterrent. It is difficult to see how this control can possibly be exercised unless these weapons are deployed separately from the conventional units and are subject to a different channel of command. This represents a revolution in NATO policy, but there is no alternative if the dangers of nuclear escalation are to be avoided. I do not believe that the current conception of dual purpose Army units capable of fighting either a conventional or a nuclear war, will work out in practice. Certainly it is very unlikely that the missiles where they have the dual capability would ever be used for conventional explosives. The missiles at present in service would be wasteful and inefficient used in a conventional role; moreover the deployment of atomic artillery is entirely different from that of conventional heavy artillery.

The atomic artillery units should therefore be organised quite separately from the conventional brigade group or divisional formations and should be available, once a political decision or directive authorising their use had been given, to support the conventional formations. The Soviet nuclear weapons seem to be organised on a similar pattern to this and it would appear that they are fully seized of the dangers of nuclear escalation. It also suggests that the use of tactical nuclear weapons by our troops would invoke immediate nuclear retaliation.

In addition to separate organisation, these special atomic units would require a separate command. I would suggest that a new senior post, Commander-in-Chief, Tactical Nuclear Weapons (TACTNUC) be created to have command over all the tactical weapons within SACEUR's command. He would be responsible to SACEUR for the deployment of the weapons and through the Supreme Commander, Nuclear Weapons (SACNUC) to the North Atlantic Council for political decisions as to their initial use. This dual responsibility or 'wearing two hats' is not unusual as most of NATO's senior officers, including SACEUR himself, have national as well as NATO responsibilities. It seems quite appropriate that the Supreme Commander and the political machinery suggested earlier for the joint political control over strategic nuclear weapons should be adopted for a similar control over tactical use.

There remains the problem of the custody of the warheads. At present the only operational tactical nuclear weapons in Europe are with American and British units. The British land forces are equipped with American missiles and American warheads. (Some British bombers in the Tactical Air Force are also equipped with nuclear bombs of American origin.) In the foreseeable future tactical nuclear weapons must be supplied by the United States—the British *Bluewater* missile will take some time to develop. Since American law forbids any transfer of nuclear warheads, all the nuclear warheads are retained in American custody. SHAPE has been engaged in drawing up a programme for the establishment of stockpiles throughout Europe to enable warheads for tactical ground-to-ground weapons to be available in the vicinity of each tactical weapon regiment's normal station. However, it is quite possible that in an emergency these regiments may be called upon to move considerable distances to their battle positions. Thus it is necessary for each non-American regiment of these weapons to have with it a small detachment of American troops charged with the custody of the warheads.

The arrangement is very similar to the agreement whereby *Thor* ballistic missiles are operated in the United Kingdom. That is the system of two keys, one held by the user country who operate the missile, the other remaining in the possession of the American forces who retain custody of the warheads. Thus since both keys are necessary to fire the weapon, there is a dual control over its use. The nuclear warheads will only be formally released to the delivery unit if SACEUR, in his dual capacity as NATO Supreme Commander and as a United States commander, gives the order. Yet it is expected that the appropriate dual author-isation, addressed to user personnel and to the United States custodian personnel, would be embodied in a single message trans-mitted by a single channel of communication.

Although these arrangements are cumbersome, it can be argued that they provide some measure of control. It is, however, doubtful if in an emergency the two key system would be effec-tive, especially if there were a break-down in the line of com-munications. And while the difficulties may not be too great now while only one nation other than the United States has its troops in Europe equipped with tactical nuclear weapons, complications seem likely when the weapons are more widely dispersed and are made available throughout the forces on the Central Front.

These complications will grow if and when Britain, and perhaps France too, have their own means of delivery together with their own nuclear warheads in Germany, or envisage the tactical use of nuclear weapons from missile sites on their own territory or from their aircraft. They may even follow the

American pattern and supply weapons to other allies while retaining custody of the warheads, thus participating in any decision to use them as America does now. In such circumstances the single control now operated *de facto* by the United States would no longer apply. And, as has already been discussed, the development of smaller weapons with low yields designed for perhaps every infantry company raises grave doubts as to the credibility of even this system of political control.

Apart from problems of control, the intention to deploy tactical nuclear weapons throughout the alliance presents political problems too. The decision to equip all the forces of the alliance with the missiles or means of delivery has already caused considerable political controversy. A relaxation of American control over the warheads or any other arrangement which led to a supply of warheads all round within the alliance, especially to Germany, would produce much more.

On military grounds and on the grounds of equality within the alliance, it is difficult to argue that the German Bundeswehr should not have its own tactical atomic weapons if they have been supplied to other members of the alliance with troops in Germany. In addition there is the strong line of argument that all German forces are automatically assigned to NATO, while the other member countries have independent national forces as well as those assigned to SACEUR. Influential circles in Germany have for a considerable time desired to equip their troops with tactical nuclear weapons and there has been much controversy in Germany itself on this question. Undoubtedly, for many Germans possession of tactical nuclear weapons, and the implied recognition of equal status in the alliance which would go with it, has the same attraction as a status symbol as possession of independent nuclear capability has for many Frenchmen. (In the case of Germany it is the desire to be accepted as an equal partner in the alliance; for France, it is a desire to preserve the status of a great power.) At the same time there is no important section of opinion in Germany that desires to go back on the renunciation of the manufacture of nuclear weapons made in the modified Brussels Treaty in 1954.

It is, however, idle to pretend that a decision to make tactical nuclear weapons available for all the forces in Europe, including the German forces, would be without political difficulties for the alliance as a whole. This would be so whether or not the warheads are subject to American custody. An indication of the problem is given in the decision in April 1961 to cancel the German order for the American long-range *Mace* missile placed during the Eisenhower Administration and the subsequent order for the much shorter-range *Pershing* missile. Certainly problems would arise in the field of arms control and limitation negotiations, and the possibility of a staged or experimental scheme for disengagement, as well as any hopes for German reunification, would be affected.

Since both the political and military needs of the situation demand the separation of the tactical nuclear units from the rest of the NATO forces, a lot of difficulties can be avoided. It is no longer necessary or desirable that these separate units should be integrated into national forces or consist of men from any one country. General Norstad has already asked for special 'fire-brigade' mobile forces to be created from the forces assigned to him. This mobile task force was established in June 1961 and is intended to be the nucleus of a larger force in which all member countries of NATO would take part. The separate nuclear artillery units I have proposed should follow this multi-national pattern—they should be NATO and not national formations and they should each consist of personnel from several countries. In this way the Americans could supply an element to each regiment or unit as an integral part of it, thus preserving the system whereby the Americans retain physical possession of the warheads. This would seem a more efficient and effective arrangement than the existing practice which adds a small American detachment to the British artillery regiments. The idea of multi-national, integrated units to dispose of tactical nuclear weapons for land forces follows the pattern of the Allied Tactical Air Forces who also have nuclear weapons.

If at the same time the control of these NATO units is through a new channel of command subject to the North Atlantic Council (or such political directives or arrangements as it makes to deal with emergency situations) for authority for initial use, the control of the weapons would in no sense be in the exclusive hands of one nation. The successful co-operation of the various national units within the Tactical Air Forces and of officers of all the member countries in the various allied headquarters gives grounds for believing that this multi-national approach is feasible, despite language and other difficulties.

Adoption within a NATO framework of this idea—which incidentally was a major feature of the rejected European Defence Community—has many advantages. In particular it gives reality to both the concept of interdependence within the alliance and the necessity of exercising joint political control over the use of tactical weapons. The proposed organisation also fulfils the requirements of the NATO strategy I have tried to expound: in short, that we should keep our tactical nuclear weapons up our sleeve and not carry them in the palm of our hand.

As with the strategic deterrent, we should not have to use the tactical deterrent first. To maintain its credibility some un-certainty as to when tactical weapons would be used should exist in the mind of a potential aggressor, particularly until such time as our conventional strength is sufficient to be a credible deterrent also. Until this happens we cannot afford to make a formal declaration of our intent never to use tactical nuclear weapons first. Nevertheless the first priority of all our countries within the alliance should be to so strengthen and reorganise our con-ventional forces that the present dangerous reliance on nuclear weapons is removed. Action towards this end will speak far louder than words. Our objective must be to have sufficient conventional strength to contain limited conventional aggression without resort to our nuclear firepower.

Henry Kissinger makes the point with great force and clarity:

Once the conventional balance of forces is restored, we could then responsibly announce that we would employ nuclear weapons only as a last resort, and even then in a manner to minimise damage. To that extent that the communists are unable to defeat the con-ventional forces of the free world without resorting to nuclear weapons, the practical effect will be to renounce the first use of nuclear weapons. Even where this is not the case, strengthened conventional forces would pose an increased risk for the aggressor and provide opportunities either for the mobilisation of additional conventional forces or for negotiations before we make the decision to use nuclear weapons. The inability to defend every area with conventional forces should not be used as an excuse for failing to build up our strength. The free world must not become a victim of asserting that if it cannot do *everything*, it will not do *anything*.[39]

NATO should adopt as its text the words of Admiral Charles R. Brown, USN, Commander-in-Chief, Allied Forces Southern Europe. In Washington in October 1958 he said:

> I have no faith in the so-called controlled use of atomic weapons. There is no dependable distinction between tactical and strategic situations. I would not recommend the use of any atomic weapon, no matter how small, when both sides have the power to destroy the world.

While we must maintain tactical nuclear capability in Europe, it must be stressed that these weapons rate a very low priority among NATO's military requirements. If this were accepted, we might then get more response to the consistent appeals for more conventional forces and ordinary soldiers—the most valuable deterrents in our system.

PART THREE

NATO Forces

Chapter VIII

LAND FORCES

For some years the major criticism of NATO strength has been directed towards the inadequacy of the ground forces in being which would be immediately available in the event of any hostilities. In particular the failure to achieve the goal of thirty divisions, assessed as the absolute minimum required by SACEUR for the defence of the Central Front, has been a major weakness of the alliance. The Assembly of Western European Union has stressed this consistently since 1956.

The consequences of nuclear parity or stalemate give the provision of adequate conventional forces a new importance and urgency. We must regard the ground forces as one of the several deterrents—and perhaps the most essential—we need to maintain to prevent war. For, as I have already tried to make clear, unless we have sufficient strength to contain a limited aggression without immediate resort to nuclear weapons, an aggressor may be tempted by the prospect of easy territorial gains to make a sudden limited attack and face us with the choice between accepting the *fait accompli* or starting a nuclear war. Adequate conventional forces are also an essential element in our protection from nuclear blackmail.

It is against the background of the new strategy demanded by the situation of nuclear parity that we must judge the adequacy of the NATO forces to discharge their tasks.

DEVELOPMENT OF NATO STRATEGY

Early NATO planning was based upon three distinct plans— the Short-Term, the Medium-Term and the Long-Term.[40] The Short- and Medium-Term plans were defence plans—the former being designed for an immediate emergency and the second being a battle plan in anticipation of the forces which were gradually being built up. The Long-Term plan was essentially a requirements plan and became the basis of the force goals recommended to the member Governments. Early planning was based on defending Europe on the Rhine. After 1950, however, a 'forward strategy' was adopted which meant defending as far east of the Rhine as possible. It was self-evident that the former strategy was unlikely to engender enthusiasm in Germany for rearmament (indeed it was also unpopular with the Dutch and the Danes), yet it was clear to the military planners that a substantial German contribution was necessary if the required number of divisions was to be assembled on the Central Front. To this extent the 'forward strategy' was thus the outcome of political rather than military considerations.

In 1952 the North Atlantic Council approved a goal of ninety-six divisions at its meeting at Lisbon.[41] This was the first approval by the member Governments of the force goals conceived in the original Long-Term Plan. It must be stressed that these divisions were not expected to be forces in being but the number that could be mobilized in thirty days. The number to be in the line and ready at all times was understood to be between thirty-five and forty divisions, about twenty-five on the Central Front, from seven to nine in the Brenner-Trieste area and two or three in Scandinavia. The rest were to be reservists, to be mobilized between a fortnight and a month after D-Day, plus contributions from the strategic reserves in the United Kingdom and the United States.

However, it seems fairly certain that many member countries regarded the fixing of the Lisbon goal as largely an academic exercise. They had little intention of implementing it and for the most part did not consider it necessary to do so. The forces in Europe were viewed as only a screen or trip-wire which would serve to trigger-off the long-range nuclear bomber force which was regarded as the real deterrent.

At this time the arithmetic, and the defence strategy, were further complicated by the accession of Greece and Turkey to the alliance. This added between twenty and twenty-five divisions to NATO strength but also greatly extended the perimeter to be defended.

From December 1954 the North Atlantic Council authorised SACEUR to base his plans on the use of atomic weapons from the beginning of hostilities. This decision was followed by a revision of the Lisbon goal to a figure of thirty divisions for the Central Front. The new target seems to have been fixed because of two considerations. First, the assumption that an all-out nuclear war would be short and would leave no time for the mobilization of reserves; hence the emphasis on forces in being. Secondly, as well as being a more realistic assessment of what the member countries would be likely to provide after allowing for the great additional strength of the twelve divisions to be provided by German rearmament, it matched the twenty-two divisions maintained by the Soviet Union in Eastern Germany, together with a reasonable allowance for such additional strength as the Russians could muster there without attracting attention. It is presumed that if there had been signs of Soviet intention to keep larger forces near the front line the target of thirty divisions would have been raised. We must also allow for the fact that Russian divisions are numerically appreciably smaller than NATO divisions, comprising at war strength 12,000 men in infantry and 10,500 men in armoured divisions.

It is thus misleading to compare the Shield force of thirty divisions with the frequently quoted figure of one hundred and seventy-five divisions at the disposal of the Soviet Union. It is also an over-simplification of the position to assume that the difference between the Lisbon goal of ninety-six divisions and the thirty divisions target of General Norstad is based solely upon the extra firepower of the atomic artillery with which the thirty divisions are to be equipped. In fact, as mentioned above, the new target requires thirty standing divisions as compared with the Lisbon twenty-five standing divisions for the Central Front. However, the adoption of the new force goal did represent a change in strategy in the light of both the existing strategic and the projected tactical nuclear capability. There was no longer any idea that there could be a non-nuclear limited war in Europe and thus the previous plans to prepare for such a contingency were abandoned.

In fact a characteristic feature of the development of nuclear capability, no doubt influenced to a considerable extent by the mounting cost of defence budgets with the dual burden of conventional and nuclear armament, was the reduction in the size of standing armies. This applied to both the Soviet Union and the NATO powers. However, as the consequences of nuclear parity have been appreciated, there has been a reversal of the trend and increased attention given to conventional forces.

MANPOWER

In December 1953 the United States announced that over the next four years she would reduce her standing forces by 18 per cent—from 3,450,000 to 2,815,000. As the Secretary of State explained in his 'massive and instant retaliation' speech a month later, it had been decided 'to depend primarily upon a great capacity to retaliate instantly, by means and at places of our own choosing'. Vice-President Nixon emphasised the purpose: 'Rather than let the communists nibble us to death all over the world in little wars, we will rely on massive mobile retaliatory power.' The British Defence White Paper of 1957 repeated the theme: 'The only existing safeguard against major aggression is the power to threaten retaliation with nuclear weapons'; and announced that British forces were to be reduced by 45 per cent from 690,000 then to 375,000 at the end of 1962.

According to Mr. Khrushchev the total strength of the Soviet forces had been reduced from 5,763,000 in 1955 to 3,623,000 in January 1960. He then announced that a further cut of 1,200,000 or 33 per cent was to be implemented in the next two years, on the grounds of the increased firepower at the disposal of Soviet forces. It is probable that the heaviest cuts have been in the ground forces. However, on 8 July 1961 Mr. Khrushchev announced that he had suspended the demobilisation announced in 1960 and proposed a substantial increase in the Soviet Union's military budget. This move and the renewed emphasis on conventional armaments were obviously related to the Soviet campaign on Berlin and a German Peace Treaty which was revived during 1961, although Mr. Khrushchev referred to 'military measures which have recently been taken by the United States and NATO'. It is only possible to speculate as to whether this was meant as a tactical move in the cold war and an indication to China that he was being tough with the West, or whether it implied a change in Russian military strategy.

Soon afterwards, on 25 July 1961, President Kennedy announced in a speech to the nation that he proposed to increase his current defence budget by 3,454 million dollars to cover increased manpower, increased airlift capacity, the retention in service of ships and planes due for retirement, and civil defence. He proposed to increase the authorised strength of the Army by 225,000 to one million men, the Navy by 29,000 (to a total of about 650,000) and the Air Force by 63,000 (to a total of about 890,000). Thus the total authorised strength of the United States armed forces is over two and a half million men. While the immediate purpose of these proposals was clearly directed to the Berlin crisis, the increase in conventional strength accords with the President's repeated emphasis on this aspect of defence policy in the situation of nuclear parity, to which reference has been made in earlier chapters. The United States Defence Budget for 1962, estimated at over 50,000 million dollars, reflects the increased costs of the build-up of both conventional and nuclear strength.

RATIO OF FORCES TO SPACE

Our problem today is to decide if the target of thirty divisions for the Central Front is sufficient in the new circumstances of nuclear parity and, if it is, what prospects there are of its being achieved and what steps should be taken to assist its attainment.

In an important study[42], Captain B. H. Liddell Hart analyses the lessons to be drawn from the experience of great armies since 1800. He shows that during this period the number of troops needed to hold a front of any given length securely has been declining steadily: 'In other words, the defence has been gaining a growing material ascendancy over the offence. Even mechanised warfare has brought no radical change in this basic trend.' A well-conducted mobile defence should be able to hold out indefinitely unless the attacking forces had an overall superiority in excess of 3 to 1. Allowing for the unequal quality of existing NATO forces, a ratio of 1 to 2 should be sufficient for them to hold their own and a ratio of 2 to 3 should provide a safe margin.

This kind of calculation seems to have been the basis of early NATO thinking; the Lisbon goal merely confirmed the requirement to have reserves to match, in proportion, the reserves available to the Soviet Union. In a sense we are back to 1949 with the emphasis on conventional forces arising from nuclear parity, but with a very important difference: whereas in the earlier days the danger was thought to be a mass invasion, today, under the ever-present threat of nuclear war, the danger is either war by miscalculation or a sudden limited attack designed to pose for us the problem of accepting a *fait accompli* or starting a nuclear war. The thirty divisions should be able to discharge these tasks adequately and to deal with anything short of an all-out conventional attack without resort to nuclear weapons. It is extremely unlikely that the Soviet Union could possibly mount an attack on the Central Front with more than forty divisions without such prior notice as to rob the operation completely of the benefit of surprise. It is even more unlikely that a mass conventional invasion would be attempted, with the knowledge that it would have the probable consequence of forcing our use of nuclear weapons and thus involving a Soviet surrender of the tremendous advantage of the first nuclear strike.

On the basis of Captain Liddell Hart's analysis, the conclusions of which I accept, it is reasonable to suppose that in the new strategy forced upon NATO by Russian nuclear capability, thirty divisions, or even less, should suffice. But numbers are not the only consideration. These divisions must be efficient, well-equipped and much more mobile than ever before. Indeed in the present situation, quality is perhaps a greater criterion than quantity.

Progress towards achieving the 'Shield' force of thirty divisions, set out in the confidential but much publicised NATO document M.C. 70, which lays down the allies' contributions to the collective defence, has been slow and has largely depended in fact upon the rate of German rearmament. French divisions have been withdrawn for use in Algeria, the British contribution has been reduced from four divisions to three and the pace of providing the German divisions has been slower than the original timetable.

Many factors can be brought forward to explain the apparent lack of concern by many member countries in fulfilling the force goals they themselves established and have many times endorsed. While individual nations have their special problems (and these are discussed later on), the overriding consideration has been the feeling that in the event of war nuclear weapons would be employed at once and that therefore the number of soldiers and their equipment were not very important. There has also been a very unrewarding controversy about the provision of atomic weapons for use on the battlefield to all the NATO units and especially concerning the position of German troops. And undoubtedly the belief, discussed in previous chapters, that nuclear capability was the qualification for carrying influence within the alliance has not inspired the non-nuclear or 'second-class' powers to make great efforts to supply their quotas of well-equipped conventional forces. So far the preoccupations of NATO strategy, first with massive retaliation with strategic nuclear weapons and now with the doctrine of using tactical atomic weapons at an early stage in any hostilities, have blunted the urgency of fulfilling the M.C. 70 tasks.

The relevance and priority of the provision of *conventional* forces have to be demonstrated if the target is to be reached. In many ways the problem hangs on the general health of the alliance. There would be no great difficulty in providing thirty divisions if everyone shared the view of General Maxwell Taylor, the former Chief of Staff of the United States Army and now one of the President's personal advisers, who described the NATO Shield as the principal deterrent to war.

CENTRAL FRONT FORCES

The existing forces on the Central Front under the command of Allied Forces Central Europe with headquarters at Fontainebleau are made up as follows:

Germany: eight divisions. (One of these divisions is assigned to Northern Europe in the event of war but is treated as part of the Central Front force for purposes of the thirty divisions goal. The final German commitment is a total of twelve divisions.)

United States: five divisions (plus the equivalent of three armoured brigades).

United Kingdom: three divisions.

France: two divisions. (The commitment is four, but two divisions have been withdrawn for use in Algeria. In fact, in June 1961 the effective French contribution was reported to be less than one division, but an additional division has been moved to Germany from Algeria.)

Belgium: two divisions.

Netherlands: two divisions.

Canada: one brigade (i.e. one-third of a division).

Thus the paper strength is twenty-three and one-third divisions (I have counted the United States strength as six divisions since the three armoured brigades seem now to be a permanent contribution) with the prospect of reaching twenty-seven and one-third divisions when all the German divisions are ready, twenty-nine and one-third if the French are able to provide their full commitment as well, and thirty and one-third if in addition the United Kingdom contribution is raised to its original four divisions.

Twenty-eight full-strength divisions with up-to-date equipment would be enough to discharge the tasks allotted to the Shield forces, but unhappily it is unlikely that the additional forces will be forthcoming in the near future. Also it must be stressed that there is reason to believe that because units are under strength and through shortages of up-to-date equipment, the present paper force of twenty-three and one-third divisions represents a fighting equivalent of no more than sixteen to nineteen divisions.

I have taken no account in the above survey of additional forces provided or to be raised because of the Berlin crisis since there is no certainty that these forces will be maintained after the ending of the emergency. The crisis has underlined the need for greater NATO conventional strength and pointed the moral of the unsatisfactory position whereby hurried and unprepared moves have to be undertaken whenever there is a worsening of the situation in central Europe.

In November 1961, General Norstad said that it had been no secret that in the Central Front, because of deficiencies in manning, equipment and supply, the recent effectiveness of NATO forces had been down to scarcely more than fifteen or sixteen divisions. However, by early in 1962, as a result of new commitments and special efforts, the number of available divisions would be raised to about twenty-five and almost all of them would be in combat readiness. One can only hope that this improvement will be maintained and that this accretion of conventional strength will prove to be permanent.

The requirement is thus as much a matter of building up the numbers and equipment of the existing forces as it is of getting the commitment of extra divisional formations. In particular there is great need to increase the mobility of the NATO divisions, especially with regard to cross-country capability, as it is considered that in these respects they fall far behind the highly mechanised Soviet divisions who certainly have the most up-to-date equipment at their disposal. In this connection it is encouraging to note that President Kennedy in his 1961 Defence Budget message to Congress drew attention to this problem: 'What is needed are entirely new types of non-nuclear weapons and equipment—with increased fire-power, mobility and communications, and more suited to the kind of tasks our limited war forces will most likely be required to perform.' It is even more satisfactory to record that an additional 122 million dollars are to be expended upon current limited warfare research and development programmes and the initiation of new programmes. Nuclear weapons have hitherto not only dominated strategic thinking; they have also absorbed almost all the effort and money directed to defence research.

An examination of the problem from the point of view of individual countries does not disclose grounds for optimism. However, before turning to this examination it is necessary to say a general word about the issue of conscription.[43] It is sometimes argued that there should be a general NATO policy to apply to all member countries concerning the type of conscription to be employed and the length of service to be demanded. In particular there is a strong opinion, well-founded on military grounds, that a twelve-month term of service is too short for a man to be trained and also contribute to an effective division within this period. If divisions in the Shield forces contain a high proportion of untrained personnel, there can be no doubt that their efficiency is much reduced.

I consider, however, that it must be left to the individual member governments to determine for themselves the ways in which they raise the necessary forces. There are many other steps towards closer co-operation and integration to which greater priority should be given. Nor is it possible to compare the defence burden undertaken by one NATO country with that of another solely or even mainly on whether there is conscription or not and on the length of conscript service. Some members (for example the United States, Britain and France) have substantial commitments outside the NATO area. Others prefer to use a greater element of regular troops or, as in the case of Britain after 1962, to rely wholly on them. The test is whether they produce the required number of trained personnel to discharge their NATO undertakings, not how they do so.

GERMAN FORCES

The German Federal Republic is the only member of the alliance whose forces are still in the state of building-up, following the decision to rearm Germany to the extent of twelve divisions taken in 1954. There is no national German general staff headquarters and all combat formations are assigned to NATO as soon as they are ready. The territorial formations, designed to protect communications and provide internal security in the rear areas, remain under national command.

The size of the Federal Armed Services has been increasing by between 50,000 and 60,000 each year and it is expected that the force goals for all services will have been attained by 1963. At the end of 1961 the forces numbered 337,000, of whom about 214,000 were in the Army, 76,000 in the Air Force, 27,000 in the Navy and about 20,000 in the territorial defence force. During 1962 three further divisions, making a total of eleven, are expected to be ready for assignment to NATO. The final total in the armed forces is envisaged as about 350,000, made up of 220,000 in the Army, 80,000 in the Air Force, 25–30,000 in the Navy and 25,000 in the territorial defence force.

Thus eight divisions have already been assigned to NATO, while the continuing build-up will add slowly to NATO strength. Similarly the build-up of the territorial forces will relieve NATO troops from these duties in the rear areas in the event of hostilities and will minimise the problems which would otherwise result from the lack of reserves.

According to Herr Strauss, the Defence Minister, a certain enduring reluctance to embrace a military career has been responsible for the fact that the *Bundeswehr* at present consists of sixty per cent conscripts and forty per cent longer service volunteers, whereas, for healthy development, the proportion should be reversed. All male citizens are liable for service, but because of the high standards set only about one in four of each year's group of nineteen-year-olds is called up. In practice, therefore, the system amounts to a form of selective service for a period of twelve months. Usually this is spent on three months' basic training, three months' technical training and six months with a unit. Over three quarters of the conscripts go into the army. It is expected that the period of call-up will be increased to eighteen months in 1962.

The build up of the armed forces in Germany has been complicated by a shortage of both warrant officers and senior NCOs and of officers of middle rank, the result of the gap of ten years when there were no forces. There is hardly a soldier today in the *Bundeswehr* in his late twenties or early thirties. There is also a problem regarding technical personnel. Although some success has been achieved in the recruitment of technicians and specialists on a long-service basis, it is in this category that the competition of industrial pay and opportunities is most difficult to overcome. The shortage of trained technical personnel cannot be remedied by conscription as the time is too short to justify the expense of training. In fact most complicated courses (e.g. radar) can only be taken by men serving on three-year or longer engagements.

Other problems have arisen, as the forces have grown in size, in connection with training areas and accommodation. This problem is peculiar to Germany because the greater part of the NATO troops are stationed in the Federal Republic, which is one of the most densely populated areas in Europe. As the German forces grow in size and the NATO force goal gets nearer to fulfilment, the difficulties become more acute. The problem is certainly more pressing now than when I first drew attention to it in 1958 in a report to the Western European Union Assembly.[44] The Assembly then recommended 'That urgent steps should be taken to provide better training areas for the forces on the Central Front, in particular through international arrangements to make suitable areas in member countries available to all forces of the alliance for periodical large-scale exercises.'

There are several aspects to this problem, and part of the difficulty lies in the traditional and understandable conflict in a democratic society between the civilian and the soldier. Local authorities and public opinion in general must realise that troops in Germany need space for their daily exercises or the efficiency of their training is greatly reduced. At the same time compensation formulae must be drawn up to provide either for lump-sum payments for the land used or quick, on-the-spot payment of claims for damage. It is important to spend more time and thought on achieving better public relations, by trying to get both soldiers and civilians to appreciate each other's point of view and problems. Other members of the alliance can help to ease the situation by making suitable land available for large annual exercises

K

or special training so as to reduce the demand on German training areas. If this were done some of the allied troops could conduct their manœuvres outside Germany. Certainly the frictions which arise deserve serious examination with a view to reducing the harm that may otherwise result to the relationships between allied peoples.

For similar reasons there has also been a problem about providing bases and training facilities for German forces outside Germany, and Herr Strauss has said that he has raised the matter many times at NATO conferences. There was much controversy when it was suggested that Germany would seek bases in Spain in 1960. Subsequently, however, Herr Strauss has said 'remarkable progress has been achieved. Now the *Bundeswehr* has bases in France, Italy and Benelux and has received a very generous offer from Britain'.[45] A West German tank battalion came to Wales in the autumn of 1961 for range firing practice, and facilities for the storage of ammunition, oil and general stores in service installations have also been arranged with the Federal German Government.

BRITISH FORCES

The United Kingdom is the only NATO power with a treaty commitment to keep a minimum number of troops in Germany, assigned to SACEUR. Under Article VI of Protocol No. II to the modified Brussels Treaty of 1954, the United Kingdom undertook to maintain on the mainland of Europe four divisions and a tactical air force 'or such other forces as the Supreme Allied Commander, Europe, regards as having equivalent fighting capacity'. She further undertook 'not to withdraw these forces against the wishes of the majority of the High Contracting Parties who shall take their decision in the knowledge of the views of the Supreme Allied Commander, Europe', with the proviso that if this undertaking 'throws at any time too great a strain on the external finances of the United Kingdom, she will . . . invite the North Atlantic Council to review the financial conditions on which the United Kingdom formations are maintained.'

The Council of Western European Union acquiesced in the withdrawal of 13,500 British troops from Germany in the financial year 1957-8 and in January 1958 authorised the withdrawal of a further 8,500. The result of these withdrawals was to reduce the commitment of 77,000 troops (about four divisions) to a total of 55,000 (about three divisions). These reductions, although approved by the procedure laid down in the Treaty, were extremely unpopular in Europe and undoubtedly contributed to the decline in British influence and prestige among the six countries with whom she was originally associated in Western European Union and who were later to set up the European Economic Community. In May 1957 the Assembly of WEU carried a motion of no confidence in the Council on the grounds that it had approved a reduction of United Kingdom forces without giving proper study to the problems involved, but it lacked the majority required to become effective.

There had been suggestions that there would be further reductions, and indeed in a British statement of 10 June 1958 the undertaking was only to maintain 55,000 men until the end of 1958 and 45,000 men until 1961. However, wiser counsels have prevailed and there have been no requests for further reductions in the level of United Kingdom troops in Germany. The Defence White Paper for 1959 said the present strength of seven brigade groups would be retained 'for the time being', which was later interpreted by Mr. Watkinson as meaning as long as seems necessary in order to keep the alliance strong, vigorous and efficient. Some British units in Germany have been below establishment but the Secretary of State for War has said that it is intended to rectify this as the all-regular army is built up.[46]

The main ground for the withdrawal of the British troops was the strain on the British balance of payments, and the problem has been closely linked with the annual bilateral Anglo-German agreements on the German contribution to support-costs. These costs have increased as a result of the revaluation of the D-mark and there was again in 1961 great pressure on British foreign exchange reserves and a serious balance of payments problem. In July 1961, the Chancellor of the Exchequer, Mr. Selwyn Lloyd, said that Britain was spending some £80 million a year in Western Europe in fulfilment of commitments to NATO and that of this sum over £65 million was going on the maintenance of British forces in Germany. Britain asked the North Atlantic Council to review the position, and in October a 'certificate of need' was issued confirming that Britain's appeal was fully justified. In addition there has been disappointment, and loss of an opportunity to earn foreign exchange, over decisions to buy American rather than British equipment. The *Nike* and *Hawk* missiles were preferred to the British *Bloodhound* for air defence throughout NATO Europe (only Sweden and Switzerland have bought *Bloodhound*); the American F 104 *Starfighter* has been chosen by the Germans and others as the NATO fighter-bomber and it seems likely that the American *Serjeant* and not the British *Blue Water* will be designated as the next generation NATO army atomic support missile.

Manpower will also cause problems for the United Kingdom in the years ahead, following the decision to end conscription and to rely entirely on volunteers and a regular army after 1962. The Government estimated in the Defence White Paper 1961 that on 1 January 1963 the numbers in the forces would be 165,000 to 180,000 in the Army, 88,000 in the Royal Navy and 135,000 in the Royal Air Force.

The reduction is largest in the army (from 230,000 at 1 April 1961) and it is the army that finds the greatest difficulty in getting the desired number of volunteers. (This is also the position in the United States and Germany.) The other services are not expected to have any great problems. It is hazardous to predict what the exact number is likely to be, as the arithmetic of voluntary recruitment and wastage is both complicated and uncertain. However, present trends suggest that if 165,000 (the lower figure) is in fact reached by 1963 the Government will be extremely satisfied. Certainly the 180,000 figure is unlikely to be attained until 1965 or after. While pay and conditions undoubtedly have a bearing on the size of a voluntary army, there is also evidence to support a view that, no matter what the pay and conditions, are, there is a limited number of men who are likely to be interested in making a career in the armed forces.

As a means of providing more manpower for the Army in the period after the ending of conscription, the Government is taking powers to retain National Servicemen for a further six months and to recall for a like period National Servicemen who have already completed their service. While this is a convenient method of selecting the particular categories of men required, it is only a stopgap expedient which has all the drawbacks of selective service and is bound to be extremely unpopular. It is not a satisfactory substitute for a reassessment of British commitments and reallocation of tasks between the three services, designed to permit them to be carried out on the basis of voluntary service.

Even if the strength of 165,000 in the army is achieved in 1963, to keep 55,000 troops in Germany then will demand a third of the total army manpower. The operation of sending British troops to Kuwait in July 1961 illustrated how tightly stretched were British resources of men and air transport. The problem of Britain's NATO and other treaty and traditional commitments can be appreciated from the following table[47] showing the present deployment of infantry battalions, before the emergency landing of troops in Kuwait, compared with the position in 1958:

	1958	1961
Europe		
Berlin and BAOR	22	20
Mediterranean		
Gibraltar, Malta, Cyprus, Cyrenaica, Tripolitania	15	7
Africa		
Kenya, Cameroons	1	$4\frac{1}{2}$*
Arabian Peninsula		
Aden, Persian Gulf	2	$1\frac{1}{2}$*
Far East		
Malaya, Singapore, Hongkong	6	4
Caribbean	1	1
	47	38

* Note: There is a detachment in the Arabian Peninsula from a battalion in Africa.

While there are many advantages in having all-regular forces and in particular in having men on a long-service engagement, as compared with a year or at most two years' service as conscripts, the size of the all-regular army has been the subject of controversy in Parliament and military circles since the decision was announced. As well as having been produced as a good political point for the 1959 election, the decision to end conscription was part of the plan to reduce defence expenditure and was taken in 1957 at a time when the policy was that 'the only existing safeguard against major aggression is the power to threaten retaliation with nuclear weapons'.[48] Conscription is very unpopular in Britain and alien to our traditions. Until after 1945, except for two months in 1939, there had never been conscription in time of peace since the naval press gangs of the eighteenth century. The continuation of conscription after 1945 was defended on the basis of equal sacrifice, all men who were medically fit being called-up, with very limited exceptions for work of national importance. This makes the idea of selective service very difficult to put across. No political party is likely to embrace it with enthusiasm although it has been suggested in some quarters and, of course, only a relatively small number of men from the age group eighteen to twenty would suffice to fill any gap left by the short-fall of volunteers. The ending of conscription has also meant the end of short-term volunteers who preferred to commit themselves for a three-year engagement in the service or regiment of their choice rather than serve for two years as a conscript in the arm of the service to which they were directed.

The desirability of cutting commitments is self-evident but it is less easy to say where. I am firmly convinced that it would be a major political error to seek further reductions in Germany, except in an emergency when British troops, as part of the strategic reserve, would be bound to be called upon. The strategic requirements of NATO demand a strengthening of the conventional forces and the return of a fourth British division to Germany would contribute much more to the alliance than the actual number of troops themselves. In defence as in most other fields, example is more eloquent than precept. However, there seems no likelihood that the British Government will reverse its decisions, and indeed influential American voices have been urging that if cuts in commitments are to be made these should be in Europe rather than east of Suez.

AMERICAN FORCES

The United States army in southern Germany is the strongest element in the Central Front Shield forces and it is unlikely that we can expect any permanent accretion of strength from America. The speeches of President Kennedy do suggest, however, that the present five divisions will remain, and this is an improvement on the prospect which developed in the last months of President Eisenhower's Administration that the American forces in Europe would be reduced. The United States has balance of payments problems too.

When taking into consideration the fact that, apart from non-NATO commitments in conventional forces, the United States has to provide by far the largest part of the nuclear weapons system, it is surely unreasonable to expect her to make a greater conventional force contribution in Europe. She has also concentrated upon building up a highly efficient strategic reserve at home, the Strategic Army Corps, consisting of three divisions prepared to move to any part of the world at short notice. This is a very important element in the West's limited-war capacity. One division can be moved in a few days, complete with weapons and equipment, and all three divisions can be transported in a short period. And although this plan indicates a considerable existing airlift capacity, one of President Kennedy's first acts was to increase the orders for airlift aircraft. A total of 129 new, longer range, modern airlift aircraft are to be delivered in 1962 instead of the previous programme of fifty. The United States also played a leading part in the building up of forces in Europe in the second half of 1961 and has brought her forces in Europe up to full strength. Additional troops have also been sent to take part in exercises.

OTHER ALLIED FORCES

French difficulties in maintaining her contribution to the Shield forces as well as carrying on the Algerian war have been considerable. Clearly no increase in her contribution can be expected until a settlement of the Algerian problem is completed. It is well known that the French army of today is one of the finest fighting forces in the world and the return of four full French divisions instead of the one or two weak divisions of recent years would mean an immense increase in the fighting potential of the NATO forces. While it is unlikely that France would wish to keep all the 600,000 men she has in Algeria under arms if circumstances permit their return from North Africa, it may be that she could increase her commitment of four divisions to NATO.

There has been doubt as to whether France would be willing to assign fresh divisions to NATO, despite the fact that the Central Front is under the command of a French general, in view of her decision not to place her Mediterranean fleet under NATO command even in time of war. It seems, however, unlikely that the same attitude will be adopted concerning land forces. France might also reflect that her influence within the alliance is likely to grow to a much greater degree if she takes the lead in remedying its greatest weakness by increasing the conventional forces rather than by developing a nuclear capability which adds nothing to the strength of the alliance.

It is difficult to see how the Belgian and Dutch Governments could increase their contributions unless they were to decide to put all their efforts into ground forces. Nor is it likely that the Luxembourg brigade that is promised upon mobilisation can be increased. The efficient Canadian motorised brigade group is also as much as can be expected of her in view of her commitments to United Nations' forces and the high cost of maintaining her troops in Europe, due in large measure to the fact that Canadian forces are the highest paid in the world.

ALLIED FORCES NORTHERN EUROPE

Although in any discussion of NATO problems attention tends to be concentrated on the Central Front, it must not be forgotten that there are three other sub-commands under SACEUR: Northern Europe, Southern Europe and the Mediterranean (which is only a maritime command). There is no publicised target for the strength of allied forces in these areas although it is presumed that the requirements were set out in the comprehensive NATO document M.C. 70. The land forces in these commands are not included in the 'thirty divisional Shield' goal.

Allied Forces Northern Europe (AFNORTH), with headquarters at Kolsaas in Norway, is responsible for the defence of Norway, Denmark, Schleswig-Holstein and the Baltic approaches. The command has at its disposal the land, naval and tactical air forces of Denmark and Norway but they are not assigned to NATO command; they are earmarked for NATO use in the event of an emergency. In addition one German division and (in the event of war) the small German navy in the Baltic are committed to AFNORTH. Denmark and Norway each contribute one division. The German division in Schleswig-Holstein, although treated administratively as part of the Central front force and included in the German commitment of twelve divisions to the Shield force, is available also, making a force of three divisions.

The German Government and their advisors have been particularly conscious of the weakness of NATO in the north since Hamburg is only 50 kilometres from the Iron Curtain and an armoured breakthrough could isolate the Schleswig-Holstein peninsular. The establishment of the new Baltic approaches command under AFNORTH, however, improves matters by placing all the forces in this area under unified command and remedies a very weak point in the command structure.

ALLIED FORCES SOUTHERN EUROPE

This sub-command (AFSOUTH) with headquarters at Naples is responsible for the defence of the Mediterranean NATO area. The command has a land frontier of about 850 miles (1,350 km.) compared with 400 miles (650 km.) on the Central front.

The land forces immediately available consist of about twenty-four divisions:

In Italy: eight divisions and five alpine brigades
In Greece: four infantry divisions and one armoured division
In Turkey: eight infantry divisions, one armoured division and four armoured brigades

A further fifteen divisions are available after varying periods of mobilisation, and in Italy there is also the United States Southern European Task Force (SETAF) which would be assigned to AFSOUTH in time of war. SETAF consists of a brigade, about 6,000 men, of special weapons units equipped with *Honest John* rockets and *Corporal* missiles.

THE ORGANISATION OF ARMY FORMATIONS

With the advent of nuclear weapons there has been much debate on the tactics and type of organisation to be adopted on a battle-field where nuclear weapons could be expected to be used by the enemy in a tactical role, and where such weapons would form an overwhelming addition to the firepower available to allied forces. It has been generally recognised that the new warfare requires the wide dispersal of troops in formations smaller than existing divisions to avoid too great destruction by nuclear attack, but still large enough to be an effective fighting force. A high degree of controlled mobility is also required to enable units to concentrate rapidly to meet an attack or to launch one, and to disperse equally rapidly afterwards. A third requirement is the ability to operate continuously at a high level of fighting efficiency without depending on regularly organised lines of communication and large supply depots, which would prove too vulnerable in a nuclear war. In short, the quest is for the smallest effective self-contained unit.

The need for rapid response in a highly mobile war, and the greater degree of initiative which subordinate commanders must display when operating at considerable distances from their own commanders, both militate in favour of shortening the channels of command and supply as far as possible. Thought has thus been given to eliminating one or more of the levels in the traditional army-corps-division-brigade-battalion chain of command.

Such studies have been conducted at SHAPE and subordinate commands and have led to general conclusions on the lines of the foregoing. SHAPE has not considered it desirable, however, to press for a standard organisation throughout Allied Command Europe, considering no doubt that on a front stretching from the North Cape to the Caucasus wide differences in climate, terrain, the technical ability of available manpower and the industrial resources of member countries would make a standard division undesirable and in practice impossible.

Within the more limited geographical area of the Central European Command, however, there must be considerable advantage in having a few standard types of organisation, and in this theatre the objections lose much of their weight. In fact the trend in all the major contributing countries is to provide for smaller self-contained units than conventional divisions, although the method of doing this has varied from one country to another.

Germany and the United Kingdom have turned to brigade groups but have not abolished the division as a major tactical entity. The United Kingdom has provided for varying numbers of brigade groups to come under the command of a divisional headquarters from time to time; the brigades must have the capability of fighting independently, but divisions must exercise control over subordinate units where possible. Belgium, France, the Netherlands and the United States have retained the division as a permanent organisation but have provided for its being split up into combat commands of varying size. All countries have introduced some armour into infantry formations, and all armoured formations continue to include infantry transported in armoured carriers.

The German army reorganisation into new-type brigade groups and divisions began at the end of 1957 after the United States pentomic division and the British brigade group formations had begun to take shape. The basic feature is a very economic use of manpower. The strength of a company was reduced from 160 to an average of 100 and that of a battalion from about 900 to an average of 650. There are two types of brigade: the armoured brigade with a peacetime strength of about 3,000 and an infantry brigade with about 4,000. The standard division consists of one armoured and two infantry brigades, and with divisional headquarters and combat and logistic support troops has a strength of between 14,000 and 15,000 men. Each brigade is, however, self-contained and is able to carry out missions on its own and to operate independently for a number of days.

Each infantry section has its own transport permanently attached to it (i.e. 'organic' transport) in the shape of tracked armoured personnel carriers (APCs) in the armoured brigade, and wheeled vehicles with across-country performance and some APCs for the infantry brigade. In this way it is claimed that reduced numbers of men in a section can carry sufficient weapons and ammunition to provide considerable fire-power and it is envisaged that in an attack by armour the accompanying infantry would normally fight from its APCs without dismounting. But as the total strength of the infantry battalions is only half that of the United States battle groups, doubt arises as to whether German units would be capable of sustained fighting over days and weeks, and the problem of replacements seems formidable although it is planned to have them immediately available. The permanent provision of transport for the infantry poses the question whether in this role some of the traditional qualities of the infantryman will be lost. The armoured brigade has only two battalions of tanks compared with the British three, and again reflects reductions in manpower.

The artillery support is partly organic—each brigade has a regiment of field guns and some anti-aircraft guns—and partly at divisional level—a regiment of medium guns and, it is envisaged, two rocket launcher units, one of the *Honest John* type. There are also anti-aircraft and reconnaissance units at divisional level. The importance of this reorganisation can be fully appreciated if one considers that a modern division, in spite of motor transport, has become an extremely slow-moving organisation both in movement and military command. The total length of a German motorised division on the march with the prescribed distances between vehicles is over 100 miles (170 km.). Under the probable conditions of modern warfare such a division no longer appears to be a useful instrument.[49]

The present British organisation is similar to the German in outline, but is stronger in manpower with infantry battalions of about 800 men comparable to those in the American armoured division. The armoured brigade is completely mechanised with an infantry battalion in APCs and three armoured regiments and a regiment of medium guns in support. The infantry battalions in the infantry brigades each have forty APCs each carrying an infantry section. The British concept of enclosed APCs is that infantry would in all cases dismount to fight. An armoured regiment, and a regiment of field guns, including a battery of medium guns, support the brigade.

In contrast to German plans, the British brigades are not permanently allocated to divisions, and there are no supporting troops permanently attached at divisional level. The British brigade group is further distinguished from the German by being stronger in manpower but less highly mechanised, and by having most conventional artillery organic to brigades (although it is understood that divisional control of fire will normally be exercised) with medium batteries as corps troops, for allocation to brigades as required.

The brigade group was officially adopted in 1958 as the basic formation of the British army but at the end of 1960 considerable modifications were made in the original structure. Many administrative responsibilities which had been placed upon the brigade group have been returned to divisional headquarters, although the teeth arms remain in the brigade group as before. The brigade group has proved extremely successful and popular with the teeth arms since it has made possible more intimate co-operation between infantry, tanks and artillery, and the continuous training together of the same regiments and battalions has resulted in a high level of co-ordination. These advantages are retained by keeping the organisation unchanged for the teeth arms while centralising the tail units higher up at divisional level. In effect this brings back the division as the controlling headquarters. The brigade group commanders will still fight their own battles, but they must look to their divisional headquarters for supplies and command.

In the United States pentomic division, the conventional brigade with its permanent headquarters, has been abolished. Only the infantry division is pentomic, in that it comprises five 'battle groups' which are large infantry battalions reinforced with heavy mortars, numbering some 1,100 men. Organic transport is available to carry a portion of the infantry; the rest normally march, although transport is available at corps level. In support is a strong battalion of medium tanks and field, medium and heavy artillery with nuclear capability. This division is too big to operate as a whole, and the 'battle groups' are organised to operate independently with a proportion of the field artillery attached.

The armoured division is completely mechanised, the four battalions of infantry travelling in APCs. These are supported by four large battalions of medium tanks and artillery with the same nuclear support as the pentomic division. This division has three roving 'combat commands' which, like the second-in-command of the pentomic division, can command any group of infantry and tank battalions. The structure of the Belgian and Dutch divisions and the experimental French divisional formation follow the American pentomic divisional pattern.

President Kennedy, however, instructed his Secretary of Defence in May 1961 'to undertake a complete reorganisation and modernisation of the Army's divisional structure, to increase its non-nuclear firepower, to improve its tactical mobility in any environment, to ensure its flexibility to meet any direct or indirect threat, to facilitate its co-ordination with our major Allies, and to provide modern mechanised divisions in Europe and new airborne brigades in both the Pacific and Europe.' As a result of this directive, the two new permanent regular Army divisions to be activated in 1962 will be organised on a new basis to give greater conventional fire-power and more mobility and flexibility. The First Armoured Division will contain six mechanised battalions and four tank battalions, and have a total strength of 15,593. The Fifth Infantry Division, with a total strength of 16,119, will have six mechanised battalions, two infantry battalions, and two tank battalions. It is presumed that this new pattern will be gradually introduced to replace the pentomic divisions.

The variations in the national formations and particularly of manpower in the different units mean that it is difficult to compare the national contributions in terms of 'divisions'. In general there has been a reduction in the number of men in each unit, although firepower has been maintained (and much increased if allowance is made for nuclear weapons). It must be recognised that this has almost certainly happened in the Soviet divisions also. Thus the smaller modern divisions cannot be compared with the former type.

Allowing for divisions of around fifteen thousand men and the necessary supply and base units, the target of thirty divisions requires a force of about six hundred thousand men.

It is implicit in the assumptions behind the reorganisation of divisional formations that any fighting is likely to be with nuclear weapons. This was certainly the case until recently, and while there are signs of some re-thinking at top level there is much evidence to suggest that there have been no changes in the strategic thinking of many military commanders in the field.

NUCLEAR EQUIPPED FORCES

The M.C. 70 NATO plan of 1957 laid down that all NATO troops should be given training in the use of atomic weapons, and this is still valid. Herr Strauss has said that[50] M.C. 70 and NATO planning for the future were based on the concept that all allied land, sea and air forces stood at the disposal of NATO; that these armed forces were to be equipped with a balanced share of conventional and nuclear weapons; and that weapons with atomic capabilities were and would remain an organic part of the armed forces concerned (not withdrawn, as suggested in some reports, and grouped in special units under American command) whereas the custody and control of atomic warheads were and would be as previously vested in American hands.

Nuclear artillery was only available in Germany to American and British units in the autumn of 1961, but there is no doubt that all NATO troops are trained and exercised on the basis that nuclear weapons will be used almost at once in the event of hostilities. German forces have been supplied with atomic launchers for training purposes and Mr. Watkinson said, in December 1961, that nuclear warheads, although not under German control, had been allocated to them on the same basis as to BAOR. Under present policy it must be anticipated that German divisions will have operational atomic artillery at their disposal, the warheads being in American custody, in 1962. Tactical weapons have been made available to other forces on the Central Front on a similar basis. I was surprised to find in 1958 that in British units in Germany, their whole strategy and tactics were conceived in nuclear terms, although the nearest nuclear artillery was hundreds of miles away at that time and the British Army units did not receive nuclear weapons of their own (subject to American custody of the warheads) until two years later. In short we had a nuclear strategy some considerable time before nuclear weapons were available to implement it. The irony is that now they are becoming available to our ground forces, there is an overwhelming case for a complete reassessment of that strategy.

There seems little doubt that the British Army in Germany is extremely dependent upon its nuclear weapons. The military correspondent of *The Times* has reported:[51]

> The nuclear artillery has been enthroned in the training manuals as the queen of the battlefield, and the infantry and the armour are now regarded as its supporting arms. With its present thinking and training, there is not much doubt that Rhine Army could react effectively with nuclear weapons. . . . Through no fault of its own, Rhine Army is not organised to react promptly with conventional weapons.

While it is obvious that if units are equipped with nuclear weapons they must receive training in their use and in the tactical situations which result from the use of nuclear weapons against them, their training should not be almost exclusively conducted on a nuclear basis. As General Norstad has said, the Shield forces must also be trained and deployed so that they can fight only with conventional weapons if required to do so.

In 1958, in reporting to the Western European Union Assembly on a visit to Germany, I said: 'Not only is it necessary for allied troops to be able to hold off conventional attacks, if necessary, while a decision is taken for the use of nuclear weapons, they must also be armed, as in the new formations at present, and *trained* so as to be able to deal with local incidents wholly by conventional means, as well as having training for nuclear war.'[52] This is as valid now as it was then.

However, in 1960, all the six major exercises with troops of the British Army in Germany, each involving one or more brigade groups, had a nuclear content. No major exercise was held on the basis that both sides had nuclear weapons but were under a restraint not to use them. Yet this seems to me precisely the most likely situation that may arise if hostilities begin.

The largest British Army manœuvres for seven years, in Exercise Spearpoint in October 1961, although beginning with only conventional exchanges, 'were conducted throughout in the tactical context of a nuclear battle.'[53] It was made clear that the British Army of the Rhine was still being trained to use tactical nuclear weapons from the beginning of operations in Europe. The exercise also revealed that serious shortages of men and equipment mean that BAOR would be incapable of defending itself even for a short time without nuclear support, even if its strategic thinking were to be changed to conform to the developing NATO policy of seeking to 'enforce a pause' by conventional means.

The emphasis on nuclear strategy in the British Rhine Army is not due to a wrong balance between nuclear and conventional weapons. Four or five atomic artillery regiments to seven regiments of conventional field artillery is not an unreasonable ratio, and although there are deficiencies in conventional armament and equipment—too few anti-tank weapons to meet a mechanised enemy and artillery of inadequate range, for example—these can and should be put right. The excessive dependence and stress on nuclear training and tactics stems much more from a firm belief that any war is bound to be fought with nuclear weapons and that they provide the only possible defence.

The United States divisions, the only other NATO ground troops equipped to fight with nuclear weapons and so equipped for a much longer period than the British, do not appear to stress the nuclear side of their armoury to the same extent. Since the Kennedy Administration took office there has been an important re-appraisal of their strategy and there is evidence to suggest that the training manuals have been revised. Yet even so it would not be surprising if these divisions did in fact rely on nuclear weapons to an excessive extent for the time being, as they certainly did prior to high-level changes in American policy. It takes a long time to reverse a doctrine that has been thoroughly absorbed into military thinking. It is also impossible to tell how far the public statements of President Kennedy and General Norstad have been translated into military directives. There is evidence, however, that US forces in Germany have been reinforced to improve their non-nuclear capabilities.

Nor can we shirk the uncomfortable fact that the political requirements of a strategy to minimise the danger of a nuclear war through miscalculation pose exceedingly difficult problems for the soldier in the field. A policy of dual capability and the ability to fight either a conventional or a nuclear war are admirable in theory but tiresome in practice. The tactical requirements and objectives vary enormously between the two kinds of war.

In deploying nuclear weapons the emphasis is on the use of space and not on holding ground. It is necessary to disperse one's forces so as to avoid giving the enemy a target for a nuclear strike while trying to force him, by skilful manœuvre, to deploy his forces in a way that opens up the possibility of making a nuclear strike against him. Atomic artillery can also deny ground to an attacker and can plug gaps in the line of defence due to insufficient conventional forces. It cannot, of course, be used in close proximity to one's own troops, and even if much smaller and 'discriminating' warheads are provided—that is, warheads accurate against relatively small targets and also able to be used in closer proximity to one's own troops—they cannot completely replace conventional artillery. With the size of existing warheads (believed to be no smaller than 1 kiloton and in many cases up to 20 kilotons in size) there is a large area of dead ground in front of defending troops in which the enemy could concentrate for a breakthrough after a dispersed approach.

THE NUCLEAR DILEMMA

There has been much controversy as to how far, if at all, atomic weapons favour the defence as against the attack, as was originally claimed when the weapons were first devised. In general it has been argued that such advantages as are claimed for the defender are at least offset by an enemy who is also equipped with nuclear weapons and has in addition overwhelming numerical superiority and is thus better able to cope with the probable extremely high casualty rate to be expected on a nuclear battlefield. Indeed it has been said that in training exercises based on a nuclear war situations, 'a good deal of training in conventional war was carried out, rather by accident, for the reason that if nuclear weapons are used at all freely the exercise comes to an end much too quickly, having run out of combatants.'[54]

Thus there is a fundamental dilemma. In facing an enemy who has a nuclear potential it is necessary to deploy on nuclear lines, even if there are restraints on using atomic weapons. Presumably the enemy would do the same. The prospect is therefore that any fighting will, or should, be conducted, in the first stages at least, with conventional weapons by troops deployed for nuclear and not conventional tactics. The dilemma arises because of the change in the rôle of the military commander in the light of political requirements. He no longer has only the traditional straightforward task of trying to defeat the enemy and defend his men. In the early stages at least, he has in addition the more sophisticated responsibility of playing a key rôle in seeking to avoid a nuclear war, even though conventional fighting has already begun. For only if the military forces succeed in achieving this pause can there be the opportunity for political intervention and only by this means can reality be given to the indisputable proposition that the question of raising the stakes should be reserved for political decision.

In my view, the conflict of responsibility between trying to safeguard their troops and defeat the enemy on the one hand and seeking to fulfil political directives on the other may well create impossibly difficult situations for the military commanders in the field. I do not suggest that they would not adhere to orders not to use nuclear weapons until express authority was given. But it is not unreasonable to suppose that faced with the prospect of being completely overrun in one area of the front, there would be a great temptation to use weapons at hand which could completely transform the local situation.

Since the physical control of the weapons themselves must naturally be at a fairly low level of command, is it not likely that perhaps one commander, unaware of the picture on the front as a whole and torn with doubts as to whether communications had in fact broken down and for that reason his orders had not been received, would fire his atomic artillery prior to the political decision for the first use of such weapons by our forces? The use of any nuclear weapons by the NATO forces might well be the signal for the unrestricted use of them by the enemy and their employment by the enemy provide in turn a general authority for NATO troops to use nuclear weapons on the battlefield. In this way the vital decision as to whether to wage nuclear war could be summarily taken out of political hands. This may seem an over-dramatic anxiety. However, my own limited experience of the battlefield in Belgium and France in 1940 and of the administrative chaos that preceded Dunkirk fortifies a belief that in the uncertainty of the actual events there is a fair chance that the plans and directives prepared in advance may not be carried out or, indeed, reach the troops for whom they were intended.

Proposals that the warheads should be stored away from the weapons until such time as their use was authorised indicate that these difficulties are recognised to some extent. But this solution contrives to achieve the worst of both worlds. The fact that the weapons are organically part of the same national formations and subject to the same command structure as the conventional forces encourages excessive reliance upon them, as does training with a heavy nuclear bias. Yet the physical separation of the two components could mean that when a nuclear strike might be wanted and authorised, failure to marry the warhead and the missile might occur. Such a scheme seems to be based on principles of military inefficiency.

Nor does American custody of the warheads provide a complete safeguard in units of other nations. The physical possession of a key or of the warhead itself by a small detachment of United States soldiers would not in an emergency deter those in physical possession of the missile, if they were determined to seize the key and fire.

The strategic requirement is that NATO forces as a whole should have both conventional and nuclear capability so that our nuclear potential can serve as a deterrent against the use by the enemy of his nuclear weapons on the battlefield. There is no merit, however, in dual purpose weapons. It is difficult to think of a more inefficient operation, in terms of either cost or of military science, than the use of, say, a *Corporal* missile with a conventional shell. In addition, the grouping of atomic artillery in order to provide the concentration of fire demanded in a conventional rôle would be to invite its destruction before it could discharge its proper function, if required, at a later stage. There would also be enormous logistics problems.

There can be only one solution to satisfy both political and military needs. As I have already suggested in Chapter VII, the nuclear element in our forces must be taken away from the conventional element and placed in separate units under a separate channel of command. It would then be abundantly clear to the military commanders (and to a potential enemy and the world at large) that they would always have to fight with conventional means unless and until they were informed, after a political decision to this effect, that tactical nuclear weapons could now be called upon. This reorganisation could scarcely fail to have a radical impact upon both military thinking and tactical planning. The fighting strength of our forces would not be impaired in any way since collectively they would still dispose of the same total conventional and nuclear capability. However, the clear separation between the two, which alone permits a realistic and practical system of joint political control, would greatly add to their deterrent purpose.

Nor is there any need for dual purpose *national* forces. The military requirement is for the NATO forces as a whole to have nuclear weapons at their disposal if given political authority to use them. Clearly if American and British divisions in NATO have atomic artillery as an organic part of their formations it is difficult to deny the same weapons to all other NATO divisions. But if the nuclear weapons are separated from divisional formations the need for atomic artillery regiments of any one nation disappears. Instead of NATO policy being directed to equip all national forces with nuclear weapons, its policy should be to have no national forces with such weapons. All the nuclear weapons should be entrusted to multi-national units, each consisting of elements of several nations. In each case the American contingent, as an integral part of the unit, could have custody of the warheads. This arrangement, as well as meeting the needs of political control and deterrent requirements, would have additional advantages in avoiding many of the problems—custody of warheads, national prestige and political difficulties—inherent in the policy of equipping all NATO forces with atomic artillery on a national basis. Equality within the alliance prevails just as well if no nation has individual control over the weapons as if all nations have them at their disposal.

It is sometimes said that we made a mistake in developing

tactical nuclear weapons, but that it is now too late to turn the clock back and we must therefore leave things as they are. These weapons must be available within the alliance. But we must interfere with the machinery of the clock since it could prove to be a time-bomb which could inadvertently trigger off a nuclear holocaust from what might otherwise have been a small war. The really difficult question of today, the decision to raise the stakes from conventional to nuclear war, must rest with political leaders and not be usurped unintentionally and unwittingly by the military.

The first mobile 'fire brigade' task force was set up in June 1961 and is intended to be the nucleus of a larger force. It is also contemplated that eventually all the member states providing forces for NATO will contribute units for this force, which is to be equipped with both conventional weapons and nuclear weapons for tactical use and to be transported by air. It is made up of units from the forces already in Germany so that there is no additional strength in numbers, but the existence of such a force capable of being moved rapidly to reinforce any trouble-spot on the NATO front is a most valuable addition to General Norstad's tactical strength. It may well prove a deterrent to sudden, limited attacks on such vulnerable positions as the island of Bornholm, the Baltic Straits, Lübeck or others on the Central Front, or Northern Norway or Greece and Turkey on the Northern and Southern fronts.

In addition the concept has the merit of applying the principle of merging units of the various national forces at battalion level, as envisaged in the European Defence Community. I have always believed that this principle was to be encouraged and I have already suggested that the idea of multi-national units on this pattern should be pursued as a means of avoiding some of the problems of nuclear weapons for tactical use.

The most extraordinary feature of the problem of the thirty divisions required for the Central Front is that it should be a problem at all. When one considers the populations of the countries involved in responsibility for this sector, or the forces which these countries were able to raise in the last war, the task of providing thirty divisions or around six hundred thousand men does not seem formidable. Indeed France has maintained in Algeria an army of greater size than that demanded by SACEUR from all the Western European countries, and the United States already contributes five of the divisions required.

If the political will to achieve the target existed there would be no great obstacle to its accomplishment. However, the United Kingdom is the only country with a clear treaty obligation to maintain any troops on the mainland of Europe at all. For all the other members of Western European Union the modified Brussels Treaty only provides maxima and does not commit them 'to build up or maintain forces at these levels but maintains their right to do so if required'. There is surely an overwhelming case for minimum levels of troops to be agreed and written into a new Protocol so that all the other WEU countries (i.e. the signatories of the abortive European Defence Community) should have the same obligation as the United Kingdom to provide a minimum force which can only be reduced with the consent of the Council of WEU.

I proposed this in 1958 and the idea was approved by the Assembly of Western European Union. The Council of Ministers reiterated their belief in the force goal of thirty divisions but declined to accept the recommendation that the Treaty should be modified to provide for it. The NATO Annual Review provides a military machinery for assessing the national contributions but so far it has failed to achieve political effect. Although M.C. 70 is a confidential document its contents as regards the thirty divisions goal and national commitments have for long been an open secret. No security considerations can thus apply. Only by stating a case to public opinion and giving public proof of the equality of sacrifice involved can either the purpose of NATO or its subsidiary objective of adequate conventional forces be attained. Certainly it would be easier in Britain to get public support for a strong British contribution to the Shield forces if there were outward and visible evidence of equal concern and binding undertakings on the part of the other member countries as to their contributions.

Chapter IX

NAVAL FORCES

With the concentration on air power demanded by nuclear strategy on the one hand and the growing need for conventional ground forces in Europe on the other, naval forces tended to diminish in importance during the 1950s. While contributing to both the Sword and the Shield they had a major rôle in neither. Indeed, during this period navies were out of fashion generally in the West.

At that time it was taken for granted that war between Russia and the NATO powers would inevitably become a global war. The main task of the naval forces was envisaged in the context of the broken-back warfare which might follow the initial nuclear exchanges, since the navies would play a crucial part in determining whether or not essential supplies and troops could be brought from the United States to a devastated Europe. This concept of a broken-back war was at variance with official NATO strategy which considered that any war would be short in duration. However, it made sense to prepare for protecting the sea-lanes because of the Soviet Union's developing submarine potential and since the United States was at this time outside the range of Soviet nuclear strike capacity.

In many ways it seemed that both in NATO planning and in the national navies there was a tendency for naval strategy to be developed quite independently of either the general NATO or national strategic concepts. It is the natural, although at times awkward, inclination of the different arms to interpret general strategic requirements in the light most favourable to themselves and the Navy seems to have been the most successful in this. Events since have proved the Navy right. This is not because of a superior assessment of the development of nuclear weapons. It is simply that the advent of nuclear parity and the consequent greater possibility of limited war demand a similar policy, in terms of men and money, to that evolved by the navy for self-preservation under earlier strategic concepts.

While the trend was international, the British Admiralty was probably the most successful in pursuing its independent strategy of heavily supporting the idea of a broken-back war. In 1955[55] the British Navy view was: 'The latest inventions may affect maritime warfare and alter the character of the forces needed to wage it but they do not diminish the need for navies. Indeed, for those who live on an island dependent on seaborne supplies, the need for a navy is all the greater.' Among its main tasks in a 'future war fought with the newest weapons of mass destruction' was 'to protect the communications necessary to support our warlike operations and to safeguard the supply lines of the allied countries'. In 1956[56] it was the same theme: 'In a global war our sea lanes would be open to attack by a massive underwater fleet and a powerful surface fleet which would be at sea with their fleet train. The main purpose of the Navy would be to retain control of the seas by destroying the enemy ships, submarines and aircraft.' Even in 1957, when the Government Defence White Paper[57] came down heavily in favour of a predominantly nuclear strategy and a smaller navy, the British Navy still maintained a virtually unchanged policy.[58] 'A global war might be fought to a quick end by the use of nuclear missiles. It might well, on the other hand, drag on, and in that event the Navy would be needed to protect our merchant ships as in the past.' In the following year, 1958, the British Admiralty surpassed itself in its claim:[59] 'Uncertainty about the course and direction of global war, which applies to all the fighting services, does not therefore restrict the rôle, the shape or the size of the future Navy.'

The development of ballistic missiles, the nuclear-powered submarine, and the present state of nuclear parity, have combined to change the picture, and it looks as if in the 1960s the balance will be tilted towards the naval arm of our services. A re-assessment of the navy's contribution to the strength of the alliance and of its capacity to meet its requirements must be made against this background.

The advent of the nuclear-powered submarine has revolutionised naval thinking. Its capacity to stay submerged for long periods has made it the ideal mobile vehicle for missiles, utilising the vastness of the oceans to protect it from pre-emptive attack. At the same time its great speed, compared to that of conventionally powered submarines, makes it a much more serious menace to merchant shipping than any craft known hitherto. There are some who predict that in time to come most naval tasks may have to be fulfilled by submerged vessels. This may come about, but it is too early to say that the need for surface vessels will not persist in the foreseeable future.

What is certainly true is that the NATO navies will play an increasingly important part in the provision of an invulnerable nuclear deterrent force, in addition to fulfilling their traditional rôle of protecting the sea lanes and permitting troops and supplies to be moved as required. They can also contribute to our preparedness to meet threats of limited war, and to the protection of our coasts.

STRATEGIC STRIKE RÔLE

The development of the *Polaris* missile submarines and their significance for our strategic forces has already been discussed in Chapter V. The United States Navy has had *Regulus I* missiles (with a range of 500 miles) in service on submarines since 1955. *Regulus II*, with a range of about 1,000 miles, is designed for use also on surface ships, for example the *Long Beach* class cruisers.

At present all *Polaris* missiles and submarines are part of the United States Navy and are subject only to the control of the President of the United States. (The proposal that some should now be assigned to NATO has been examined in Chapter VI.) Although Britain has one nuclear submarine launched and another on order, these are designed for anti-submarine work as 'hunter-killers' and not for carrying missiles. France has announced plans to build nuclear missile submarines in the late 1960s.

Strategic striking power is also available from aircraft carriers, which form the nucleus of the United States First, Second, Sixth and Seventh Fleets. The Second Fleet, which operates from the east coast of the United States and is also designated NATO Striking Fleet Atlantic, and the Sixth Fleet which operates in the Mediterranean are assigned important tasks in the NATO strike plan. Until the *Polaris* submarine fleet is built up—at the end of 1961 only six such submarines were fully operational—the aircraft carrier will remain the navy's main contribution to delivery of the strategic deterrent. The general belief that the days of the manned bomber as the most effective means for delivery of strategic weapons are numbered means, however, that the future of the aircraft carrier too is uncertain. It has been suggested that missiles might be launched from surface ships. Obviously this idea is preferable to 'soft' fixed-site missile bases, but the ships concerned could too easily be tracked by enemy submarines or aircraft to give anything like the degree of invulnerability against surprise attack attained by *Polaris*-type submarines.

The navy has also a conventional strike capacity, but this is of decreasing value. The bombardment of ports or installations by battleships or even heavy cruisers is a thing of the past, certainly within the NATO area.

While considering the implications for our striking power and our strategy of nuclear-powered missile submarines we must also take into account the consequences of similar developments in the Soviet Union. It has been widely reported that the Soviet Navy includes a number of atomic-powered submarines with equipment for launching rockets against ground targets, even if there is doubt as to whether they have as yet the range and undersea firing characteristics of *Polaris*. Admiral Jerauld Wright, then SACLANT, said in November 1959:

> We have conclusive evidence that the Soviets are constructing ballistic missile submarines, and will be able to launch via the seas a significant threat against NATO within a year, with a serious threat developing by 1963. We have conclusive evidence that they are showing an increased interest in the east coast of North America, a key area, and an industrial complex of first importance, not only to America but to our NATO alliance.

The decision of the Soviet Union to build a large number of submarines occasioned surprise in the West, since it was taken at a time when both sides were thinking that any war involving NATO and the Soviet Union would lead quickly to a global nuclear conflict. However, as I have pointed out in discussing Soviet strategy and forces, she was careful not to neglect her conventional capability, even at the time when she was making an all-out effort to develop nuclear capability. The geographical position of Russia, together with memories of the effectiveness of German submarines, caused the Soviet Navy to concentrate on submarines and destroyers rather than on aircraft carriers and big ships. For a landlocked country Russia has an enormous and very modern navy (at 1,600,000 tons it is second in size only to the United States Navy and has been constructed almost entirely since 1945). The technological revolution and the search for an invulnerable deterrent which have since taken place, and which could hardly have been foreseen when the decision to increase submarine strength was taken for other reasons, have given the Soviet Navy a great uncovenanted advantage.

Many experts have argued that defence against Soviet missile-launching submarines should have the highest priority in NATO naval defence policy. It is extremely difficult, however, to see how this could be done effectively. Submarine detection is far from perfect and the factors which commend *Polaris* submarines as an invulnerable vehicle for our Western deterrent apply equally to Soviet submarines. Even if the present imperfect, but extremely costly, anti-submarine equipment can be afforded against the danger of Soviet missile submarines operating in coastal waters, it is doubtful if it could be justified as a defence against surprise attack. Any Soviet submarines detected near the coast in peacetime cannot be attacked before they have launched their missiles, as there is no means of knowing that this is their intention. To go to great expense to be in a position to destroy them immediately afterwards seems hardly worth while. It seems more logical to give priority in the allocation of anti-submarine equipment to those forces protecting the convoy routes, where enemy submarines would be concentrated and therefore more easily destroyed. This may not be the American attitude. They may prefer to see their anti-submarine forces patrol their own coasts, since even in a conventional war they would always be on tenterhooks wondering if the next submarine would carry a nuclear missile. One can appreciate the dilemma facing the Americans. But the hard fact is that in the present state of development of anti-submarine equipment, an American decision to give priority to protecting her own coasts would make the protection of merchant shipping virtually impossible.

PROTECTION OF SEA LANES

All the European nations depend on a heavy tonnage of sea-borne traffic to keep their economies going. The Atlantic Ocean, the North Sea, the Channel, the Baltic Sea and the Mediterranean are all of vital importance. If the Soviet Union succeeded in imposing an effective blockade, Europe would starve.

Two possibilities can be visualised. First, total war in the form of annihilating nuclear blows followed by a long drawn-out phase of fighting, i.e. the broken-back war. The Soviet Union formerly considered that a general war would be likely to involve long campaigns, which explains their interest in building up forces to disrupt Western sea communications. In present circumstances such a war is not considered a very likely contingency, but obviously the possibility cannot be discounted altogether.

The second possibility is a Soviet blockade of Western sea-traffic without a nuclear war. Undoubtedly the greatest nuisance value of Soviet submarines would be reaped in a limited war situation, and a blockade would present a serious dilemma to the West. It has been suggested that the West should immediately initiate nuclear war in retaliation to such a blockade, and pressure for a nuclear strike on the submarine bases would be very great. But this raises all the problems of nuclear escalation posed in earlier chapters and does not seem to be a practicable or a credible solution—at least in the early stages—in view of the Soviet capacity for nuclear retaliation.

In either broken-back or limited war, protection of shipping is necessary. Merchant ships would have to be escorted by a fleet equipped with anti-aircraft and anti-submarine weapons. Experience during the last war indicates that below a certain speed, ships are safer in convoys. Merchant ships today move at speeds which compare unfavourably with those of conventional submarines and are much below the very high speeds of nuclear-powered submarines. Thus convoys would be the universal rule. The navy believes that very large convoys would get through, provided they were not subjected to nuclear attack, e.g. from missiles. While a large convoy does present an attractive target for nuclear attack, it seems unlikely that the enemy would take the risk of nuclear escalation involved. If it is decided to launch a nuclear war, it would be a surrender of the nuclear initiative to make the first strike upon ships at sea, no matter how large the convoy.

Undoubtedly effective protection of our sea lanes is a task of great magnitude. In contrast to the situation on land, the attacker on the sea needs far less resources to achieve success while the defender must have proportionally much stronger forces at his disposal to ensure effective defence. For example, in the first twenty-one months of the Second World War, the Germany Navy had less than forty submarines available, and only an average of twelve on operational patrol in the Atlantic and North Sea. Nevertheless these comparatively small forces caused dislocation and considerable losses of merchant shipping. Even at the height of the Battle of the Atlantic the German submarines never numbered more than 200, and rarely were there more than fifty on active operations at any one time in this theatre.

The strength of the Soviet submarine fleet has been variously estimated as about 450, more than ten times as big as the German submarine fleet in 1939, and probably two-thirds of them are long-range ocean-going craft. The Soviet Union might choose to deploy about 100 of these submarines in the Atlantic and North Sea. Of this 100, one half might be expected to be on operational patrol while the other half would be in home bases for supply and refitting. Of the fifty thus cruising in the Atlantic, some might be off the American coast, participating in the nuclear strategic strike, some might be used to ward off allied submarine attacks on the Russian coasts, some might be in the North Sea and some on the main Atlantic sea routes. It should be remembered that of the twelve million tons of allied shipping destroyed in the last war, eleven and a half million tons were destroyed by submarines alone. The Western shipping tonnage has increased by 55 per cent since 1939 and amounted to ninety-eight million tons in 1955. It is probably still larger today in view of the new fleet of big tankers constructed since the Suez crisis.

To afford protection against this threat anti-submarine forces must be concentrated at the points where merchant shipping is particularly dense and where enemy submarines would therefore be most numerous. The only method of fighting submarines at present is by hunting them down with destroyers and anti-submarine submarines, as well as with land- and sea-based aircraft. The development of atomic depth charges will favour the defence as they may be able to destroy a submarine at 600 yards distance. Anti-submarine submarines present an effective defence weapon provided they have the latest equipment including, in particular, detection devices (long-range *Sonar*). This is not at present the case with the submarines of most NATO member states.

Concern to provide the most effective counter to the submarine threat caused SACLANT (then Admiral Wright) to set up in 1959 the SACLANT Anti-Submarine Warfare Research Centre at La Spezia, an Italian naval port. It is now getting thoroughly into its stride and it is hoped that substantial technical advances will come from its work. Although it is a naval establishment and under SACLANT command, it also has the services of eminent civilian scientists. In addition to doing work designed to increase the operational range and efficiency of *Sonar* (Sound and Navigation Ranging), pure research is undertaken in the neglected field of oceanography. There is also a section concerned with operation analysis, the task of devising the most fruitful combination of methods for the real objective—killing submarines. The Centre reports on its work twice a year to a Scientific Advisory Council on which serve scientists from nine NATO countries. They are responsible for advising SACLANT and also their own Defence Ministers on any developments. The Centre has a vital part to play in anti-submarine defences and is an excellent example of NATO co-operation and consultation and of preventing wasteful duplication of effort. It should also go some way to remedy the shortage of scientists experienced in the neglected field of anti-submarine warfare. At present it seems that much more has been done in atmospheric exploration than on the sea bed and the establishment of the La Spezia centre should mean increased scientific study of the problems with resulting operational advantages.

It goes almost without saying that one of the primary tasks of the navy is to escort troops and their heavy equipment to the scene of any action and if necessary give them air cover until air bases can be established ashore. This function is particularly important in Southern Europe, for example, where the sea is the best means of communication between the NATO countries concerned—Italy, Greece and Turkey.

LIMITED WARFARE

Is a limited naval war in Europe a likely contingency at the present time? The following circumstances can be envisaged in which the navy would have to intervene: attacks on offshore islands, like Bornholm, or even one of the large Danish islands; amphibious localised operations against a coast-line; blockade of a single sea lane, such as the Baltic Sea or even the Mediterranean. As such attacks are unlikely to justify strategic nuclear retaliation, the navy would need limited war capabilities. There is also the danger of hostilities in which neither the Soviet Union nor the NATO alliance as a whole are directly concerned—for example in the Near East—where naval action would be required.

Soviet naval writers have recently begun to examine problems of seaborne landing operations. In the event of war—total or limited—seaborne as well as airborne assaults on the Danish and Norwegian coasts and on the Turkish Straits might have to be faced. In Europe, however, air action would perhaps be more effective in preventing an invasion and it is important to ensure that available air forces can be concentrated quickly against such a threat without difficulties over command and control.

Although naval headquarters have been slow to prepare for the possibility of a limited war, this has not raised any particular difficulties from the point of view of equipment, as most of the units in the NATO navies are of the conventional type and are therefore well suited for limited war operations. An integrated force for such a contingency might be created around light aircraft carriers and, for landing operations, commando-carriers. The commando-carrier, of which the British HMS *Bulwark* is the first model, carries a full marine commando with their equipment and transport and helicopters to lift them swiftly from ship to shore. Her value was proved in the Kuwait operation in July 1961. Her success has been followed by the decision to convert HMS *Albion* for commission as a commando-carrier with a larger military force. She will be ready in 1962 and will thereafter rotate with HMS *Bulwark* between the British Eastern and Western Fleets.[60] These commando-carriers are particularly suited to the tasks which may arise on the periphery of NATO territory and reduce the need for bases.

COASTAL DEFENCE

This last task of the navy in nuclear and non-nuclear warfare is not a responsibility of allied commands; it is entirely in the hands of national authorities. This is unsatisfactory, since defence against amphibious assault must be the concern of the whole alliance. The coastal defence of Denmark, for example, is clearly not just her own responsibility. Little is known of how satisfactorily member nations discharge their duties, except for the warning given by SACLANT that national authorities are not devoting sufficient attention to it.

THE NAVAL COMMAND STRUCTURE

The naval command structure is highly complicated. Three supreme commanders participate: SACEUR, Commander-in-Chief Channel, and SACLANT.

(i) *SACEUR*

SACEUR and his naval deputy have naval responsibilities in all the four subordinate commands:

Northern Europe Command—HQ Kolsaas (Oslo) has a Commander Allied Naval Forces, Northern Europe, responsible for the Norwegian and Danish naval forces as well as the German naval forces stationed in the Baltic Sea;

Central Europe Command—HQ Fontainebleau—has a Commander Allied Naval Forces, Central Europe, responsible for part of the Dutch and all the German naval forces stationed in the North Sea;

Southern Europe Command—HQ Naples—has a Naval Striking and Support Forces Command, consisting of the United States Sixth Fleet which will be assigned to Southern Europe Command in the event of war.

Mediterranean Command—HQ Malta—is a purely maritime command with subordinate commanders of the Gibraltar-Mediterranean, Western Mediterranean, Central Mediterranean, South-Eastern Mediterranean, Eastern Mediterranean and North-Eastern Mediterranean areas. It consists of the naval and maritime air forces of the NATO powers (except the United States Sixth Fleet) in the Mediterranean.

(ii) *Commander-in-Chief Channel*

The Channel Command, which was established in February 1952, is subject to the Channel Committee consisting of the naval Chiefs-of-Staff of Belgium, France, the Netherlands and the United Kingdom. The Command was originally exercised jointly by the Allied Commander-in-Chief Channel and the Allied Maritime Air Commander-in-Chief Channel. In 1961 the Allied Maritime Air Commander-in-Chief Channel became the Maritime

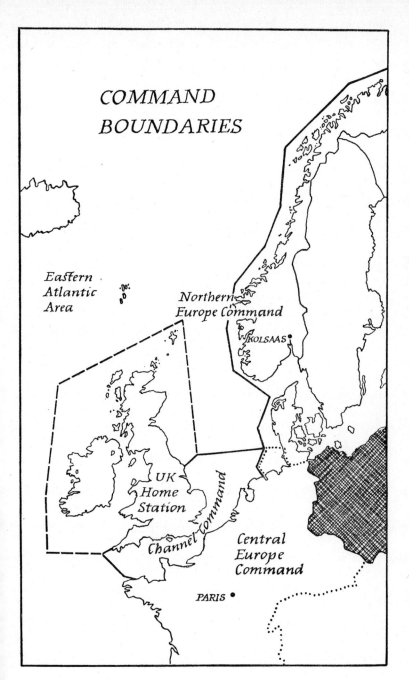

COMMAND
BOUNDARIES

Eastern
Atlantic
Area

Northern
Europe Command

•KOLSAAS

UK
Home
Station

Channel Command

Central
Europe
Command

PARIS •

M

Air Adviser to the Allied Commander-in-Chief in this area. This Command covers the English Channel and the southern North Sea, extending to the middle of the Jutland peninsula. There are five subordinate commands for various sub-areas of the Channel, two located in British ports, one in a Dutch port and two in French ports.

(iii) SACLANT

SACLANT's Command extends from the coastal waters of North America to those of Europe and Africa except for the Channel, the British Isles and the southern North Sea. There are at present three subordinate commands:

Western Atlantic Area—HQ Norfolk (USA);

Eastern Atlantic Area, under the joint command of the Commander-in-Chief and the Air Commander-in-Chief Eastern Atlantic Area—HQ Northwood (England). (In practice the Air Commander-in-Chief Eastern Atlantic Area is the same person as the Allied Maritime Air Adviser to the Commander-in-Chief Channel.) There are six sub-area commands, including a Command Submarine Force, Eastern Atlantic Area at Gosport (UK);

Strike Fleet Atlantic Command—HQ Norfolk (USA).

The fourth command—IBERLANT—was planned to cover the western approaches to the Straits of Gibraltar from the Bay of Biscay in the north, west to the Azores and south to the region of Dakar. Because of political difficulties, the permanent headquarters of this command has not yet been set up in Lisbon, although it was provisionally activated during exercises in 1960.

Before embarking upon a brief survey of the tasks of the various NATO naval commands and the adequacy of the forces available to discharge them, it is necessary to stress that any attempt to draw conclusions presents great difficulty. This is due to the different, and even conflicting, requirements of NATO and national demands in a number of important details. Also, we must avoid the error of assessing maritime problems in isolation. It is easy to make a case for more of this and that without reference to priorities and without remembering that the needs of all the services must come from the same defence budgets and the same pool of men and materials. On the other hand suggestions aimed at making better use of existing resources or achieving more effective defence for the same sum of money should command attention.

CHANNEL COMMAND

The forces available to the Channel Command are the smaller units of the four participating countries (the United Kingdom, France, Belgium and the Netherlands) but these are earmarked for assignment only after the declaration of an emergency. A few naval air squadrons are also earmarked for assignment to the Command. Nuclear weapons do not appear to be available in the area.

The primary mission of Allied Command Channel is to protect merchant shipping in the area in the event of hostilities. The question of providing alternative means and sites other than main ports for discharging merchant ships appears still to be under consideration. The danger is that merchant ships might be caught at the moment of evacuation in the fallout of nuclear bombs. Nothing has yet been done, however, to provide merchant shipping with anti-fallout devices, as these are costly and are not considered to be a good commercial investment by shipowners. Insufficient attention has been paid to this aspect of our defences, especially since most of our naval planning is on the basis of a nuclear attack. The Governments concerned should take steps to assist in the provision of anti-fallout equipment.

THE ATLANTIC AREA

Forces available to the Atlantic Command include almost the entire Atlantic fleets of both the United States and the United Kingdom, as well as ships from Canada, Denmark, France, the Netherlands, Norway and Portugal. SACLANT is also anxious to have a German contribution. American, British and Dutch units alone make up the strike fleet, which is composed of aircraft carriers, cruisers, guided missile ships and submarines. This strike fleet comes under the direct command of SACLANT. The ships earmarked for the Eastern Atlantic Area are smaller surface units. The Submarine Command, Eastern Atlantic Area, will have at its disposal in case of emergency American, British, French and Dutch submarines for anti-submarine warfare. The Air Commander, Eastern Atlantic Area, will have under his command American, French, British and Portuguese air squadrons, using bases from Norway to Portugal. Nuclear weapons appear to be available and would be relied upon to deal with any threat from enemy cruisers.

In SACLANT's view, the primary task in this area is to participate in the strategic strike; the second task is to protect shipping from submarines. In the initial phase, the main threat would come from submarines which would already have reached their area of operation, such as the south-western access to the Channel. In view of this danger, it would have to be decided whether the ships removed from harbours should be taken across the Atlantic or whether they should be dispersed in anchorages in Western Europe. In the first case the ships would have to be convoyed by escort destroyers under cover of long-range, shore-based patrol planes.

While anti-submarine forces are not strong enough, their strength should be sufficient to protect the strike fleet forces and to save a certain percentage of merchant shipping. It appears that the main area of operations would be the area beginning at the south-western exit of the Channel. If the Eastern Atlantic Command has to concentrate the bulk of its units in this area, and the Channel Command its units in the Channel itself, few NATO forces would appear to be available for the North Sea. Moreover its division between two commands (SACLANT in the north and Channel in the south) makes effective arrangements for its defence the more difficult. The resulting weakness of this North Sea pocket for SACLANT is discussed later in the context of changes needed in the command structure.

In case of emergency, it is considered that SACLANT's forces would be too weak to fulfil all the tasks entrusted to them simultaneously; they might suffice, however, if these tasks could be fulfilled consecutively. The general idea is that the bulk of these forces, and in particular the anti-submarine units, would first have to be used to defend the American and Canadian coasts against enemy submarines equipped with missiles. Since the European countries could be covered by Soviet ground-based MRBMs there would be little danger of submarines operating off their coasts for this purpose. There would therefore be little risk in concentrating SACLANT's units off the North American coast. Once this task was fulfilled, these units would have to create a barrier against enemy submarines coming through the waters between Greenland, Iceland and the Faroes into the Atlantic to obstruct allied shipping. It seems reasonable to suppose that Soviet submarines earmarked to attack the sea lanes would not make their way into the Atlantic before a nuclear exchange had been completed. This nuclear exchange would, in any case, interrupt allied shipping which could only resume operations after the first phase was over. When Russia has nuclear-powered submarines at her disposal in sufficient numbers a second barrier may be necessary in the Pacific, although insufficient forces are available at present for such a task.

The above discussion is based on the assumption that the primary task of SACLANT is to participate in the strategic nuclear strike and that any war in which naval forces will be engaged in the Atlantic area will involve nuclear weapons. It is not yet clear to what extent this strategy has been affected by the change of emphasis in strategic thinking both within NATO and in the United States.

In the more likely event of any hostilities between NATO countries and the Soviet bloc beginning on a conventional basis, we are faced with the difficult question of whether we could cope with a blockade without resort to nuclear retaliation. This dilemma is posed in the earlier consideration of the rôle of naval forces and the answer is far from clear. However, there would be time for full consultation between the NATO powers since no one would want to embark upon immediate nuclear retaliation after the first submarine attack. Ironically, in this situation the fact that NATO forces are insufficient to provide adequate protection to our merchant ships may itself be a deterrent. The Soviet Union must recognise that the more successful she is in destroying our shipping, the greater the risk of nuclear retaliation. Unless she desires a nuclear war, the risks involved by submarine operations in the Atlantic are surely not worth while. The problem is quite different from that posed by lack of conventional strength on land, which might expose us to nuclear blackmail and tempt Russia to snatch easy gains. These considerations cannot apply on the high seas. Thus it seems unlikely that there will be an Atlantic blockade unless there is also a nuclear conflict.

THE BALTIC SEA

The Baltic Sea perhaps presents NATO's most acute naval problem. Western forces there are weak. They include some units of the Danish Navy, consisting of two coastal destroyers, six frigates and four submarines; some units of the Norwegian Navy, consisting of six destroyers, ten frigates and eight submarines; and some units of the German Navy, consisting of twelve destroyers, six frigates and twelve submarines as well as two minelayers and some coastal minesweepers. The mission of the NATO fleet in the north is mainly to keep the Russians in the Baltic by controlling the straits between Denmark and Sweden and Norway.

A major difficulty is the command structure which results in the junction of Channel Command, SACLANT, and two sub-commands of SACEUR in this key area. These matters are further discussed below as part of the general command structure problem.

The Soviet Baltic Fleet is the largest Soviet sea force with about eight modern cruisers and a large share of all the other components of the Soviet Navy, including submarines. Its objects would be to clear the Baltic Sea and, once having gained superiority, to occupy the Danish Islands, Jutland and possibly Southern Norway, by airborne and seaborne assaults. Once the exit of the Baltic Sea had been freed, submarines would be sent into the North Sea and the Channel to interrupt communications.

THE MEDITERRANEAN

Like the Baltic Sea forces, those in the Mediterranean come under SACEUR's command. Since the United States Sixth Fleet with its strategic strike capability is the most powerful element in the allied forces in the area, the major task of the other units is to protect it. The Sixth Fleet consists of three aircraft carriers (eighty-five planes), three cruisers, sixteen destroyers and one attack carrier, and an amphibious force of marines with their tanks, helicopters and artillery. It has its own service force of oil tankers and maintenance vessels which enables it to remain at sea almost indefinitely. Other units include the British Mediterranean Fleet (one aircraft carrier, several cruisers, destroyers and frigates as well as minesweepers and submarines); part of the French Mediterranean Fleet (a total of 70,000 tons: two aircraft carriers, one anti-aircraft cruiser, twenty-five destroyers and fast frigates, minelayers and sweepers and about fifteen submarines); the Italian Navy (one guided missile light cruiser in construction, four to five light cruisers, some twenty-five destroyers and frigates, eight submarines); and the Greek and Turkish naval forces.

The French decided in 1959, however, to retain under national command the part of the French Navy previously earmarked for

NATO in case of war. Apart from the other political considerations, the basis of French objections to assigning the French fleet was that in their view the role of the Navy should be to keep free the passage from the north to the south of the Mediterranean (i.e. from France to North Africa), whereas NATO policy was and is to maintain free passage from west to east and vice versa. Although it is likely to be retained as a NATO base, the uncertain future of Algeria affects the port of Mers-el-Kebir, one of the biggest bases in the western Mediterranean. Uncertainty persists too over France being able to retain her base at Bizerta.

The enemy threat in the Mediterranean is constituted by the Soviet Black Sea Fleet of about ten cruisers, thirty destroyers and fifty submarines, the Soviet forces stationed in Albanian ports (although increasing coolness between the two countries suggests that the Soviet Union is unlikely to retain for long the use of these facilities) and the forces of any State which might support the Soviet bloc in case of war—for example, the United Arab Republic, which has already received a number of Soviet submarines. The Soviet objective at the outbreak of war would be to seize the Turkish Straits and break through into the Mediterranean to support the action of the submarines already operating in these waters. The main Western goal, therefore, would be to close the Turkish Straits, destroy possible bases for Soviet submarines in the Mediterranean and trace submarines already operating there.

NATO *versus* NATIONAL REQUIREMENTS

At first sight, one of the greatest weaknesses in naval defence is the fact that, in contrast to SACEUR, the naval headquarters have no forces assigned to them in peacetime. Forces are only earmarked for assignment in case of emergency. A time lag is to be feared between the first alert and the assignment of the various forces to each command, possibly of up to twenty-four hours. During that time the allied commanders could only command the forces of their own countries (usually they hold a national as well as a NATO command) and the allied defence plans could not be set in motion. Furthermore, the earmarked units might not be in the theatre of operations at the time of the emergency, which would mean the loss of more time before they became available for their required task. The transfer of command from national to allied authorities at the outbreak of war likewise presents obvious drawbacks, since, apart from occasional exercises, the allied commanders have no experience of the units assigned to them. When this problem was considered by the Defence Committee of Western European Union they came to the conclusion that the same principle of assignment in peacetime should be applied to naval forces earmarked for naval commands as already applies to ground and air forces committed to SACEUR.

From a NATO point of view I am sure this judgment is right; but further reflection prompts doubts as to whether so comprehensive an assignment of forces is feasible. Many of the problems of the NATO alliance arise from the fact that it is considered by member governments to be an alliance of sovereign states for a particular purpose in a defined area but without a general common policy. The United States, Britain, France, the Netherlands and Portugal all have commitments in other parts of the world besides the NATO area and are obliged to keep part of their forces outside NATO command. They must be able to supplement their local forces quickly if the need occurs. Warships are built to operate away from their bases for months, and, with normal amounts of fuel, can be moved immediately over thousands of miles. Therefore the navy is always the first available reserve of armed forces for action anywhere in the world. This remains true despite the increased provision of air transport.

Yet while conceding that there are insuperable difficulties in seeking as extensive an assignment of forces to SACLANT as now applies to SACEUR, I am not wholly convinced that the present position is satisfactory. It is surely not necessarily a case of all or nothing? At the moment no NATO naval commander has a single ship in his command in his NATO capacity, although in most cases the NATO command is duplicated with a national command and in this latter capacity the commander would have national naval forces available. In this connection it seems especially important that units of the strategic strike fleet should be permanently placed under the command structure of NATO; it cannot, surely, be maintained that nuclear strike forces could be used by one nation without an almost certain involvement of the alliance as a whole. It is also desirable that the nucleus of a NATO anti-submarine force should be set up in the Atlantic by permanent assignment of some units, since the priority demanded by anti-submarine measures deserves the fullest multi-national co-operation. The establishment by SACLANT of the NATO research centre at La Spezia was a step in the right direction.

Another argument has been put against the assignment of naval forces: because the high seas are free and open to vessels of all nations, it is quite possible that an international incident might occur in the Atlantic between NATO ships and those of the Soviet Union. There have been such incidents—for example, the cutting of a supply cable by a Soviet trawler off the Canadian coast. If this happens to a ship under national command there are political directives as to what to do, or the commander can rapidly acquire such political guidance. But in NATO at present there is no political authority from whom SACLANT could seek advice. Difficulties might accordingly arise.

This seems a valid objection in existing circumstances, but it is not insuperable. If, for other reasons, it is desired to have assigned naval forces, the NATO Council must issue political instructions to cover such contingencies or delegate a power of decision to the Secretary-General. Indeed they should do so in any event, since an incident might equally well occur during combined exercises when ships are technically under NATO command.

A strong consideration in favour of the principle of at least a proportion of assigned forces is simply that without its acceptance we shall not move towards balanced collective forces. In addition the reason why SACEUR has succeeded in getting a bigger slice than SACLANT of his allocation of infrastructure funds and why the existing command structure creates special naval problems is probably the present absence of assigned forces in the naval commands. If there are forces in being within the commands they must have the necessary installations and a satisfactory military framework in which to work; and members of the alliance cannot avoid tackling the problems involved. But so long as forces are only earmarked, there is not the same incentive to put the needs of the alliance before national considerations. The Western European Union Defence Committee were satisfied after examination of the problems that, while the forces earmarked for the naval commands in case of emergency have attained a high degree of efficiency and training, their strength is not sufficient to meet their allotted tasks. Indeed while NATO naval forces consist only of units allotted by nations whose composition is largely determined by national and not NATO considerations, it is difficult to see how adequate naval forces for NATO requirements can be built up. Arguments for collective as distinct from individual defence efforts, seem equally convincing on sea as on land or in the air.

Admiral Sir William Davis, former NATO Commander-in-Chief Eastern Atlantic Area, poses the problem:

> Briefly then, NATO is making great efforts to keep abreast of modern developments and these are meeting with success. But the acutest problem facing NATO today, not only in the maritime sphere, is quantity rather than quality, and this points again and again to the need for ensuring the very best value is obtained for the effort and money expended. Is it wise for all NATO nations to continue to have 'all-purpose' navies with the cost involved in having small numbers of widely differing classes of ships? Would it not be best to extend the example of the Belgians, who concentrate in minesweeping craft only, and are rapidly becoming experts in this field of warfare?[61]

This is, of course, the logical answer. Although there must be some compromise between national responsibilities and NATO requirements, there is scope for a better utilisation of resources. Only by seeking to avoid duplication of effort can we begin to get full value for money spent on NATO defence. This is particularly important when, inevitably, we are bound not to have as many resources for naval tasks as are needed. Many members of the alliance can and should afford to make bigger contributions. As Rear-Admiral Nuboer has argued:

> We Dutch will have to carry our part of the heavier naval expenses. Our task is the protection of the sea lanes towards our harbours, the most important entrances of Western Europe. These lanes cross the Atlantic. We would therefore have to make a bigger contribution towards submarine hunting groups and that would cost more money than we spend now. But, as well as the Belgians and the Norwegians, we pay less than half for our defence, per capita, than the French and the British, and just over one-third of the amount paid by the Canadians. The Americans pay more than six times more, and if we look around we surely have not less to lose![62]

There is much to be said for allocating specific tasks to the various member countries and encouraging them to concentrate on producing specialised units.

The lack of integration of the supply services of the various nations is also very disappointing. Under present circumstances, ships of different nationality operating under an allied command in the event of war would depend on their own supply system and it would be difficult for a destroyer of x to be refuelled by a refuelling ship of y. Apart from financial considerations, this system leads to duplication and waste of physical resources. In peacetime it should be possible to avoid such waste by accounting procedures or bilateral agreements. Within the NATO alliance as a whole, logistics is a national responsibility. Both operational requirements and the objective of obtaining the best return from available defence resources, demand the surrender of sovereignty in this field and the establishment of a joint supply service.

Infrastructure has made less progress in these two naval areas than in SACEUR's Command. It is nonsensical for the installation of common bases or airfields to be held up or even abandoned because of arguments about the rent to be paid for the use of the land. As the facilities are normally used by all the nations participating in the command, the usual NATO principle of sharing the cost of maintenance between the host country and the user country is not applicable. The best arrangement would be to set up a common pool to provide for these maintenance costs as well as to finance initial infrastructure costs, but a general re-examination of the finance and procedure of infrastructure in these naval commands is required to avoid delays in the provision of necessary infrastructure and to ensure an equitable sharing of the burden among the members of the alliance.

WEAKNESS OF THE COMMAND STRUCTURE

The Command structure contains three weak points:

(i) *The Baltic and North Sea*

The defence of one of the most dangerous areas, the Baltic and North Sea, is split up under the three Supreme Commanders: SACEUR, SACLANT and Channel (see map page 163). The Baltic Sea is in SACEUR's Command and the North Sea is divided between SACLANT and Channel Command. The dividing line between SACEUR and SACLANT seems to be the Skagerrak; between SACLANT and Channel a line in the North Sea mid-way across the Jutland peninsula, which creates for SACLANT the so-called North Sea pocket. And the Baltic Sea, although under the supreme command of SACEUR, was formerly divided between two commands: the German naval forces in the Baltic Sea and German ground and air forces north of the Elbe line came under the Commander-in-Chief Northern Europe; the German naval forces in the North Sea and all the ground and air forces south of the Elbe came under the Commander-in-Chief Central Europe. There was only one word to describe this situation: chaotic.

The creation, under SACEUR's Allied Forces Northern Europe Command, of a new Baltic Approaches Command (COMBALTAP) in December 1961, eliminates most of the anomalies in the particularly dangerous area of the Baltic Straits. The effect of this new Command is to bring under unified control the land forces in Jutland and Schleswig-Holstein and the Danish Islands, air forces north of the Elbe and naval forces in the Baltic. It means that in the event of war (and for manœuvres) one Command is charged with the defence of Denmark, northern Germany and the approaches to the Baltic.

The Command has a Danish Commander with a German deputy and its headquarters will probably be established at Karup in Jutland. There are four subordinate commands: land forces in Jutland and Schleswig-Holstein (under Danish alternating with German command); land forces Danish islands (Danish commander); air forces (Danish Commander); and naval forces, Baltic approaches (under German alternating with Danish command). Thus the Command will always have a Danish Commander and three out of the four service chiefs will be Danish. One-third of the staff officers will be German, the rest are to be drawn from Denmark and other NATO countries.[63]

This great improvement of the command structure within SACEUR's territory removes one of the main weaknesses in command in this area; but the difficulties which flow from the junction of the three Supreme Command boundaries remain. It is to be hoped that the rationalisation achieved so far will be completed by a re-drawing of the boundaries between the Supreme Commands.

(ii) *Channel Command*

The second weak point is the delimitation between SACLANT and Commander-in-Chief Channel, which raises problems particularly in the North Sea and Eastern Atlantic areas. It is highly questionable whether there is a case for maintaining Channel Command at all. It was set up in the first place mainly for political reasons—there are no military reasons justifying the existence of two supreme naval commands, with all the dangers inherent in such an organisation. In fact the military authorities have succeeded in reducing the disadvantages to some extent by entrusting a single commander with authority in several commands. For example, the posts of Air Commander-in-Chief Eastern Atlantic Area and Allied Maritime Air Advisor to the Commander-in-Chief Channel are held by the same man. A high degree of flexibility has thus been introduced in the command structure and commanders are able to use forces assigned to the various commands where the need arises and not according to the delimitation of areas. Nevertheless the situation is highly unsatisfactory; a general rationalisation of the command structure is needed.

(iii) *The Mediterranean*

The third weak point in the command structure is the Mediterranean where, for political reasons, it was found convenient to create a purely maritime Mediterranean Command alongside the Southern Europe Command which includes land, naval and air elements. Far and away the strongest naval force in the Mediterranean is the United States Sixth Fleet, which in the event of hostilities is assigned to Southern Europe Command. Yet all the other naval and maritime air forces in the Mediterranean, whose main task is to protect the Sixth Fleet, are divided among six sub-area commands under a separate regional commander.

Further difficulty arises from the attitude taken by the French Government. Although the French Government does not exclude that its naval forces which were earmarked for assignment to NATO in case of war might be used for joint operations with the other NATO forces, it has renounced the agreement by which they would have been made subject to NATO command immediately on the outbreak of hostilities.

ALTERNATIVE SOLUTIONS

The overall command structure, in order to operate efficiently, calls for rationalisation. Several alternative plans are possible:

(i) A single command could be created for Northern and Central Europe with a command subordinate to it for naval forces embracing the Baltic Sea, the North Sea and the Channel; a command subordinate to it for ground forces between the northern tip of Norway and the Alps; and a third command for air forces which would control aircraft over the whole area. A Southern European Command, organised on the same lines, would be responsible for ground, air and naval forces from the Alps to the North-African coasts;

(ii) SACEUR could be made responsible for the defence of the entire Western European land mass, including the two inland seas—the Baltic and the Mediterranean—the subordinate commands being limited to two only, i.e. a Northern Command stretching from Northern Norway to the Alps and a Southern Command stretching from the Alps to North Africa; SACLANT to be made responsible for the naval striking and sea lane defence operations in the whole of the Atlantic, including the North Sea and the Channel. He might have several subordinate commands, one for the North Sea, one for the Channel, one for the Spanish-French waters and one for the North African waters;

(iii) another proposal is that SACLANT should have authority over all seas, including the Mediterranean, the Channel (including British territorial waters) and the North Sea;

(iv) while maintaining the present organisation of SACEUR and SACLANT, Channel Command responsibility could be extended to embrace the whole of the North Sea.

While there is almost unanimous agreement that the present command structure is highly unsatisfactory, it is quite another matter to get agreement on any alternative scheme. After I first put forward various proposals to the Western European Union Assembly in 1959[64] there appeared signs that some action was to be taken. But by the end of 1961 only the new Baltic Command had emerged. Rationalisation of any organisation is a delicate and complex task and I do not underestimate the difficulties with which the NATO authorities will have to contend. But this is no excuse for their shelving the problem.

While it is impossible to lay down firmly what the basis for a new structure should be without access to classified sources for all the political and military factors one needs to take into account in deciding so complicated a question, I earnestly hope a new structure will be forthcoming and that it will give defence considerations priority over political aspirations and national susceptibilities. For example, if the Channel Committee is really only retained (as is sometimes argued) so as to give Belgium and the Netherlands direct access to the Standing Group in Washington, the prospects for a command structure in that area which makes sense on military grounds are not bright. The fact that such political considerations may still be important is also a reflection on the North Atlantic Council's failure to create among member states a sufficient feeling of equal participation in the political and military decisions of the alliance. A rational and efficient command structure is essential to the effective operation of the NATO forces and it is up to the North Atlantic Council to shoulder their responsibilities and tackle this problem.

Chapter X

TACTICAL AIR FORCES

NATO air forces consist of the Second and Fourth Allied Tactical Air Forces (ATAFs) in Germany (in the Central Europe Command) and the Fifth ATAF in Northern Italy and Sixth ATAF in Greece and Turkey (in Southern Europe Command). The strategic nuclear air potential of the alliance is not subject to NATO control and remains under the national control of the United States and Great Britain. Air defence is still largely a national responsibility with SACEUR, Regional and ATAF Commanders having only 'co-ordinating authority', although the decision to set up a unified system marks a great advance in this field.

The ATAFs' mission is to gain air superiority, to give air support to ground forces and to co-ordinate air defence. In case of emergency, the ATAFs will attack tactical targets in Eastern Europe and attempt to neutralise the enemy's potential air capabilities. Some of the ATAFs' tactical aircraft have a nuclear capability. Except for some British aircraft carrying British nuclear bombs, all the nuclear bombs and warheads are, as everywhere within NATO, under American custody. Reconnaissance tasks include low-level photography and visual inspection.

There seems to have been little change in the missions assigned to the tactical air forces in the light of the changed military and political situation resulting from nuclear parity and mutual deterrence.

General Norstad's request for *Polaris* missiles to replace in due course the manned bomber element of his air forces underlines the fact that among the missions of the ATAFs substantial emphasis is put on participation in the atomic strike plan. On military grounds, there is an overwhelming case for giving top priority in the initial stages of a conflict to the destruction of the enemy's tactical air forces and to interdiction attacks behind his lines with the aim of preventing his resources being moved into the battle area. Attacking the enemy's tactical air forces and destroying communications targets in his rear areas are undoubtedly the most satisfactory operations that air forces can perform by way of giving support to ground troops. Air superiority in the theatre of operations can best be won by striking the enemy's air bases, and nuclear weapons are unquestionably the most effective for this purpose.

Unhappily, while this approach fitted the previous concept of a generalised nuclear war, it does not match the political requirements of avoiding nuclear escalation and attempting to compel a 'pause' in a limited war situation. In fact, in considering the whole problem of nuclear weapons within the alliance the rôle of the tactical air forces poses the biggest dilemma and the greatest conflict between military requirements and political control.

PROBLEMS OF NUCLEAR INTERDICTION

If the tactical air forces are to engage—as military considerations would dictate—in nuclear interdiction on enemy airfields or lines of communication as soon as any hostilities begin, there is little point in seeking to restrain the ground forces from immediate resort to nuclear weapons. For the bombing with nuclear weapons of targets well behind the enemy lines, whether airfields or railway junctions, would surely invite immediate nuclear retaliation and remove any possibility of enforcing a 'pause' to allow for political action.

It is true, of course, that in existing circumstances nuclear weapons would not be used without the express authority of SACEUR; and the fact that the air forces are well removed from the immediate area of probable hostilities makes the implementation of political control easier than with ground forces. But the increasing provision of nuclear capability—V-bombers and long-range missiles—in the tactical air forces poses the question as to what their mission is intended to be in the event of any hostilities.

It is also true that the manned aircraft is an ideal dual-purpose weapon, unlike atomic artillery and missiles, and is equally capable of either a conventional or a nuclear rôle. But it has a limited life, and there would be grave doubts about committing the tactical air forces wholly to conventional interdiction at the beginning of any fighting. Tasks which could be discharged by

N

two or three planes with nuclear weapons would require perhaps a hundred with conventional weapons, with the consequent much greater risk (in terms of numbers) to men and machines.

Some of the aircraft of the tactical airforces must in any case be used to give close support to the ground troops. But the dive-bomber type of attack in front of their own troops and close air defence of their own forward defended localities are also likely to prove expensive in terms of losses of aircraft and personnel. The expert regards this as a most inefficient and ineffective use of air forces and it would be difficult to justify the heavy commitment of our forces for this purpose.

Thus it could well happen that a full commitment of the tactical air forces to conventional interdiction and ground support operations might result in their being unable to undertake their nuclear missions should these become necessary at a later stage. Missiles, as for example the *Mace*, would have no effective part to play in a conventional rôle.

Without rehearsing the arguments of previous chapters as to the need for stricter political control and the avoidance of nuclear escalation, there seems an inescapable conclusion that the missions and rôle of the tactical air forces need to be reassessed as a matter of urgency by the North Atlantic Council. If SACEUR and the military authorities are given tasks within NATO plans they must have the means to carry them out. It is the plans which must be revised, so that all tasks assigned are in keeping with the strategic and tactical requirements resulting from the state of nuclear parity.

The tactical air forces should be made to fit into the structure postulated in Chapter VII. Conditional on a decision to place the strategic air forces and missiles in Europe under NATO control, the long-range targets at present assigned to the tactical air forces should be taken away and given to the strategic forces. This may involve a transfer of the missiles and some aircraft at present included in the tactical forces. The strategic forces should be under a separate command from SACEUR. I have suggested a new Supreme Commander for Nuclear Weapons (SACNUC) subject to the political control and direction of the NATO Council.

A more detailed political control of the use of nuclear weapons by the remaining tactical air forces is also required. It is not sufficient that they be given authorisation for the initial use of nuclear bombs without regard also to the nature and location of the targets to be attacked. It would seem practicable to draw up several categories of targets—'A', 'B', 'C'—so that the first use of nuclear weapons authorised would cover targets in category 'A' only; a second and separate authority would be required for targets in category 'B' and a third for targets in category 'C'. The purpose of the categories would be to try to equate military objectives with the political objective of attempting to control the level of nuclear escalation. It is conceded that the crucial decision is probably whether to employ *any* nuclear weapons, and that once any are used it may well prove impossible to avoid an all-out nuclear war. We cannot, however, be sure; and thus it is prudent to plan on the basis that some control may be possible, since it will be manifestly impossible to devise such a system should the worst happen and we find ourselves at war.

It is also desirable that the use of the tactical air forces should be correlated with the tactical use of the atomic artillery on the battlefield. Both should therefore be subject to the same channel of command. I have suggested the designation of a new Commander-in-Chief for Tactical Nuclear Weapons (TACTNUC) for the control of army atomic weapons and I consider the best arrangement would be for him to have charge of the tactical air forces as well. He would be responsible to SACEUR for their deployment and operational control and through a new Supreme Commander, Nuclear Weapons (SACNUC) to the North Atlantic Council for political authority for the use of nuclear weapons.

EXISTING FORCES

The Second ATAF is composed of tactical air forces from Great Britain, Belgium, the Netherlands and Germany. It consists of a fully-integrated headquarters command and national wings stationed on aerodromes in the northern German area. Second ATAF has a British Commander-in-Chief who also has the post of Commander-in-Chief of the Royal Air Force Element, itself re-named Royal Air Force Germany. The Fourth ATAF is composed of American, Canadian, French and German forces and is commanded by the Commander, United States Air Forces Europe.

The Second ATAF is closely linked with the Northern Army Group and liaison is ensured by the Offensive Operations Centre situated in the vicinity of the Army Group Command Centre.

The Fourth ATAF maintains similar liaison for this purpose with the Central Army Group. The offensive and reconnaissance tasks are controlled by the Joint Command Operations Centre which has various tactical operations under its command.

These ATAFs together consist of about 3,000 aircraft of which the United States fighter-bombers and the British *Canberras*, *Vulcans* and *Valiants* have a nuclear capability and range which would cover Eastern Russia. The composition of both ATAFs is, however, extremely varied as nations are free to assign whichever aircraft they choose. Within the Second ATAF there are three types of offensive aircraft and four types of reconnaissance aircraft. Within the Fourth ATAF there are American, Canadian and French aircraft flying side by side. The build-up of the German contribution to both ATAFs is still relatively slow.

Training is basically a national responsibility, but ATAF operational standards are set to which individual crews are trained. Low altitude training presents a problem because of the shortage of facilities and the lack of air-to-air and surface-to-air firing ranges. The German Air Force has found special difficulty in training for these reasons and also because of the lack of a nucleus of trained pilots. It has been obliged to seek such training facilities in other NATO countries. Training flights too near the Iron Curtain are obviously undesirable and these restrictions have added to the problem.

The fact that logistics is a national responsibility and the Commanders-in-Chief have only advisory powers is a source of weakness to both ATAFs. In view of the great variety of aircraft in service no standardisation is possible although the introduction of the American F 104 by Holland, Belgium, Germany and Canada into their ATAF contributions is a step in the direction of standardisation. Even within a single ATAF interchangeability of squadrons is very limited. The various units are dependent upon their own aerodromes and their own national supply depots, which makes free deployment impossible and restricts mobility. Steps have, however, been taken to minimise the difficulties as far as possible. A fair degree of cross-servicing has been obtained and the object is to ensure that all airfields can at least refuel and give first-aid to any type of aircraft. The lack of standardised aircraft communication equipment also creates problems. United States aircraft are equipped with UHF

(Ultra High Frequency) radio and British aircraft with VHF (Very High Frequency). This has meant equipping airfields with both systems, which is both costly and unsatisfactory.

Lack of compatibility of equipment and procedures is even more pronounced between the two ATAFs: although the dividing line between the Second and the Fourth ATAFs in Germany is entirely artificial, it has acquired the importance of a frontier. The differences in procedures and equipment create particular difficulties for the German Air Force, which is divided between the two ATAFs. The efficiency of both ATAFs would also be increased by a revision of the command structure and areas.

The Fifth ATAF in Northern Italy consists of about 400 aircraft of F 84F, F 84G and F 86K types. Modernisation of the available aircraft is planned with the Italian G 91, selected as the NATO jet light strike reconnaissance aircraft for direct support of ground forces, and the American F 104 *Starfighter,* to be produced in Europe. In addition there are three battalions of *Nike* surface-to-air missiles to which will be added four battalions of *Hawk* missiles, at present being manufactured under NATO joint production arrangements.

The Sixth ATAF, with Headquarters at Izmir, Turkey, is divided into the Greek Twenty-Eighth TAF and the Turkish First, Second and Third TAF. About 750 aircraft are available, consisting mainly of F 84 and F 86 types. These are eventually to be replaced by F 100 aircraft and a few of this type are already in service.

It is possible to spend vast sums of money on air defence and yet add little to our security. The main requirement in Central Europe is to have a single system for the whole area since otherwise no measures can be satisfactory technically. This means that a single concept of the air defence battle must be agreed throughout the region; that similar, or at least compatible, ground radar and data handling equipment must be developed throughout the region; that these ground radars must be specifically suited to the weapons systems they will control; and that the whole organisation must function as a unity under one commander.

Although air defence has always been a national responsibility within NATO, in December 1957 it was proposed that an integrated system should be established under SACEUR. Unfortunately France was opposed to the scheme and because of her geographical position, it was impossible to have any kind of European system without her.

However, in September 1960 a compromise was reached whereby a unified system of command and operational control was established, with effect from 1 May 1961, for Western European air defences, including the United Kingdom, and for an early warning system over the whole NATO area. General de Gaulle's objections were met by 'unifying' as distinct from 'integrating' (a word which has been banished from the French military vocabulary) the French air forces with those of the other nations concerned in the forward area, i.e. in the zone on either side of the Franco-German frontier. The greater part of France remains under French national control, but this agreement means that it will now be possible to have a unified system in the key forward area.

Mr. Watkinson, in announcing the British participation in the scheme, said:

> I am arranging for General Norstad to be given formal notice of the assignment of Fighter Command to NATO in accordance with the decision on unified air defence taken last year by the North Atlantic Council. The assignment will take effect from 1 May 1961. It will improve the air defence capability of the whole area including the United Kingdom.
>
> The Fighter Command forces assigned to SACEUR will be the air defence fighter squadrons and the operational units of the *Bloodhound* Mark 1 SAGW system and of the control and reporting system. The size, composition, rôle and deployment of these forces will remain matters for our own decision.
>
> Air Marshal Sir Hector McGregor, the Air Officer Commanding-in-Chief, Fighter Command, is being nominated for appointment by SACEUR as Commander, United Kingdom Air Defence Region. SACEUR's responsibilities for air defence in the United Kingdom region will be exercised through the Commander.

After confirming that the purpose of the unified air defence system was to provide defence in depth, he went on 'We now get the great advantage of the forward radar coverage and the forward fighter screen far further forward in Europe, as part of our NATO air defence.'[65]

CURRENT DEVELOPMENTS

Air defence plans provide for a gradual phasing out of the day fighters and a progressive increase in the number of all-weather fighters and surface-to-air missiles. The missiles chosen are the United States *Nike Ajax* and *Nike Hercules* against high-altitude aircraft and the United States *Hawk* against low-flying aircraft. The United States *Nike Zeus,* under development as an anti-missile missile, is unlikely to be available for a considerable time. *Hawk* missiles are being produced jointly by French, German, Belgian, Italian and Dutch companies under American licence. The decision to adopt the *Hawk* for this purpose was a great disappointment to the United Kingdom which has produced its own comparable surface-to-air *Bloodhound* missile (which has been ordered by Sweden and Switzerland). The British Army has its own surface-to-air missile—the *Thunderbird*.

The *Sidewinder* (United States Navy) air-to-air guided missile is being produced on the same basis as the *Hawk* for fighter equipment. The British equivalent is *Firestreak,* with which the British *Javelins* and *Lightnings* are already equipped. Mark 2 *Lightnings* are being introduced in 1961–2 and the Mark 3 *Lightnings* on order will carry an improved air-to-air guided weapon *Red Top*.

Much progress has been made in the provision of an early warning system and of a 4,000-mile radar chain from Norway to Turkey. The NATO system is linked with the British Fighter Command and the North American Air Defence Command (NORAD) in the United States. NORAD has developed a comprehensive network of warning and detection systems. The Distant Early Warning (DEW) line of radar stations runs across the continent in the Canadian Arctic and Alaska. In addition there is a mid-Canada line and a third Pinetree line near the United States-Canadian border. South of these lines is a network of radar covering the whole of the United States.

Early warning of missiles is dependent upon the Ballistic Missile Early Warning System (BMEWS). Huge radar screens in the shape of a parabolic section the size of a football pitch have been developed which can detect a missile as far away as 3,000 miles. Two stations have been completed, at Thule in Greenland and Clear in Alaska. A third, at Fylingdales Moor in Yorkshire, England, is expected to be completed in 1962. The Jodrell Bank radio telescope has been adapted to assist in the detection of ballistic missiles until Fylingdales is ready. The data from the detection system must be assessed and evaluated with great speed and a new electronic data-processing system has been installed. This is the Semi-Automatic Ground Environment (SAGE) system.

Shortly after the BMEWS system was brought into use, there was an anxious moment when the rising moon was for a moment interpreted as a mass missile attack. The new SAGE system rejected the data, although the manual system which was operating concurrently was less easily convinced. However, no alert was called in this case and the incident confirms that the danger of a false alert arising from faulty identification of objects observed is very slim.[66]

To complement the BMEWS system the United States has under development a Missile Defence Alarm System (MIDAS). The MIDAS system will consist of a number of space satellites equipped with infra-red apparatus to detect ballistic missiles in early stages of their flight. Information recorded in the satellites will be relayed back to readout stations. One such station is to be constructed at Kirkbride in Cumberland, England, and this will enable the British, and thus the NATO, air defence system to receive the information simultaneously with the North American system.

These early warning systems can only give a limited period of notice—estimates vary from four to thirty minutes—and of course depend upon the type and location of the attack. It has been declared both in the United States and in the United Kingdom that no counter measures would be authorised on the evidence of these systems alone. They should, however, suffice to enable us to get most of our aircraft off the ground in anticipation of the attack. To this end the extra minutes' warning to be provided by the MIDAS system are of great value. In addition the search for the most efficient and comprehensive warning system provides tangible evidence of our declared intention not to initiate a surprise attack and of our concern to maintain a second and not a first strike capability.

With the increasing emphasis on mobility, one of the obvious deficiencies of NATO forces at present is the lack of adequate air transport for both men and supplies. There seem to be no transport aircraft assigned to SACEUR at all, and such as are made available are wholly on a national basis. It has been stated that the new mobile 'fire-brigades' are to be fully air transportable, and clearly they must be if they are to fulfil their purpose. Presumably the necessary air transport will be supplied by the countries whose troops are assigned to these units, permanently on call.

It seems to me that the ATAFs should be supplied with some transport aircraft, assigned to them in the same way as bombers, fighters and reconnaissance aircraft are now assigned. But over and above this there is a strong case for a general provision of transport aircraft at the disposal of SACEUR. The rapid movement of troops or crucial stores may be of the greatest importance. The development of short take-off and landing (STOL) aircraft will increase the utility of air transport still further, but a beginning should be made now without waiting for STOL aircraft to come into service.

In my view consideration should be given to the establishment of a Transport Command within NATO of aircraft assigned to SACEUR and wholly within his control. Obviously difficulties of supply arise from the existing situation whereby logistics are a national responsibility and the military commanders have very limited powers to re-allocate supplies within their commands. These problems are discussed in the next chapter. But, since one decision rests on another, as is so often the case, if there is a genuine attempt to untangle the logistic difficulties the setting up of a Transport Command would be quite feasible. Moreover apart from its own merits, such a system would also assist in remedying some of the logistic weaknesses.

Consideration of the allied tactical air forces and related matters repeats familiar themes which have now become a refrain. First, the rôle of the NATO air forces needs to be re-assessed in the light of changed strategic concepts. Secondly, in this field as in others, despite the highly successful integration of officers of many nations in the ATAF administration, there is a reluctance on the part of member nations to view defence from the viewpoint of the alliance as a whole.

Chapter XI

INFRASTRUCTURE AND LOGISTICS

Ever since Napoleon's famous aphorism about armies marching on their stomachs, the importance of logistics for military operations has been well appreciated. Today, of course, the complicated demands of our forces are much more exacting than the food, boots and ammunition of a hundred and fifty years ago. But Montaigne's dictum, *Il faut être toujours botté et prêt à partir,* still serves as a text for logisticians.

Thus no discussion of the capability of NATO forces is very meaningful unless it is also related to their equipment and supplies. It is claimed in French military text-books that there are twenty-two definitions of logistics. It is perhaps an oversimplification, therefore, to say that logistics covers the equipping of troops, moving them into combat position and supplying all their military and physical needs but this definition suffices to indicate the kind of problems that must be dealt with. Clearly movement and transport are key elements of any logistic planning, although fixed installations are obviously also necessary.

Unhappily a survey of the logistic situation within the alliance discloses a number of serious problems and shortcomings, and it is impossible to say today that NATO forces are fully ready to go. In considering this state of affairs, however, it is important to make a clear distinction between the infrastructure or static facilities which come within the NATO infrastructure programme, and all other logistic requirements which are wholly a national responsibility. The infrastructure programme has made good progress whereas achievements in other respects fall far short of what is required. The explanation lies in the fact that the initiative for infrastructure projects comes from the Supreme Commanders, who are able to allocate priorities based on overall military requirements, and that these projects are financed from a common pool.

The infrastructure programme is an arrangement whereby certain static facilities, for example airfields, communications networks and ammunition storage, are provided in NATO countries for the use of the alliance as a whole. The host country provides the site, and the materials and construction work are provided by tendering in which firms in all NATO countries can compete. The work is financed from a pool to which each country contributes on a percentage basis.

The achievements under this programme have been very considerable. About £1,000 million has been allocated, roughly in the proportion of 50 per cent for airfields, 20 per cent for communications installations, 10 per cent for the pipeline system and 20 per cent for headquarters and missile sites. Although only about one-third of the projects authorised have been completed, this includes 160 airfields, 4,600 miles of pipeline and 26,500 miles of signal communications. Two outstanding achievements are the construction of a fuel pipeline network and the development of a communications system throughout central Europe, from Norway to Turkey.

A NATO petroleum fuel pipeline network is already in operation. Fuel requirements of all forces are standardised. These fuels are now all transported by the network from certain ports to the general line of the Rhine and beyond. The fuels for national units assigned to allied commands are supplied or procured by the country concerned at the terminal port of its choice and corresponding quantities are supplied to that country's forces at the selected eastern terminal. There is a NATO Pipeline Committee which is responsible for the overall direction of this network, and in 1957 a Central Europe Operating Agency was established to be responsible for its operation.

The need of Allied Command Europe for a reliable, secure and instantaneous means of communication has been met by the decision to construct ACE HIGH, a communications system utilising the Tropospheric Forward Scatter principle. When completed it will be the world's largest communications system to be designed, engineered and installed at one time as a single integrated unit. A portion of the system is already functioning and it is expected to be fully operational in 1962. A unique feature of this scheme is that, because it covers most of the member states, it had SHAPE acting as the host country.

The present formula for sharing the cost, although revised several times, is quite arbitrary. Lord Ismay, the first Secretary-General, has explained how it was first reached:

> They dumped the whole problem in my lap, so I called in three assistant secretaries-general, and each of us drew up our own list of what we thought the percentage of sharing should be, and then we averaged them out. I couldn't for the life of me possibly say on what basis I acted, except I tried to take into account all sorts of things like the ability to pay and whether the building would be going on in a country so that it would benefit from the construction and the money spent.
>
> Then we got into the Council meeting in April of 1953, and everybody around the table thought it was a jolly good distribution except for his own, which they thought was too high. Anyway, we went round the table and finally got agreement of each to take what was given within 1·8 per cent of the total, and then we simply divided up that 1·8 per cent among the fourteen, and that's all there was to it. That's why all the shares are in those funny percentage amounts.[67]

The percentage division of infrastructure costs agreed in 1956 is as follows:

Belgium	4·39	Luxembourg	0·17
Canada	6·15	Netherlands	3·51
Denmark	2·63	Norway	2·19
France	11·87	Portugal	0·28
Germany	13·72	Turkey	1·75
Greece	0·87	United Kingdom	9·88
Italy	5·61	United States	36·98

In February 1961 a revision of these figures was reported which increased Germany's share to about 20 per cent and the United Kingdom's to 10·5 per cent while reducing the United States' share to about 30 per cent, Greece's to 0·67 and Turkey's to 1·1 per cent.

While this arbitrary division of costs works reasonably well for an annual programme of about £100 million, the formula would not be acceptable if it were sought to apply it to much bigger sums, e.g. logistics as well. The same considerations apply to foreign exchange problems which inevitably arise because some members have few or no installations on their territories. In addition there have been great problems of delay in the cumbersome procedure of finding the sites and letting the contracts.

SACEUR's programme, partly, no doubt, because of the crucial character of the Central Front and the fact that he has actual forces in being assigned to him in peacetime, has advanced much faster than the more modest allocation to SACLANT. While it would not be practicable to extend the formula and machinery of infrastructure in their existing form to the wider field of logistics, there is much to be said for extending the principle of burden-sharing involved.

It is significant, and a justification of the alliance, that in every field that is left wholly to member nations the shortcomings are more serious than where there is a combined NATO policy.* Logistics is no exception to the rule, as a visit to any NATO command makes plain. There is no dramatic way of remedying matters: it is the old story of lack of resources and political will. But it does seem indefensible for a nation to assign its forces to the alliance and then deny those forces adequate means to discharge their tasks in the event of hostilities.

Logistics has traditionally been the Cinderella of military science. Operational plans remain on paper and do not involve expenditure until the emergency begins, whereas logistic plans require immediate translation into materials and money. In addition, although operational plans are drawn up to meet all kinds of contingencies, only one set of plans is likely to be put into effect. The logistic support on the other hand must be prepared for all possible contingencies and able to meet the demands of any operational plans. The changes in NATO strategy and the requirements to prepare for either conventional or nuclear hostilities and for either limited or global war have added substantially to supply problems. Improvisation is no substitute for organisation.

The main weakness has been a reluctance on the part of member nations to face the problem. It is a familiar attitude, aptly summed up by Montaigne three hundred and fifty years ago:

It is a fond fashion of the Nobility and Gentry of our age, never to betake themselves to arms, except upon some urgent and extreme necessity, and to quit them as soon as they perceive the least hope or

* I am indebted to Mr. Frans Goedhart for permission to use material contained in his report to the WEU Assembly in October 1960 (*Document* 180).

appearance that the danger is past. Whence ensue many disorders and inconveniences. For, everyone running and calling for his arms when the alarm is given, some have not yet buckled their cuirass when their fellows are already defeated.

The major difficulties, which seem common to most commands, are (i) the need to give military commanders greater authority over logistics; (ii) lack of standardisation; (iii) the inadequate level of stocks; and (iv) the great need for more mobility and flexibility.

At present in peacetime the allied commanders have no power to direct the logistic support on which they depend—in fact, their authority in this field amounts to little more than the right to give advice. This fact, which stems from the responsibility for logistics being entirely national, is a denial of the military principle that logistics is a function of command. NATO commanders have no control over supplies or stocks or installations. In addition they have to contend with a wide diversity of equipment, weapons and vehicles. Their dependence upon national supply lines imposes severe restrictions on the lateral movement of troops within their commands. In war, their power is limited to the reallocation of supplies within the combat zone, although most of the stores must of necessity be held further to the rear. At present they often find difficulty even in obtaining full information about the level and location of the stocks on which they must rely.

There are, of course, difficulties in handing over to a military commander (who might be of another nationality) the power to order supplies to meet an operational plan which did not take account of the cost and of the logistic problems for individual member countries. There are constitutional problems, since control of expenditure rests with the respective Parliaments. Also, there is well-founded unwillingness to allow military commanders to become powerful political figures. But there is scope for a considerable increase in the powers of NATO military commanders without invoking these difficulties. The obvious need to extend the power of allied commanders in this field in the interests of military efficiency depends, first, upon the building up of adequate contributions by all the nations involved. For unless all member countries make a sufficient contribution to the pool to meet the requirement of their own armed forces, there would be a tendency for some to feel that their shortcomings could be offset from the supplies furnished by others. This points to the need for a common logistics pool to which nations would contribute on an agreed basis and which would be controlled and directed by the military commanders. This suggestion is examined more fully later on.

It seems essential for supply and transport to be organised on an Army Group basis. (This can only be done, of course, if the principle of a pool is accepted.) As has been demonstrated in exercises, the present arrangement whereby in the Northern Army Group, for example, there are four separate national logistic organisations, makes rational organisation impossible. There can be no logic in the arrangement which separates operational control of forces from control of their supplies.

A fundamental change in NATO policy is required to permit proper authority in the field of logistics to be given to allied commanders. They should have full authority over logistic resources, including power in the event of war to re-allocate supplies in the communications zone as well as in the combat zone and in time of peace to plan these resources.

Unquestionably one of the basic difficulties in devising an adequate logistics system for NATO forces is the diversity of weapons and equipment in service as well as the variations in organisation found in the combat units of the different nations. The very large total sum spent annually by the alliance on arms and equipment poses the obvious question whether there would not be great savings, or the acquisition of much more for the same expenditure, if there were an agreed production of standard equipment based on a rational division of labour between the member countries. The economic advantages are self-evident and it must be stressed that over and above these considerations there are very strong military arguments for standardisation. I have little doubt that the Warsaw Pact forces do not have the same logistic problems that arise from the diversified equipment and organisational variation of NATO.

Much work has in fact been done, both in WEU and in NATO, to achieve more standardisation but the results have hardly been commensurate with the effort expended. While some progress has been achieved, the situation as a whole has tended to get worse rather than better, because originally there was a measure of artificial standardisation due to a number of countries using American

weapons and equipment supplied under the military aid programme. As these obsolete items have been replaced in many
cases by a variety of models selected from different countries, the
tendency has been to increase rather than reduce the types of
ammunition, spare parts, etc., required. Everyone believes in
standardisation—provided that his own product is adopted as
the standard model. Even when an agreement is made to standardise an item of equipment, some years elapse before military
efficiency and ease of logistic support are improved. For example,
the Belgian FN rifle was adopted as a standard item of NATO
equipment seven or eight years before the British troops in
Germany were equipped with it.

There are three stages in the development of any item of military equipment, and these are the same whether it is a rifle or an
aeroplane. First, there is the specification of operational requirement—the military characteristics it must have to fulfil the function demanded of it; secondly, there is the stage of preparing the
final blueprint after a lengthy process of research and development; finally there is the production stage. Little can be done
about existing equipment, or about the next generation of
weapons already at the production or even the blueprint stage.
Any attempt at standardisation has to be aimed at the next-
generation-but-one of weapons. This has been the approach of
both the NATO and the WEU Armaments Committees.

The Standing Armaments Committee of WEU* succeeded in
establishing a very good procedure which was later adopted by
the NATO Armaments Committee, thus showing NATO how the
problem of common production could best be tackled and
obliging it to take the problem seriously. However, in terms of
actual achievement, both as regards standardisation and common
arms production, we are still a long way from the objectives set
out in the resolution of the Ministers in setting up the Committee
in 1955, of 'increasing the efficiency of the forces of the countries
of Western European Union and improving their logistics; and
of seeking the best methods of using the resources available to
these countries for equipping and supplying their forces and
sharing tasks in the best interests of all.' At first glance this seems
hard to understand, since the diversity of national wealth and

---

* For an assessment of its work and problems, see the report of Vice-Admiral
John Hughes-Hallett, M.P., to the Assembly of WEU. March 1960 (*Document* 164).

technical development is much less between the seven members of WEU than between the fifteen members of NATO and it should accordingly be easier to get a regional agreement than agreement within the alliance as a whole. Indeed, it is widely held in the arms industry that the transfer of projects from WEU to NATO often leads merely to their being taken over by American industry. It must be admitted, however, that the WEU Standing Armaments Committee is hampered in its work by the general reluctance to take any action which could lead to the impression of WEU forming a caucus within the alliance, with the result that projects of any importance are referred to the NATO Armaments Committee. At present the WEU Committee's activities are largely confined to joint European research and development projects and to attempts to standardise minor items of equipment.

It cannot be claimed that the NATO Armaments Committee has achieved a great deal. Many projects have foundered at the operational requirement stage—the tank is a prime example—because it has proved impossible to get agreement between the member countries on the military characteristics required. In the case of the light fighter, in default of agreement among the different nations concerning which of several national designs to adopt, SHAPE had to lay down the specification and the Italian Fiat *G 91* was finally adopted as the standard aircraft. Moreover, even where a NATO specification has been laid down, it is rarely adopted by all the member countries. Herr Strauss has acidly remarked that where there is a NATO standard weapon it is only adopted by Germany (who is only now developing an armaments industry and is anxious to equip her forces only with NATO standard weapons) and the country of origin.

To get results, drastic steps need to be taken and agreement must be reached at the top political level. It has been suggested that different nations should be allocated particular weapons to develop for the whole alliance; for example, guided missiles to the United States, vertical take-off aircraft to the United Kingdom and infantry weapons to Germany. This is an excellent idea; but when one considers how difficult it is to get agreement on requirements even within one country, as the history of British military aircraft illustrates, and how considerable modification of the original design, even after production has started, tends to be the rule rather than the exception, the magnitude of the problem becomes apparent. One must also take into account national interests and different national military concepts, and the powerful influence exerted by private armaments firms (and especially American ones) looking for business.

Some measure of common production has been achieved, for example the *Hawk* ground-to-air missile and the F 104 *Starfighter*. While this standardisation is good, it is not the general answer to the problem for European countries to adopt and manufacture under licence items of American equipment already in existence and produced without regard to the procedure for establishing NATO military requirements. This practice causes friction within the alliance, as some countries feel that their own designs do not get proper consideration, and in the long run is bound to have serious consequences for the technical development of European industries. Unless the United States is prepared to co-operate to a greater extent in the research and development of new weapons, the cost of which for complex weapons is beyond the means of individual European countries, the system will not work on a NATO basis. The outcome is bound to be an increased demand to agree specifications and make common production arrangements on a European basis only.

A new pattern of international collaboration, encouraged by NATO, emerged at the end of 1961 when it was announced that several international consortia had been formed to submit joint proposals for the NATO specification for vertical take-off and landing aircraft. These include a consortium of Dassault and Sud Aviation in France working with Boeing in the United States and the British Aircraft Corporation (basing their design on the *Mirage III*); a consortium of seven companies from Britain, France, Holland, Germany, Belgium and the United States (basing their design on the Hawker *P 1127*); and the British Short Brothers working with American Lockheed on a VTOL version of the F *104*.

While inevitably, and rightly, the Armaments Committees have largely concerned themselves with new weapons, from the point of view of logistics the most urgent standardisation required is that of ammunition. For even if nations insist on producing their own weapons, if they could to a larger extent than now use the same ammunition it would ease supply problems considerably. Ammunition and explosives amount to 50 per cent by weight of the total supplies required daily by a division on active operations and thus a relatively modest measure of agreement would bring great practical benefit to the operational efficiency of our troops.

Although there is no clear information about the level of stocks made available to the NATO Commands because of the complications of a system based on national supply arrangements, it is undoubted that few member countries have fulfilled their obligations. Some critical items are in very short supply and the geographical distribution of stocks is very unsatisfactory.

In 1957 the Ministers of Defence fixed the level of stocks to be maintained at ninety days' supply as it was agreed that this was the minimum period in which any re-supply could be effected in the event of nuclear hostilities. The bulk of these supplies would, of course, be well dispersed outside the combat zone.

The British Minister of Defence, Mr. Watkinson, has suggested that because of the difficulties involved in meeting the ninety-day level of stocks, it would be more realistic to set a lower target of thirty days. This does not represent as great a reduction as would appear at first sight, since the rate of consumption of stocks is not even and must be reckoned to be much greater in the early days of any fighting. According to the consumption rates laid down by SACEUR, twice as much would be consumed in the first thirty days as in the last sixty days. Thus to achieve a thirty-day supply level would demand two-thirds of the stocks demanded by the ninety-day level. One must also take into account that the new organisational structure of smaller, self-contained fighting units has increased the supplies they will require to carry.

As a first step to remedying the logistics shortfall, it would be worth while setting the new thirty-day level as a target to be attained by a fixed date, say within twelve months. Money is the main problem, and there is no doubt that many member countries would find difficulty in financing the necessary build-up of stocks. To give an indication of what is involved, it was estimated that in 1959 the cost to Belgium, France, the Netherlands and the United Kingdom of bringing their existing stocks up to the ninety-day goal would amount to 500 million dollars, or 6 per cent of the combined defence expenditure of the countries concerned. However, since this building-up of stocks is so essential, from the point of view of both operational efficiency and providing a sound basis for any improved supply procedure which may be agreed by the member nations, it should surely be possible as a temporary measure for some means to be devised of assisting members of the alliance who find themselves in special financial difficulties while a more satisfactory arrangement is under consideration. Perhaps loans could be raised for this purpose, either within the alliance or through other international institutions?

The greatest problem of the present logistics system, apart from the difficulties imposed by national as distinct from allied responsibility, is that it is still fundamentally based upon the logistics system of the occupation forces set up after 1945. It lacks cross-country mobility and is too closely tied to a fixed depot system. It is too dependent upon civilian resources for labour and transport. These shortcomings would be serious in case of nuclear warfare: road and rail movement will be disrupted; major bridges, communications centres and depots will be destroyed; refugees will impede or halt military movement; and troops will become isolated on the battlefield.

The development of aircraft with VTOL (vertical take-off and landing) and STOL (short take-off and landing) capability will be a useful step forward. But even when these aircraft are available, they will only provide mobility for a relatively small proportion of forces. The general transport problem requires substantial action to remedy it now, without waiting for these aircraft to come into service. The suggestion made in the previous chapter for a NATO Transport Command is here extremely relevant. More helicopters, particularly of the crane type, and mobile bridging equipment are also required. Unless a good deal is done to make available more equipment of modern design, the logistics system will be unable to provide the mobility and flexibility demanded by operational plans.

Many proposals have been made and studied by the military authorities for improving the organisation of logistics. But only a radical approach will provide the logistic support required to achieve the military objective of creating integrated and efficient fighting formations. It is no use having international forces under one command unless there is an international logistics system to support them under the same command. Logistics problems underline the conflict between national interests and the interests of the alliance as a whole which is found time after time in a detailed analysis of the NATO forces. This is emphasised by the comparison between the progress achieved in infrastructure projects, based on NATO initiative and common financing, with the logistics system dependent upon a national choice of priorities.

It is readily appreciated that the common organisation and financing of infrastructure projects is a relatively simple operation compared to the provision of an allied logistics system. The practical problems and the much greater amount of money involved, with the consequent strain on foreign exchange for some members, undoubtedly fortify national objections to an integrated system based on common financing and NATO control.

Thus to solve logistic difficulties it may be necessary to view them in a wider context and to include foreign exchange problems arising from support costs and the purchase of weapons and equipment by one member country from another. Only by taking an overall view can one establish the equality of burden which is the essential basis for the interdependence and common effort required to ensure the success of an alliance of independent nations.

The rejected European Defence Community Treaty did provide for a common defence budget to be prepared by the international Board of Commissioners, and in order to avoid disturbances in the balance of payments of member countries, the Board was ordinarily required to spend between 85 per cent and 115 per cent of the contribution of each member state in the territory of that state. Without the surrender of national sovereignty implicit in the European Defence Community it is not feasible to expect so far-reaching an arrangement to be acceptable in NATO. But at least some part of a scheme of this sort is necessary to provide adequate logistics support to the troops we have assigned to the allied commands as well as to resolve the hardships of balance of payments deficits arising from defence commitments and to ease the frictions of arms purchasing.

NATO should establish a fund from which it would procure the necessary supplies, spending the money in the various countries in proportion to their contributions. This fund could be extended to provide also for an independent NATO Transport Command for air transport and for such other items as are militarily necessary but difficult to arrange on a national supply basis. If infrastructure contributions, purchases of arms and equipment, and allowances for maintaining troops in another member's country were also taken into account, a rough balance could be struck so that no country's balance of payments suffered unduly. For example, the foreign exchange cost of the United Kingdom's troops in Germany might be offset by purchases of supplies and equipment from Britain by the fund.

I do not suggest that this proposition satisfies all possible objections. In particular I anticipate many problems in working out the proportions to be paid by the member countries and real difficulties in assessing those contributions in the light of the non-NATO commitments of some countries. The accounting procedures would also be cumbersome and complicated. But since there is not much point in setting up an integrated military alliance in terms of men and then denying them the means to make the military operations effective, I do not see any alternative to tackling the logistics problem on a NATO-wide basis.

PART FOUR

What Next for NATO?

Chapter XII

DISARMAMENT AND ARMS CONTROL

One cannot properly consider military strategy and foreign policy without relating them to hopes of disarmament, since these are three facets of the same problem. Indeed part of the story of the failures of disarmament negotiations can be found in the fact that disarmament has been treated too much as an isolated problem and too little as an integral part of defence policy. The scope of this book does not permit a detailed analysis of the problems of arms control and disarmament or an attempt to disentangle the threads of the labyrinthine negotiations which have been pursued intermittently since the end of the last war. But some discussion of the problems is essential if we are to get NATO's future tasks correctly in perspective.

It has often been taken as axiomatic that increases in military strength imply increases in security. But, on the contrary, we can reach a point where adding more and more weapons to our armoury does not necessarily increase our military security. Increased deterrence of an all-out aggression through greater capacity to meet it may be offset by increased danger of war by accident. Stability and a slowing down of the arms race will contribute more to our security in the long run. As well as the quantity, the *kind* of weapons has a direct bearing on this aspect of security.

Weapons systems and military strategy tend to be devised without any regard to political purpose. The policy of producing smaller and smaller atomic weapons, for example the *Davy Crockett*, seems to have been approved without consideration of the difficulties it may present in terms of political control or of the dangers of nuclear escalation. The same is true of the military concept of 'a bigger bang for a buck'.

To separate arms control policy from defence policy is as

sensible as, in the case of a husband and wife with a joint income, charging the husband with the duty of saving while the wife has unrestricted freedom to spend. Unless there is some joint control over the decisions to spend it is unlikely that they will make much progress in saving. Similarly unless there are joint decisions by those responsible for arms control and those in charge of defence policy there is unlikely to be any significant progress towards a halt in the arms race or towards disarmament. We must seek to maintain efficient defence forces to meet all likely contingencies but with a view to creating conditions for the reduction of armaments which is the only sure path to security. We cannot assume that it is possible to reach and maintain a stable balance of military power; the process of continuous technological innovation means that we depend upon a 'delicate balance of terror'. The characteristic of the arms race is that, like Alice, we have to run faster and faster to stay in the same place.

The recent development of a growing literature on this subject, especially in the United States, is a welcome sign, although the arguments of the experts are often rather too sophisticated to be translated into political practice. Governments and Members of Parliament have to be much more concerned with public opinion than with logic and mathematical analysis. Much of the discussion has centred around the new concept of 'arms control' while 'disarmament', although still more usually employed in political language, is losing ground. Thus it is necessary to define our terms, since the words seem frequently to be employed with varying shades of meaning and the difference is more than mere semantics. Mr. Hedley Bull[68] has defined them as follows:

> *Disarmament* is the reduction or abolition of armaments. It may be unilateral or multilateral; general or local; comprehensive or partial; controlled or uncontrolled.
> *Arms control* is restraint internationally exercised upon armaments policy, whether in respect of the level of armaments, their character, deployment or use.

I shall follow these definitions.

It will be seen that there is nothing mutually contradictory about the two terms: there is no basis for the supposition that to believe in arms control is to be against disarmament. Indeed the most desirable form of arms control is disarmament, i.e. a reduction in the level of armaments. As is so often the case in politics, part of the difficulty and confusion arises from both words having acquired emotional overtones. To the old-fashioned military mind 'disarmament' conjures up woolly-minded 'do-gooders' who want to send the country's representatives 'naked into the Conference room'; whereas to many people, rightly disturbed at the dangers of the arms race, it is an article of faith. On the other hand, 'arms control' has acquired a false connotation; it is often wrongly assumed that because arms control is concerned with the stability of deterrence, its advocates do not want to see a reduction of armaments at all.

'Arms control' is understood to imply an integration of arms control policy with foreign and military policy, whereas it is usually felt that 'disarmament' can be abstracted from the political background and from military strategy. The use of the word 'control' is helpful since it points the essential condition that any agreements in this field must be subject to adequate safeguards to ensure that they are carried out. But linguistically 'control' presents difficulties, since in French and Russian it means exclusively 'examination' or 'inspection' whereas in English it also includes 'direction' or 'supervision'. This was revealed by a comparison of the Russian and English texts of Mr. Khrushchev's disarmament speech to the United Nations General Assembly in September 1960. Care must be taken to avoid allowing this difference of meaning to bedevil disarmament discussions in the way the difference between the English and French definitions of 'federation' has confused the issue of political integration in Europe.

However, although they are not incompatible, the two concepts do tend to symbolise fundamental differences in approach to the problem. Arms control aims at limited agreements for specific purposes, as, for example, a nuclear test ban, in the hope that as a result of the experience gained and the increased mutual confidence further progress will be possible. The doctrine of general and comprehensive disarmament, whose greatest exponent is Philip Noel-Baker,[69] aims at a single treaty leading by stages from lesser to more drastic measures over a period of years. Such plans were put forward by both sides during the ten-nation disarmament discussions of 1960.

Unfortunately the idea of disarmament as a means of reducing the danger of war is not so simple in the nuclear era. It never was easy to achieve but at least a layman could follow the proposals since the issues were always about the number of men, the size of ships and the abolition of heavy bombers, etc. Today a wealth of technical information is required to show how many inspections are the minimum to render a nuclear testing agreement reasonably safe. Whereas in matters of arms control the policy decisions and the balancing of the risks involved must remain in political hands, now more than ever Ministers—and public opinion—must rely on technical and military advice as to the feasibility of proposals put before them. In a sense the concept of arms control is a child of the nuclear age. With conventional forces, greater security always depended upon reductions in the level of forces and armaments. But today measures designed to prevent the spread of nuclear weapons, to safeguard against surprise attack or to ban nuclear testing are clearly advantageous although no reduction in the present level of armaments is necessarily involved.

The nuclear age has also served to lay increased emphasis on the importance of the inspection and control of any disarmament or arms control agreement. The ease with which a few nuclear weapons can be hidden, together with their vast power of destruction, mean that an immense advantage would be conferred on any country which did not carry out fully a treaty to destroy all nuclear weapons. And this new technological trend has been reinforced by mutual suspicions arising from the ideological divisions of the cold war. No agreements can be contemplated by either side which do not provide safeguards against evasion by the other. In fact the extent and means of inspection have been the issues on which negotiations have foundered hitherto.

Inspection and control systems are likely to prove very costly. It has been estimated that it would cost over 1,000 million dollars to build a network of twenty-one seismographic detector stations in the Soviet Union, required for policing a nuclear weapons test ban. It would cost 5,000 million dollars for a worldwide network of these stations.[70] While the cost should prove much less than the cost of maintaining defence forces, and in any event no one would wish to sacrifice additional security on financial grounds, it must be recognised that in the nuclear age disarmament will not mean a total net gain to the taxpayer of the whole of the previous defence budgets.

Partial measures will not by themselves halt the arms race; but they may help to reduce the fever, which is a necessary preliminary to beginning a cure of the disease. And there is no logical reason why the pursuit of general and comprehensive disarmament should deter agreement about partial measures, provided these measures do not upset the balance of power or lead away from the ultimate goal. We have to get what we can. The irony of our present situation is that if we could get back to the point where disarmament negotiations began in the 1930s, we should feel we had virtually achieved disarmament.

It would seem more reasonable to suppose that partial arms control measures could be agreed and the inspection procedure worked out more easily than the achievement of a grand design to deal with everything. And, although the Western proposals of 1960 were set in a general and comprehensive framework, in effect they were partial measures since it was made clear that the early stages could be negotiated separately. The Soviet Union, on the other hand, insisted that the different stages of its plan were inseparable and that they must all be carried out within a fixed period. We may well consider that the Soviet Union is not seriously intent upon any kind of arms control or disarmament agreement and that her purpose is only to make good propaganda. This may be so, of course: the more grandiose and far-reaching the disarmament proposals are, the better reception they will get throughout the world. But we cannot be sure and we must therefore negotiate on this basis to put Soviet sincerity to the test. At best we may be proved wrong in our suspicions and get an agreement; at worst we shall, for a change, achieve some good propaganda by making it absolutely clear that it is the Soviet Union and not the West that is dragging her feet.

This approach seems to be the basis of the American proposals, following the joint statement of agreed principles for disarmament negotiations by the United States and the Soviet Union filed with the United Nations on the eve of the Assembly meeting in September 1961. In the speech in which he challenged the Soviet Union to a peace race, not an arms race, President Kennedy said:

> The programme to be presented to this Assembly—for general and complete disarmament under effective international control—moves to bridge the gap between those who insist on a gradual approach and those who talk only of the final and total achievement. . . . It

would achieve, under the eye of an international disarmament organ-
ization, a steady reduction in forces, both nuclear and conventional,
until it has abolished all armies and all weapons except those needed
for internal order and a new United Nations peace force. And it
starts that process now, today, even as the talks begin.

Despite this joint statement of agreed principles and the
encouraging advance represented by United States and Soviet
agreement on the membership of the new 18-power disarmament
committee and on the decision to resume negotiations in March
1962, it is too soon to predict any agreement on practical disarmament measures. The United States plan has less emphasis,
as compared with earlier Western plans, on the linking of specific
measures within each stage. It suggests immediate implementation
as soon as agreement is reached on a particular step. On the other
hand, the Soviet Union insists on agreement on complete disarmament before implementation can begin. As before, the
question of control is likely to prove a major obstacle and in
particular America's understandable concern to have inspection
arrangements to cover the armed forces and weapons to be retained as well as for those to be done away with. The Soviet
Union's renewed demand for an uninspected nuclear test ban is
an indication of the difficulties to be encountered.

Mr. Khrushchev has advocated 'total disarmament' since
1959 as Mr. Litvinov had done in the old League of Nations in
1932. It is true that in each case a reservation was made for
internal security forces, and in totalitarian countries and those
with dissident overseas territories the demand for such forces
could be quite high. But even with this allowance, as Mr. Bull
argues with ruthless logic, there is no force in the argument that
'total disarmament' will make war impossible.

> The objection that proposals for it are impracticable, however, con-
> cedes too much to the idea of total disarmament. The objection to it
> is not that it is impracticable, but that there can be, in principle,
> nothing of the kind: the physical capacity for organised violence is
> inherent in human society. Even the most thorough-going dis-
> armament treaty must leave nations with the capacity to wage war
> on a primitive level; and, moreover, with the capacity to raise this
> level, to re-establish what has been dis-established, to remember or
> to re-invent what has been laid aside.[71]

All the stocks of nuclear bombs can be destroyed, but unless we shoot all the scientists and burn their books we cannot abolish the 'know-how' of making new bombs very quickly.

Mr. Khrushchev's sincerity may be open to question, particularly in the light of the Soviet *volte face* on nuclear testing: it is widely believed that he changed his mind because he could not be sure that China would renounce her right to become a nuclear power. One cannot see Mr. Khrushchev agreeing, when it comes to the point, to 'total disarmament' either unless China agreed too, and this would appear even less likely than her acceptance of a nuclear test ban. On the other hand, his reluctance to admit inspection of the Soviet Union except as part of a substantial disarmament agreement leading to general and complete disarmament is understandable. Mr. Finletter, United States Ambassador to NATO, has said:

> The plan we propose must be fair in that it shall recognise legitimate Russian insistence on keeping the inspection and control at reasonable levels during the early stage when the amount of disarmament is small. We must not expect the Russians to give up their closed society and the military secrecy it gives them without a *quid pro quo*.[72]

General and comprehensive disarmament also raises the problems of how it can be enforced, how order will be maintained in the world and how to deal with a situation if it is discovered that a country has not destroyed all its nuclear weapons. Since we cannot expect to have an international police force under a world authority to enforce partial arms control measures or even the early stages of a general and comprehensive disarmament agreement, what is to happen if a violation of an agreement is detected? While there has been much discussion about inspection and control procedures, there has been comparatively little concern expressed about the enforcement of agreements.[73] What political and military consequences can be expected to follow a breach of an arms control agreement or a refusal to allow the agreed control procedures to be carried out? For it is not sufficient that any violation will be detected; there must also be sanctions which will counter any advantage which may accrue from the violation. World opinion and the prospect of condemnatory resolutions by the United Nations may be a deterrent for a democratic government but it is far from certain that they would inhibit a totalitarian regime. Moreover world opinion, like public opinion in an individual country, tends to have a short memory. If the only effect of a detected violation is to re-start the arms race abated by the agreement, the 'guilty' nation would not be penalised while the world would be back in the present state of tension.

It is impossible to envisage a disarmed world without an international police force with sufficient military power at its disposal to deal with any defaulting country. It is significant that in the 1959–60 negotiations the Russians agreed to a United Nations police force, reversing their previous policy. But how is the police force to be controlled—a matter of crucial importance in any society? With the present ideological cleavages and the power of veto, it is highly optimistic to suppose that the United Nations in its present form could perform this task effectively, or that its powers could be suitably revised by agreement of the member nations. We need a world authority, a world government, to direct such a police force in a fully disarmed world.

There can be no early prospect of any significant moves in this direction while nations cling to their sovereignty even within their own defensive alliances, and while nationalism is the dominant political force in Asia and Africa. We must not imagine that the neutral and uncommitted countries will automatically agree to such proposals. They clamour for the great powers to disarm; but it does not follow that they are ready to give up their own armaments or to abandon their own local arms races. Chastity is no virtue if it emanates from impotence. And if there were such sweetness and light in the world that nations were willing to set up a world authority which none could control and to delegate to it the most cherished attributes of national sovereignty as well as the means of overwhelming destruction, would disarmament still be a problem? Would not the mutual suspicions which feed the arms race have long since disappeared?

With customary perspicacity Mr. Khrushchev seems to have anticipated this political chicken-and-egg argument as to which comes first, world government or disarmament, and has made his position clear. He accepts the logic of an international police force and a world authority to control it, and he has stated his terms—terms which are utterly inconsistent with the ideals of world government and the principle of democracy but which accord with communist philosophy and Soviet confidence that their system will ultimately triumph. Mr. Khrushchev insists upon having a veto in any international authority or control administration. This is the real meaning of the Troika proposal. The proposal was not simply directed at the late Secretary-General of the United Nations or at the proposed single neutral administrator for the nuclear test ban treaty. Mr. Khrushchev was announcing that the only kind of world authority in which he could be interested is one controlled by a tripartite board, tied to the unanimity rule and with one of the three seats always filled by a Soviet nominee. The American-Russian agreement for U Thant to take over as Secretary-General of the United Nations in October 1961, following the tragic death of Mr. Hammarskjöld, does not mean Soviet abandonment of the Troika principle.

Mr. Walter Lippmann gives an account of his discussions with Mr. Khrushchev on this point:

He would not accept a single neutral administrator. Why? Because, he said, while there are neutral countries, there are no neutral men. You would not accept a communist administrator and I cannot accept a non-communist administrator. I will never entrust the security of the Soviet Union to any foreigner. We cannot have another Hammarskjöld, no matter where he comes from among the neutral countries. I found this enlightening. It was plain to me that here is a new dogma, that there are no neutral men. After all, the Soviet Union had accepted Trygve Lie and Hammarskjöld. The Soviet Government has now come to the conclusion that there can be no such thing as an impartial civil servant in this deeply divided world, and that the kind of political celibacy which the British theory of the civil service calls for is in international affairs a fiction. This new dogma has long consequences. It means that there can be international co-operation only if, in the administration as well as in the policy making, the Soviet Union has a veto.[74]

Mr. Khrushchev may change his mind and his terms. But we must recognise that we have a fundamental ideological impasse as well as a disarmament impasse. He believes communism is right and will triumph. We believe the same about democracy. In the cold war, both our military policy, based on the doctrine of deterrence, and our political policy are in the final analysis acts of faith. But this does not mean that all negotiation with the Soviet Union is hopeless and that we should give up trying.

Both the Soviet Union and the West have a common interest in restricting the spread of nuclear weapons, in reducing the risks of

P

nuclear escalation and in safeguarding against surprise attack. If, despite our best efforts, we make no progress towards general disarmament, we must seek to reduce tension and achieve a measure of stability by partial measures.

The resumption of nuclear testing by the Soviet Union was, however, a bitter blow to hopes of progress in this direction. The fact that the resumption took place on the eve of the Belgrade conference of non-aligned nations was even more disturbing. It suggests that Mr. Khrushchev is quite indifferent to world opinion and that he considers intimidation more effective than persuasion in the neutral world. The Soviet Union, unlike the West, is not dependent on the goodwill of the uncommitted nations. No doubt Mr. Khrushchev calculates correctly that Afro-Asian obsession with anti-colonialism and their fear of Soviet strength will prevent any significant defections to the West. The Russian refusal of the Anglo-American proposal for a mutual ban on atmospheric testing, without inspection or control, was a further disappointment.

The special nature of nuclear tests is such that there is a good case for the West renouncing them unilaterally. The main disadvantage of this course is that it would encourage Mr. Khrushchev to assume that he can get everything for nothing, through our unilateral action, provided that he is sufficiently obdurate and waits long enough. Equally if the Soviet Union is able to carry out tests and then resume the moratorium, it makes the whole concept of a ban meaningless and could give her a decisive military advantage. Unless we can get a test ban there seems little hope of any other type of arms control agreement; and, as President Kennedy has stressed, an end of nuclear tests of all kinds is a logical beginning to a programme for general disarmament.

The health hazards of atmospheric nuclear tests are so serious that we should be prepared to take great risks in respect of control and inspection to achieve an agreement to end testing. Atmospheric tests are self-policing and the value of underground tests, which would escape detection unless there was a proper system of inspection, is open to argument. There is good evidence to suggest that the Russians have never been interested in low-yield nuclear warheads and the development of miniature atomic weapons. As we have seen, these weapons also merit low priority in the defence strategy the West should adopt to ensure political control over the use of nuclear weapons and to avoid the dangers of escalation. The military risk that the Soviet Union may have illicit and undetected underground tests does not appear to be excessive.

On the other hand, the banning of tests by the Soviet Union, the United States and Britain is not satisfactory as an end in itself. Such an agreement would not restrict the production of more nuclear weapons or reduce existing stocks. It is also most unlikely that other countries—France, for example—would accept a test ban unless it were designed to lead on to a prohibition of production of nuclear weapons and reductions in stockpiles. For these purposes, of course, inspection and control procedures would be of crucial importance. Thus any relaxation of Western demands for inspection in order to halt the tests must not create precedents for further agreements.

Against the background of all the difficulties, what should we do? What kind of policy do we need? To begin with, we must in our own countries and collectively in NATO agree on two things: we must make the pursuit of arms control and disarmament a central aim of both our military and our political policies; and we must establish machinery, designed to implement this aim, for co-ordinating the work of scientists and the military as well as of the Foreign Offices. Too often we have treated disarmament questions as just one aspect of international affairs and left Foreign Ministers to produce plans and counter-plans without over much concern as to whether they fitted our defence requirements or were relevant to the political aims of the West. There has been little consultation within the alliance on these problems. This attitude probably accounts for the fact that we have so often gone back on our own proposals and that generally we have been badly out-gunned in the propaganda war.

Consistently governments have given far more attention to disarmament as an objective in their political programmes than they have devoted energy and study to achieving it in their administrations. However, President Kennedy's pronouncements have sounded a new note and the formation of a new Disarmament Agency in the United States is an encouraging step in the direction of translating his words into political action.

Prima facie there should be more chance of reaching military stability and making progress towards disarmament in times of relative tranquillity than at times of tension. Yet we must not rule out that crises pose the dangers more acutely than periods of international harmony and as a result can lead to a 'crash' arms control programme, as Professor Schelling has pointed out:

> Neither we nor the Russians at the present time take arms control terribly seriously; we do not view it as an alternative to a war that is imminent. But it is not impossible to imagine crises in which the likelihood of immediate war would become a grave preoccupation. . . . It is perfectly conceivable that in a real crisis there would be a sudden and drastic change in the attitudes of both sides towards arms control. 'Preventive arms control' might begin to look like a risky but attractive alternative to a possibly inevitable pre-emptive war. Sudden and drastic 'measures to safeguard against surprise attack' might have to be negotiated on an acutely demanding time schedule.[75]

If such opportunities should come during or as a result of the Berlin crisis we are ill-equipped to take them. We still need to develop a sound strategic policy for the defence of NATO. As a pre-requisite to any agreements we must redress the nuclear-conventional balance as stability in a situation of mutual deterrence demands. We must remove from Mr. Khrushchev the temptation of easy gains, minimise his chances of subversion and give him no opportunity to play off one ally against another. We can achieve these purposes if only we will adopt the right military and political policies. In particular we must avoid putting him in a position of having to choose between surrender or war, whilst keeping out of this kind of situation ourselves. His playing of the Berlin crisis suggests that Mr. Khrushchev is himself not unaware of this danger.

Within NATO, without depending on agreement with the Soviet Union, we can help to make the wider problems of nuclear escalation and the spread of nuclear weapons less acute by getting our own position right in these respects. The proposals made in previous chapters for joint political control of nuclear weapons are designed to meet the needs of arms control as well as the requirements of NATO's military and political policies. We need these policies also to minimise the danger of stumbling into nuclear war by accident. In this connection there is much to be said for the suggestion that there should be a direct telephone line between the White House and the Kremlin, to be used only in emergency, to explain if some mistake occurs and to prevent a precipitate response from the other side. This is perhaps the simplest and cheapest proposal for arms control.

There is scope also for political approaches which may prepare the way for both political settlements and arms control and disarmament possibilities. Disarmament agreements must be negotiated under the auspices of the United Nations; yet China, whose adherence is an essential condition of any general agreement, is not admitted to the United Nations. Just as any arms control proposals must, to succeed, preserve the military balance, so stability must be expressed in political as well as in military terms. The removal of causes of political tensions may justify some reductions in military strength. We have to weigh all the advantages and disadvantages to decide the balance. It is on this basis that we must judge the proposals made for disengagement and the unification of Germany, which, although separate problems, are in terms of practical politics inseparably linked.

The idea of reducing tension in Europe by 'disengagement', the mutual withdrawal of NATO and Soviet forces from their existing proximity in Germany and the establishment of a neutral and politically independent zone between them, was first put forward as long ago as 1952 by Dr. Pfleiderer, the late German Ambassador in Belgrade. The van Zeeland plan for a demilitarised zone was developed in 1953 and disengagement became a controversial political issue in 1954 when Colonel von Bonin advocated a plan for German rearmament independently of NATO, involving the withdrawal of NATO forces behind the Rhine. In July 1955 Sir Anthony Eden suggested at the Heads of Government Conference at Geneva the possibility of a demilitarised zone between East and West, although later developments revealed that he had in mind an experiment in local disarmament and not the total disengagement of Soviet and NATO forces.

In the next two or three years a number of variations on these themes were put forward. Early in 1957 Mr. Gaitskell put forward his plan for a disengaged zone to be created by the gradual withdrawal of foreign forces from East and West Germany, Poland, Czechoslovakia and Hungary. The level of national arms within the area was to be fixed and controlled and the territorial integrity of the countries within the zone was to be guaranteed by a European Security Treaty. German reunification would be agreed and guaranteed by the Four Powers and the countries within the area would withdraw from NATO and the Warsaw Pact. This was approved as official Labour Party policy and the German Social Democratic Party also came out strongly in favour of disengagement in 1957. Later that year the Polish Foreign Minister, M. Rapacki, proposed a plan for a nuclear free zone in Central Europe and expanded it to include also a controlled reduction of conventional forces in the zone. His plan, which did not provide for German reunification, received the support of the Soviet Union. His proposals were followed by those of Mr. Kennan, former United States Ambassador to Moscow, which went much further than the Gaitskell plan and advocated the withdrawal of American forces from Europe.

Official reaction to these ideas—from NATO Governments and military authorities alike—was extremely hostile and it is doubtful if any serious examination was made of their political and military implications by the North Atlantic Council or by individual members. It was too easy to prefer the *status quo* without acknowledging, as is now all too evident, the precarious foundation on which it rested. Disengagement became a dirty word in political circles and the plethora of plans permitted its objectives to be distorted beyond recognition. Some of the plans were put forward as measures of arms control, some concentrated on solutions of the political problems and others aimed at both objectives. Thus there was no agreed definition of disengagement. The Berlin crisis in the autumn of 1961 produced a revival of interest in disengagement proposals. A final judgment, however, as to the value of any plan and as to whether it maintained the balance of political and military power, must depend upon the details. As yet even the principles involved have not been accepted by the NATO powers.

In assessing disengagement today we must recognise that its military and political implications must be judged in the light of the new strategy demanded by mutual deterrence and not against the background of massive retaliation by which it was judged in 1958. The change in NATO strategy invalidates any previous conclusions as to the military consequences then expected to flow from its adoption. It is equally important to consider the concept of a mutual withdrawal of forces in the wider context of general disarmament. Any form of disengagement would pose awkward problems for NATO; but it will be a great error if, for this reason, proposals are dismissed out of hand as they were before. The difficulties must be compared not with the *status quo* but with the alternatives which are likely to present themselves in the absence of East-West agreements to attain political and military stability.

It is idle to expect that the Soviet Union would agree to the reunification of Germany, and the certain loss of the communist regime in East Germany, without a substantial *quid pro quo*. Similarly she would not withdraw her troops from Poland, Hungary and Czechoslovakia, with the possible desertion of the first two from the communist empire, without corresponding concessions.

From the NATO point of view a neutral zone in Europe would represent great advantages provided that (*a*) it was part of an acceptable plan for the reunification of Germany; (*b*) there was a firm commitment on the part of the United States to maintain her forces in Europe; (*c*) it was possible to station sufficient NATO troops in the Low Countries and France to preserve NATO's conventional strength and (*d*) that West Germany continued to remain within the European Economic Community. Whether a unified Germany would provide stability in Europe is perhaps open to argument and much would depend upon the terms. It is, however, indisputable that we cannot expect stability while Germany remains divided. And, in return for Western support for reunification, we are entitled to insist that a reunified Germany accepts the Oder-Neisse line without equivocation. Franco-German rapprochement is one of the most hopeful developments of recent years and if this were followed by German-Polish rapprochement many fears would be set at rest.

No progress can be attained in any of these directions unless to begin with there is agreement among the members of NATO. We cannot expect to negotiate successful arms control or disarmament arrangements with the Soviet Union unless we can first get agreement among ourselves upon the strategy and guiding principles for the alliance as a whole. If arms control and disarmament are viewed, as they must be, as part of defence and foreign policies, it is clear that the NATO alliance has a crucial part to play in the co-ordination of the policies of member governments and in determining the right military strategy, as well as in persuading

Mr. Khrushchev by its solidarity and strength that it is worth his while to make agreements.

Future generations will judge the success or failure of NATO not so much on its military organisation as on its achievements in facilitating measures of disarmament, described by the United Nations in a resolution adopted unanimously by its eighty-two members on 20 November 1959 as 'the most important question facing the world today'.

Chapter XIII

THE MILITARY TASKS

Defence policy is a matter of priorities. The essence of my criticism of NATO is that it has not got its military priorities right.

As so often in life, it is the dramatic and spectacular proposal which catches the headlines whereas it is uninspiring routine work that makes the difference between efficiency and incompetence. The effective strength of the alliance is more likely to be enhanced by an integrated logistics system than by the acquisition of five or fifty *Polaris* submarines.

Few travellers by civil airlines can fail to have asked themselves whether there is any point in all the efforts that are now being made to develop a supersonic airliner. If the object is to get from one place to another more quickly, could not much more time be saved by reducing the thirty or forty-five minutes one must report before take-off, the delay in collecting baggage and clearing customs, the frequent delays before the plane is in the air? Also could not more be done to reduce the time taken to get from the airport to the town? But there is, of course, the factor of prestige. If one airline could get a supersonic liner then the others would have to have one too. Similarly with the passengers: status would demand that they 'fly supersonic' in order to keep up with their neighbours. I am sure we shall soon get a supersonic airliner. I am equally sure that the waiting time and ground travel time at each end of the journey will increase proportionately to the reduction in flying time.

The same factors apply to the NATO alliance. Prestige and the spectacular, symbolised by nuclear weapons, have tended to blunt our urgency in dealing with less exciting matters which would more surely and immediately increase our security. There is no prestige in having the best level of stocks within the alliance and nothing dramatic in maintaining a full complement of signallers in an infantry division in Germany. But we have to make up our mind whether we want the most effective set of defence arrangements we can get for our money or whether we really prefer to pursue independent national policies whilst paying token tribute to the NATO alliance.

The first task is to get our nuclear doctrine right. This cannot be left to be a matter of debate between generals or military commentators or even as a theme for political speeches and pamphlets. It is a classic example of the complete interconnection of military and political problems. An appropriate strategy to match the epoch of mutual deterrence must be agreed by the North Atlantic Council and clear directives transmitted to the allied military authorities. The new doctrine must then be laid down throughout the whole military hierarchy. All remaining vestiges of the old philosophy of massive retaliation must be swept away since, apart from military dangers and political uncertainty, while they linger it is impossible to expect the co-operation and enthusiasm required from members of the alliance to furnish sufficient conventional forces.

In previous chapters I have suggested what must be done to give military substance to a sound nuclear doctrine derived from political considerations. European technology is unlikely to be able to make a significant contribution in this field in the foreseeable future and maintenance of the nuclear deterrent must therefore remain the special responsibility of the United States. As well as bearing this military burden, the United States must also take a political initiative within the alliance if effective allied political control over strategy, essential to the cohesion of NATO, is to be achieved. For it is important to recognise, as is all too rarely done, that although NATO depends upon American nuclear power, the nuclear force of the United States as at present constituted is purely a national force. It is open to the same political criticisms that can be applied to Great Britain, France and the next NATO country, even if it is in a different military category by virtue of its much greater power, invulnerability and flexibility.

Without American co-operation we cannot hope to resolve the *Nth* power problem or, more accurately, as Albert Wohlstetter has pointed out, the *N-plus 1* country problem:

So far as long-run world stability is concerned, the Nth country tends to think of the problem as beginning with *N-plus 1*. The original irony intended by the label 'Nth power problem' was seated precisely in the fact that the United States and the Soviet Union thought of the trouble as the third-power problem, Great Britain thought of it as the fourth-power problem, France as the fifth-power problem and so on. Each new or prospective nuclear power thinks of the problem as that of stopping the next country after itself. This is the N-plus 1 country problem.[76]

All nuclear weapons in Europe, big and small, should be assigned to the alliance in the same way that the divisions in Germany are so assigned. And this must apply equally to America, Britain, France and any other member acquiring nuclear power status. Political control over the whole range of nuclear weapons would be exercised by the North Atlantic Council through a new Supreme Commander who would exercise overriding military control in the nuclear field.

In order to make political control effective in the case of tactical nuclear weapons and to avoid dangers of unpremeditated nuclear escalation, I have suggested that the nuclear weapons of the alliance available for tactical use on the battlefield should be organised separately from the conventional artillery and be subject to a separate allied channel of command under a new Commander-in-Chief for Tactical Nuclear Weapons. He would be under the direction of two supreme commanders—SACEUR for the deployment and military operations of his units and the new Supreme Commander for Nuclear Weapons for authority for the initial use of his various types of weapons. A separate authorisation would be required for each category of nuclear weapon, so as to limit escalation as far as possible.

I have further proposed that the new allied atomic artillery units should be, like the present tactical air forces and General Norstad's new mobile fire-brigade force, multi-national in personnel and organisation. If there are no national atomic artillery units, there should be no awkward problems of national prestige, equality within the alliance and custody of warheads. The organisation would also match the intention that the use of nuclear weapons should be controlled by the alliance and not by individual members of it.

To meet this requirement it is also necessary to reassess the rôle of the allied tactical air forces. Clearly if they are to undertake nuclear interdiction bombing in response to conventional attack, there is no point in worrying about the use of tactical nuclear weapons on the battlefield itself. I have suggested that long-range tasks, for which *Polaris* or similar missiles are required by SACEUR under current plans, should be transferred to the strategic air forces. This would obviate the need for such missiles to be allocated to SACEUR. The use of nuclear weapons by the ATAFs for their remaining tasks would be controlled by the same channel of command suggested for the battlefield tactical weapons.

If this principle of joint political control over the use of nuclear weapons is accepted and implemented, there is hope that the most intransigent problem of the NATO forces can be resolved. Within the alliance, although not at present within NATO control, we have no shortage of nuclear power. The military problem concerns the maintenance of means of delivery which will survive a pre-emptive attack and also be capable of penetrating enemy defences.

The nuclear strategy demanded by a state of nuclear parity only makes sense if the nuclear capability is complemented by conventional strength which is sufficient to deal with any likely contingency short of all-out aggression. The old concept of the Sword and the Shield, the nuclear strike forces to be brought into decisive play like a gladiator's sword once the enemy's blow has been parried by the conventional forces of his shield, is outmoded. War will not happen like that. A massive Russian conventional attack, which seemed the most acute danger when NATO was created, is no longer credible because the risk of nuclear retaliation by the West cannot be discounted. If the Russians decide deliberately to embark upon all-out war, they will surely use their nuclear striking force from the outset so as to gain the maximum advantage from the element of surprise. The analogy of the Sword and the Shield should be buried along with the doctrine of massive nuclear retaliation on which it depended.

NATO nuclear capability must be designed to strike the second blow. And it must be supported by adequate conventional means to protect us against nuclear blackmail and to deal with the most likely cause of hostilities—mistake or miscalculation. Instead of *the* deterrent—American strategic nuclear power—we need a series of deterrents so that we have an appropriate response to any type of aggression and can meet conventional attack with conventional defence. Thus the soldier in uniform has become

as important a part of the deterrent as the nuclear weapons, large
or small. And the provision of more well-equipped and well-
trained divisions, which has not been given its due priority because of the natural and proper concern about nuclear weapons,
is the prime function of the European members of the alliance.

The problems and prospects of obtaining the conventional force
required to meet the needs of the new strategy have been examined
in earlier chapters. Essentially it is a matter of political will and
not of insuperable military difficulties. It is absurd to suppose, for
example, that there need be any great problem in raising a force
of six hundred thousand men for Central Europe. In part the
European countries have become used to getting their defence
on the cheap and have been encouraged to feel that the only force
that mattered was strategic nuclear air power, which was not their
concern. Most NATO countries welcomed the increased firepower
of atomic weapons as a pretext for reducing the unpopular and
expensive manpower demanded by purely conventional forces;
and they did this well before the atomic artillery was likely to be
available. And few countries have allowed their obligations to
the alliance to inhibit the free pursuit of what they alone deem to
be their national interests, even if it has meant denuding their
agreed contribution to the NATO forces.

The United Kingdom has been much criticised because she has
reduced the size of her forces at the disposal of NATO and I do
not seek to defend her policy. But it must be remembered that
she is the only NATO member who has treaty obligations to maintain a minimum force available to SACEUR and who requires the
consent of her partners in the alliance before any withdrawals can
take place. Other countries can withdraw their troops without
incurring the same publicity.

The essence of the new strategy demanded by mutual deterrence is that there shall be a ready mobilised conventional capability to deal with unexpected sources of friction—a rising in
East Germany, for example. It is not sufficient for NATO divisions
in Germany to be augmented to meet a critical situation and then
allowed to lapse to their former inadequate level. Indeed when it
was announced that steps were to be taken, including the return
of a French division, to bring up to strength NATO forces in
Germany in response to the mounting tension over Berlin, Mr.
Khrushchev was able to use this as a pretext for much more

drastic measures of his own. There seems to be an overwhelming case for a binding commitment on all the allies, similar to that undertaken by the United Kingdom, to assign a minimum strength to SACEUR and to maintain it unless permission to reduce it is granted by other members of the alliance. If the overriding issue of control of nuclear strategy and weapons can be resolved to the satisfaction of the non-nuclear members of the alliance, one of the major factors militating against the provision of adequate conventional forces will be removed. As part of such a settlement a new protocol on the foregoing lines should be negotiated.

But it is not simply a requirement of men. It will not suffice merely to fulfil the goal of thirty divisions and leave it at that. The forces at the disposal of SACEUR must be welded into an effective and integrated organisation. This demands in turn an integrated logistics system and an adequate level of stocks. Despite having assigned their troops to the allied commanders, there are few signs that the member countries are prepared to give the commanders a like authority over the means with which their troops must fight. Variations in organisation and equipment also add substantially to the military problem of creating efficient military formations from the components of several nations.

As I have already suggested in Chapter XI, there is a strong case for extending the principle of common financing, now applied to infrastructure, over a wider field so that the military commanders, acting under the direction of the North Atlantic Council, can have some funds at their disposal to supplement the contributions in kind of the individual countries. A contribution of one per cent of their gross national income from the member countries would make available over seven thousand million dollars a year. If NATO as such had a fund of something like this size at its disposal each year, it would be much easier to obtain the air transport and logistic support necessary if its forces are to have the mobility and flexibility required to give them corresponding capability to the highly mechanised and mobile divisions of the Soviet Union.

The standardisation and the supply of arms is another field in which national interests have been allowed to override the interests of the alliance as a whole. We are a long way from the principle of a rational economic division of labour on the research, development and manufacture of new arms and equipment. Any nation's reluctance to be dependent upon foreign military equipment is understandable; but unless we overcome it we shall get neither the standardisation necessary for allied military efficiency nor the maximum protection for the minimum expenditure.

Besides the governments pursuing independent national policies in this field, there is the added complication of private commercial interests. I would prefer to see all arms research and manufacture conducted by governmental enterprise and not by private concerns. However, since no company in this industry can exist without government orders and finance, it should not be too difficult for the national governments to require the cooperation of their private arms firms provided they have the political will to do so. Unless and until this is done, we shall not make significant progress towards remedying what is acknowledged to be a grave source of weakness in our forces.

In NATO's early days there was much talk of subordinating national military interests to the goal of a truly international 'Balanced Collective Force'. It is perhaps not surprising that in a field so close to national interest as defence, achievement has fallen far short of early aspirations. The slogan has changed to 'Interdependence', but in terms of military fact the performance has moved even further from the goal of integrated defence. Yet it is in this direction, unspectacular and vexatious though it is, that we must look for the greatest accretion to the strength of the alliance at the lowest cost. In considering NATO's naval strength it has been pointed out how absurd it is for each naval power to seek to provide a whole range of hardware instead of adopting the principle of division of labour and making a specialised contribution, thus building up balanced collective forces for the alliance as a whole. In the naval field the conflict of NATO and national requirements and obligations is particularly evident since all the major NATO naval powers have substantial commitments outside the NATO area and cannot follow Belgium's admirable example of concentrating on one type of vessel (in her case, mine-sweeping craft). However, a good deal of duplication could be avoided without neglect of non-NATO responsibilities if there was more concern to build balanced collective forces for the alliance.

The naval forces of NATO rate a lower priority than the provision of an invulnerable nuclear strike force and adequate ground conventional forces in Europe. It seems very unlikely that any hostilities in the NATO area will start at sea and in this sense naval forces, except for their increasing contribution to the invulnerability of the strategic nuclear striking force, have a less clear rôle to play as a deterrent against war or nuclear blackmail. However, should hostilities begin, either as a result of a mistake or miscalculation in Europe or by an all-out nuclear attack, the Soviet submarine strength and its menace to allied shipping in the Atlantic would create grave problems and common prudence demands that we minimise naval shortcomings. As a means of providing more balanced forces and better naval defence I have suggested that some forces should be assigned to the NATO Commands, especially SACLANT, in peace-time. The lack of naval forces in being within NATO and the uncertainty about forces which are only eaamarked account, in my opinion, for many existing naval problems. So long as forces exist only on paper, there is not the same pressure to complete infrastructure projects or to rationalise the command structure, and the whole of naval thinking, outside the staffs of NATO headquarters, tends to concentrate on national and not NATO strategy.

Finally in the question of a revision of the Command structure and the boundaries between the Commands and sub-commands, we come to a matter which can contribute to the strength of the alliance with no additional expenditure at all. It is widely recognised that the existing Command structure is unsatisfactory and that it was designed on grounds of political expediency rather than military science. Yet little or nothing seems to be happening to put it right. National interests and prestige make great difficulties in devising a command system which will satisfy each nation and nevertheless contrive to make operational sense. In this case military efficiency should have precedence over political expediency.

Member countries must ask themselves whether they believe in collective defence or not. If they do, their approach to defence should be conditioned by what is needed by NATO rather than by what happens to suit their national plans. The ideal would be for NATO requirements to be drawn up by the allied Commanders in conjunction with the Military Committee and then the tasks divided among the various member countries. At present most countries plan their defence expenditure and equipment on a national basis and then consider, in the Annual Review procedure, what they can assign or earmark to the alliance.

Obviously for all the principal countries of NATO there is the problem of commitments outside the NATO area and this poses difficult questions, requiring political rather than military solutions. It is now generally agreed that NATO's interests are much wider than its defined area and that the menace which draws the Atlantic powers together, in the words of the statement issued by the North Atlantic Council after its Oslo meeting in May 1961, 'is now not only military, but also has world-wide political, economic, scientific and psychological aspects'. Thus the commitments undertaken outside NATO by some of its members ought to make at least an indirect contribution to the strength and purpose of the alliance, and there is no reason why these obligations should not be freely discussed within the alliance and account taken of them in allocating tasks and in assessing each member's contribution. If a country is unwilling to discuss its non-NATO responsibilities with its NATO allies, it would seem *prima facie* that this country doubts their relevance to the objects of the alliance and is pursuing them from entirely national interests.

While many members of the alliance have fallen down on their commitments and in this or that direction have patently pursued national interests which have conflicted with the purpose of the alliance, only France has unmistakably made clear her reluctance to accept the principles of collective effort and integration without which no military alliance can function efficiently. In withdrawing troops from Germany, in her decision to withhold her Mediterranean fleet from NATO command in time of war, in declining to have American aircraft with nuclear weapons on French airfields and in her refusal to join a fully integrated system of air defence in Europe, France has insisted on placing national sovereignty before effective defence. Apart from the substantial strength and wisdom a fully co-operative France could bring to the alliance, her key geographical position means that no rational plans for the defence of NATO territory are possible without her participation. France more than any other member has the power to determine whether or not NATO becomes an effective system of collective defence. The cause of these difficulties is once again to be found more in the political than in the military field, and the proposals I have made for the operation and control of nuclear weapons should remove many, if not all, French objections to the existing structure of NATO. Certainly it can safely be said that unless

Q

France is a willing partner, NATO cannot achieve its purpose.

The insistence on national sovereignty, often in small rather than big things, and the concern to maintain national defence forces rather than provide a specialised contribution to the balanced forces of the alliance, would make sense if independent national defence were a viable alternative to a collective defence system like NATO. But surely no country really believes it could alone provide for its own defence in the 1960s—not even the United States? And how does our security benefit by the setting up of a collective defence system which is then denied the men and equipment and money needed to make it effective? If these simple, and to me undeniable, principles were translated into practice by the member Governments, the strength of the alliance would be transformed almost overnight.

Chapter XIV

WHAT KIND OF NATO?

There are more opinions about what NATO is and what it should become than there are members of the alliance. Some consider it interferes too much with the political independence of its members; others see it as the blueprint for an Atlantic Community or Union and as such consider it too narrow in its outlook and too conscious of national susceptibilities. Should its activities be limited exclusively to the defence field, or, at the other extreme, should they extend over the whole field of the political and economic relations of its members with one another and with the rest of the world?

The Treaty offers no guide as it was drawn wide enough to permit NATO to develop in almost any direction. Article II talks of peaceful and friendly international relations, free institutions and economic collaboration while Article III is concerned with the maintenance and development of individual and collective capacity to resist armed attack. These two objectives are not, of course, mutually exclusive; but it is doubtful if both can be achieved by an organisation of sovereign states bound by the rule of unanimity. Certainly neither purpose is carried out very efficiently at the present time.

When NATO was formed in 1949 it was designed to meet a military threat, primarily in Europe. As well as the communist success in Czechoslovakia and the Soviet blockade of Berlin, there was concern for the political stability of the NATO countries on the continent, prompted by the large communist parties in Italy and France. West Germany was an unknown quantity as she began to move away from the economic twilight of the immediate post-war period after the currency reforms. The immediate tasks were to rebuild the war-shattered European economies and to ensure the permanent commitment of the United States to

Europe. Inevitably both in military and economic terms NATO depended to an overwhelming extent on the United States and, in lesser degree, upon Britain. This was the basis of the Anglo-American alliance which was essential for the birth and weaning of NATO but which caused so much friction and resentment as NATO reached its adolescence.

In its early days NATO was very much concerned with the economic problems of rearmament and the need to work out machinery for the equitable sharing of the economic burdens of defence. During the winter of 1951–2 a special committee examined these economic problems. The British Government at this time was anxious to wind up the Organisation for European Economic Co-operation (OEEC) and transfer its functions to NATO. In the event, however, the general climate of opinion (especially in the United States) made this idea impracticable and it was only possible to get agreement on a cost-sharing formula for the administrative expenses of NATO headquarters and, in 1952, for the modest infrastructure programme.

By 1956, before the Sputnik burst upon the world to advertise Russia's immense progress in rocket technology, the economic progress and military strength of the alliance appeared satisfactory. Interest turned towards widening the scope of NATO and presenting a more positive image in the neutral world which was beginning to show its importance. Accordingly in May of that year, to emphasize its non-military functions, the North Atlantic Council set up a Committee consisting of the Foreign Ministers of Canada, Italy and Norway—Mr. Lester Pearson, M. Gaetano Martino and Mr. Halvard Lange—'to advise the Council on ways and means to improve and extend NATO co-operation in non-military fields and to develop greater unity within the Atlantic Community'. In between their appointment and their report there occurred the Suez episode when Britain and France felt unable to consult the North Atlantic Council before resorting to armed intervention. Although Egypt did not fall within the NATO area, some members felt strongly that such consultation should have taken place and indeed it was soon evident that the British and French action might involve other members and also have repercussions within NATO territory.

The Report of this Committee of Three was approved by the Council in December 1956. With Suez in mind, they declared that

unless the NATO countries could achieve common policies by full
and timely consultation on issues of common concern the very
framework of Atlantic co-operation would be endangered. They
went on to stress that the basis of NATO was the political obligation which member governments had undertaken for collective
defence. The best deterrent against military aggression lay in the
entire acceptance by all the NATO governments of this political
commitment. Changes in national policy or strategy which affected
the coalition should be made only after collective consideration.

The requirements of consultation were admirably stated:

> It is easy to profess devotion to the principle of political—or
> economic—consultation in NATO. It is difficult, and has in fact been
> shown to be impossible, if the proper conviction is lacking to con-
> vert the profession into practice. Consultation within an alliance
> means more than exchange of information, though that is necessary.
> It means more than letting the NATO Council know about national
> decisions that have already been taken; or trying to enlist support for
> those decisions. It means the discussion of problems collectively in
> the early stages of policy formation, and before national positions
> become fixed. At best, this will result in collective decisions on
> matters of common interest affecting the alliance. At least, it will
> ensure that no action is taken by one member without a knowledge
> of the views of the others.[77]

The recommendations of the Committee were adopted. And
NATO's move into the political arena was given impetus by the
choice of M. Spaak as Secretary-General to succeed Lord Ismay
in May 1957. M. Spaak is very much committed to the whole idea
of Western political integration and there is little doubt that
during his four years of office he sought to provide the leadership
to move the alliance in this direction as well as to broaden the
scope of its activities. It is also widely accepted that the lack of
sufficient achievement in these objectives contributed to his
decision to resign as Secretary-General and return to Belgian
politics. For despite the advice of the Committee and the great
political experience and skill of M. Spaak, the political cohesion
of the alliance has not advanced. NATO good offices did contribute
to the settlement of the Cyprus problem, but this was an isolated
case; no success was achieved with the Icelandic fishery dispute,
for example. In 1961 it was fashionable to talk of its malaise; disarray is perhaps not too strong a term.

Before attempting to prescribe what seems necessary to restore the alliance to political health and vigour, it is useful to sketch in the background to the present state of affairs. The world, and particularly the balance of power within it, has undergone fundamental changes within the last decade. The emergence of nearly forty independent states in Africa, Asia and the Middle East has added a new and complicating factor to the balance of power. At the same time, within the alliances as well as between them, there has been a significant shift of power. Inside NATO, while America remains the most powerful single member nation, the growth in economic strength of the European members and the establishment of the European Economic Community mean that European political and military bargaining power is now vastly stronger than in the early years of NATO history. Similarly while the Soviet Union remains the strongest of the communist countries, she is increasingly obliged to pay attention to China. In both cases the concept of coalition is becoming more important. Finally, while military technology has developed at a staggering rate in both America and Russia, the consequence of Russia's emergence as a nuclear power equal to or, in certain fields, ahead of the United States has profoundly altered the picture.

Most of the newly independent countries have internal economic and political problems to grapple with and they have a common desire to be neutral in the cold war between East and West. But the emergence of these countries has affected the balance of forces within the United Nations, since on any issue their votes can be decisive. Thus the point of view and probable reactions of the 'uncommitted' nations is a factor which can never be omitted from consideration of any major international problem and their support has great propaganda value. Unhappily it is in relation to Afro-Asian problems that there has been the most conflict between members of NATO.

Considering the high proportion of colonial and ex-colonial powers in the alliance, this is hardly surprising. Even though all the colonial powers with the exception of Portugal are committed to the principle of independence for their overseas territories, the policies they apply and their attitude towards nationalism and their relations with the emerging states differ markedly. The simple truth that people prefer to govern themselves badly rather than be governed well by someone else has been hard to swallow.

The United States has been slow to accept the desire of Afro-Asian countries to remain neutral and has mistakenly believed that enough economic aid could sustain corrupt and unpopular but pro-American régimes in power. Equally Americans, while being candid critics of the imperialist blunders of their European partners, have failed to discern that the world-wide publicity inevitably given to incidents involving colour prejudice, and even the housing problems in Washington of the representatives of the new countries, have a harmful effect on NATO's image in Afro-Asian eyes.

Although the non-colonial powers of the alliance—and often those not involved in a particular dispute, since it is always easier to perceive one's neighbour's shortcomings than one's own—have sought to avoid being tarred with the imperialist brush, it is undeniable that problems such as Suez, Algeria, South Africa, Cuba, the Congo, Angola and Bizerta have created a bad image for NATO in the neutral world. The sins of one member are invariably visited upon the alliance as a whole. The voting of NATO members in different lobbies on these issues in the United Nations only serves to display NATO's disunity and engender friction between members. It does not repair the damage done to NATO's standing.

While the emergence of new and mainly neutral nations has been a source of embarrassment to NATO, the political instability and need for capital of these countries have proved a happy hunting-ground for the Soviet Union. After Suez we saw Soviet influence grow in the Middle East, and the Congo troubles provided an opportunity to meddle in Africa. By supporting nationalist movements and by supplying arms and offering favourable terms for capital equipment and trade, Russia has been able to gain a substantial foothold in what were formerly European spheres of influence. This successful 'peaceful competition' has been another thorn in the flesh of the alliance, yet its success has been achieved at the expense of only a tiny contribution to the needs of the under-developed countries, compared to the large sums so expended by the West and particularly by the United States.

An unfavourable factor for the Soviet Union has been the rise in the power and influence of China, which poses a threat to the acceptance of Russia as the unchallenged leader of world communism. Already among the uncommitted nations and within the communist alliance there has been some competition between the Soviet and the Chinese concepts, both in ideology and in the strategy to be pursued in the cold war against the West. As China resolves her economic problems her military strength and influence must be expected to grow faster. We are, however, in no position to exploit the differences within the communist world in the way Mr. Khrushchev makes capital out of the frictions within NATO. Although the non-recognition of communist China and the refusal to admit her to the United Nations are cardinal errors of policy, it would be wrong to imagine we shall drive a wedge between China and Russia to our advantage by a change of attitude now. Nevertheless, there is an overwhelming case for Communist China's admission to the United Nations.

In contrast to the privacy afforded by the closed society, which means we often only find out about communist quarrels long after the event, the differences within NATO are all too apparent. The growing economic strength and unity of the European Economic Community should provide additional power to NATO —'the Six' now produce more steel than the United States and the mark has become stronger than the dollar. But in fact the additional economic strength has been offset by increasing political divisions. France and Germany have been more concerned with their power within the alliance than with the effectiveness of the alliance as a whole. Britain has clung obstinately to her badge of nuclear capability without recognising the relevance of her V-bombers to the discord in NATO and their irrelevance to its military strength. The unquestioned benefits of the Economic Community have been dissipated, in political and military terms, by the division of Europe into two camps—'the Six' and 'the Seven'—with NATO members on both sides of the argument and with the United States on the side-lines, her inclination favouring the Six because of her own history and with her match-making efforts suspected by both parties.

Whatever the outcome, Britain's application to join the Community must have profound consequences for Europe.

British membership of the Community, and, as a result, the membership also of all or most of the EFTA countries, must have far-reaching political as well as economic consequences. Already the political discussions among the Six and talk of defence consultations among them presage an important change in the relations of European members of NATO to one another and to the United States. It is not clear how, if at all, the neutral members of EFTA can be fitted into the arrangements, but it is unmistakable that the ending of the economic division of Europe would have an impact on the alliance. It is bound to lead to a closer co-ordination of foreign policy and to greater military integration, both important elements for strengthening NATO. On the other hand, should the negotiations fail, the resultant permanent rift and the hard feelings engendered must have a most adverse consequence for NATO and may indeed threaten its effective survival. This situation imposes a great test upon the statesmanship of all parties involved and not least of the United States, for whom the outcome is also of great moment.

Part of the difficulties within NATO can be traced to the lack of effective leadership during much of the 1950s from the United States. Undoubtedly there will always be resentment and jealousy of American wealth and power; but the European countries will more readily accept American leadership than allow one of their number to usurp the first position. One has the feeling from time to time that American political leaders have been afraid of unpopularity and have not learned the lesson that it is impossible to be rich and powerful and popular. Britain learned in her years of pre-eminence that unpopularity is an unavoidable price to be paid for world leadership. Particularly after the illness and death of Mr. Dulles, the lack of American leadership left a power-vacuum within the alliance. The type of diplomacy which, in an attempt to fill the vacuum, preceded the abortive Summit Conference of 1960, must ultimately impose impossible strains on NATO. First Mr. Macmillan and then other Western leaders had personal initiatives and the more successful these were in terms of relations with Russia the more unpopular they were with their NATO colleagues. The unprecedented diplomatic scramble in the last months of the Eisenhower Administration certainly did nothing to help matters. However, apart from the Cuban aberration (and the right lessons appear to have been drawn from this), President Kennedy has given evidence of his concern for the political unity of the alliance and promises to supply the leadership it requires.

The final factor—military technology—goes to the root of both the military and political troubles of the alliance. The rapid evolution of Soviet nuclear power, first destroying the American monopoly and later suggesting that Russia might have or develop a significant lead in this field, changed the whole balance of power between East and West and undermined NATO's existing strategy. The tangible proof of Soviet prowess in rocketry furnished by the first Sputnik, alarmed the Western world and in December 1957, as a demonstration of unity, the North Atlantic Council met for the first time at the level of Heads of Government. The immediate consequence was a move to restore the political cohesion of the alliance after the Suez disaster, which had produced the unbeliev-able result of the United States and the Soviet Union joining forces in the United Nations against Britain and France. But, as usually happens once the immediate crisis passes, as the shock of the Sputnik wore off the old differences reasserted themselves. There was now an additional point of controversy: it was quite clear that the United States would be in the front line of a nuclear war and doubts began to be expressed about her willing-ness to come to the aid of Europe if it meant exposing her cities to nuclear retaliation. The urge for independent nuclear weapons in Europe was thus strengthened and became another, and major, cause of difference within the alliance.

The problems of NATO can be compounded into nuclear wea-pons and national sovereignty, two sides of the same coin. I have suggested ways of dealing with the control and use of nuclear weapons which would go far to meet the problem. No progress can be expected towards fashioning NATO into an integrated military and political alliance until the nuclear weapons nettle is firmly grasped. This must be the first priority. But beyond this objective we need to make up our minds as to what NATO can and should do. Its *raison d'etre* is a means of providing efficient collective defence. This requires not only an effective military organisation in being but also concern for future security and in particular a co-ordination of the policies of its members towards negotiations with the Soviet Union, arms control and the obliga-tion to reduce both the dangers of nuclear anarchy and nuclear escalation. Some aspects of disarmament and arms control pro-blems and NATO's contribution to their solution have been dis-cussed in Chapter XII. It is crucially important for NATO to have the objective of reducing armaments by multilateral agree-ments as well as of fulfilling its task of providing effective military strength to deter war until and unless general disarmament can be achieved.

NATO's function, then, is essentially that of a defensive alliance, construing defence in its widest meaning. Since foreign, defence and disarmament policies are so closely interwoven—and much of the success of the Soviet Union comes from her recognition and implementation of this principle—if not a common foreign policy at least a well co-ordinated one is a pre-requisite for a sound military organisation. It is essential, however, to guard against the natural tendency to make up for shortcomings in one direction by publicising ambitious plans for other fields of endeavour—that is, by developing the non-military aspects of the alliance at the expense of collective defence efforts.

It is, of course, much more difficult for NATO to stick to its defence last now than it was when it first came into being. Germany remains the most intractable political and military problem and is still the key issue between NATO and the Soviet bloc. The position has been held in Europe; but while the major military threat remains there, the major ideological challenge is now outside Europe. And in fighting this ideological battle the West is at a great disadvantage. The countries in the area usually have first-hand experience of European imperialism and want to break their dependence upon Europe as a sign of their independence and to express their nationalism which was fostered by such anti-imperialist sentiments. On the other hand, the communist form of imperialism is quite new to them and Soviet support and encouragement, apparently disinterested, can be readily allied to nationalism and the violent economic and social change which is a natural characteristic of new régimes.

The communist talent for making trouble has full scope for its activities on the periphery of the NATO area and outside it and here NATO as such is powerless to intervene, although the possible consequence of a global war imposes limitations on the extent of communist-inspired and Soviet-supported moves in these areas. This fact causes the attractive thesis to be advanced that NATO should develop the capacity and machinery to counter these moves by assuming world-wide responsibilities and by acting as an agency to co-ordinate trading policies and economic aid to underdeveloped countries. Clearly NATO countries cannot be concerned only with what goes on in NATO territory and cannot be indifferent to developments in other parts of the world which at best lead to a weakening of the Western position and at worst threaten to erupt into war. But it is a mistake to suppose that NATO itself can be refashioned into a suitable instrument to deal with these problems.

NATO will carry the stamp of a military alliance no matter what may be done to change its character. As such it would not be acceptable as a vehicle for dealing with the newly independent countries who value their neutrality in the cold war as highly as their new independence. We must come to terms with this fact. As Henry Kissinger has pointed out,[78] there is a parallel in American history. In the first one hundred and fifty years of American history no conceivable British policy could have produced an Anglo-American alliance. Neither the invasion of Belgium in 1914 nor the aggression against Poland in 1939 seemed to Americans at the time sufficient to justify the surrender of their neutrality. Attempts to widen the scope of NATO in the economic field or to change it from being a regional military alliance would produce many difficulties and no tangible results.

The best that can be achieved within NATO is for there to be the prior political consultation recommended by the Committee of Three so that members can co-ordinate their individual policies, and for all NATO members to recognise that their shortcomings are certain to reflect upon the alliance as a whole. On the military side, there is much to be said for informal consultations between NATO and the other Treaty Organisations in which NATO members are involved—CENTO (the Central Treaty Organisation of Pakistan, Persia, Turkey and the United Kingdom) and SEATO (the South-East Asia Treaty Organisation of Australia, France, New Zealand, Pakistan, the Philippine Republic, Thailand, the United Kingdom and the United States). At the same time it would assist if within NATO there were recognition and frank discussion of the economic and military responsibilities of its members outside the NATO area and due account taken of these responsibilities in assessing their contribution to NATO itself.

And just as it would be a mistake, as the Committee of Three pointed out, for NATO to try and duplicate the work of other international bodies in the economic sphere, the same is true of the political sphere too. There is no point in seeking to make

NATO a kind of select United Nations—the kind of body some people might like the United Nations to be. We need to strengthen the United Nations as much as possible, not to undermine such authority as it has or to invade the few fields, such as technical aid, where it works well. And while the enlargement of the European Economic Community (assuming the negotiations with Britain are successful) may prove an important step towards an Atlantic Community and ultimately world government, it is much too early to envisage these ideas in practical terms. Indeed if NATO were to neglect its proper function of deterring war in favour of promoting an Atlantic federation, any hopes of a better scheme of things in the future might rapidly disappear. If member nations are reluctant to give up enough national sovereignty to make NATO work well under its present constitution, it is unrealistic to suppose that more ambitious proposals involving an even further surrender of sovereignty will get very far. Constitutional innovation is no substitute for political will.

NATO is ill-equipped to play a significant rôle in the wider political and economic sphere. It is an alliance of sovereign states ranging from the United States whose power is the backbone of the alliance to Iceland who has no armed forces at all. Like the United Nations, it can do no more than its members are agreed upon; and while the United Nations has suffered from the power of veto conferred upon the original 'Big Five' members, in NATO the rule of unanimity gives a veto to every member. NATO has little independent authority and its reliance upon its individual members for all its needs is even more marked in its political than in its military functions. The Secretariat has no Ambassadors or organisation to supply independent information. It has no inflow of telegrams and reports such as is found in a national foreign office. This weakness has, of course, a parallel in the military field since military Intelligence in NATO is also a matter for the individual countries, so that the Standing Group and other military organs have to content themselves with accepting and co-ordinating what comes to them from national sources.[79] SACEUR and some other allied commanders have political advisers but these are supplied by their national governments and must rely upon national sources of information.

There have been suggestions for changing the unanimity rule and for providing for an inner leading group within the North

Atlantic Council. President de Gaulle is keen on having a three-power directorate within NATO. Other suggestions have been made for a kind of NATO 'Security Council' or executive body with a two-thirds majority rule. It may well be that some changes on these lines may become desirable. But what is wanted at the present juncture is not so much new machinery as a new attitude by some members towards the requirements of the alliance under its existing flexible constitution. Dr. Stikker, the new Secretary-General, has confirmed that no revision of the Treaty is needed and that the Secretariat and Council could easily allow for a widening and deepening of their functions. A modest surrender of sovereignty would suffice to revolutionise both the military and political practice of the alliance, particularly if it took the form of implementing the policy I have advocated concerning the control and use of nuclear weapons.

Indeed it is hard to appreciate why there should be so much difficulty about national sovereignty and why there is always so much reluctance to give *de jure* recognition to what has already been given *de facto* acceptance. The creation of NATO was a result of the sober realisation that no individual country, however powerful, could provide effective defence for her own people by her own independent efforts. This is just as true today. The unprecedented decision to place troops under the control of allied commanders in time of peace was a tacit recognition of the fact that national sovereignty could no longer be equated with effective defence. Already today national parliaments cannot control the actions of their governments in NATO. The British Government refuses in Parliament to say in advance what its attitude will be to items on the agenda of the North Atlantic Council, and after the Council has met it declines to go beyond the official communiqué. Doubtless other member governments are equally uninformative.

These developments are a necessary outcome of private meetings: avoidance of publicity and inspired journalistic guesses are essential concomitants of mutual confidence and frank discussion. Otherwise one may as well follow the United Nations practice and hold meetings in front of the television cameras. Secret diplomacy is not harmful as a means of reaching agreement; the danger comes from keeping secret the agreements or undertakings reached. In the field of military policy strict secrecy is

essential if the plans are to be worth while. Democracy is safe-
guarded if the conclusions of diplomacy are made public; the
citizen is not deprived of his rights if he is not given a detailed
account of the negotiations. In fact unless this principle can be
established it is idle to have political consultations between allies
at all.

Having ceded the substance of national sovereignty in the
unavoidable surrender of the task of defending one's country,
there is little logic in denying it proper form. But one cannot
ignore the fact that nationalism exists in Europe as in Africa and
Asia (although of course in a far less virulent form), and therefore
a deliberate act of surrendering sovereignty in a limited field can
cause considerable emotional disturbance in a country while
control over many sectors of policy can be ceded relatively pain-
lessly so long as the shadow of constitutional form is preserved
intact. Thus no matter what decisions are taken by the member
Governments, any surrender of sovereignty depends upon the
support of public opinion. And this support will not be forthcoming unless NATO's aims and purposes are understood and
accepted. Getting public opinion behind NATO's policies is primarily a matter for the member countries and I believe this is
best done by a direct avowal of its defence functions, not by
attempting to dress up its non-military activities.

To this end I would urge very strongly that there should be a
properly constituted NATO Parliamentary Assembly. The unofficial Conference of NATO Parliamentarians has since 1955 done
some useful work in helping to get support for the alliance; but it
lacks the authority as well as the machinery to become an effective Parliamentary assembly. Although I must declare prejudices
in the matter, I would say that it has done a much less effective
job than the Assembly of Western European Union in scrutinising
the policies of the alliance and promoting the public discussion
about them necessary to get popular support. If, as I hope, Britain
becomes a full member of the European Economic Community,
which has its own Parliamentary Assembly, it would seem likely
that Western European Union, or at least its Assembly, will be
disbanded. In this case the need for an official NATO Parliamentary
assembly will be even greater. An unofficial body, lacking an
adequate secretariat and having no regular committee meetings
between plenary sessions cannot fill this need.

An official NATO Assembly on the model of the WEU Assembly would fulfil the double rôle of exercising some Parliamentary supervision over the activities of the alliance as well as of providing a means of fostering Parliamentary interest and gathering an informed public opinion behind the purposes of NATO. I do not suggest that the assembly should have executive powers. But it should have similar authority to the present WEU Assembly to pass resolutions and receive replies thereon from the Council and to request information. The practice of the WEU committees of having off-the-record meetings with the Council and with national Ministers of Defence should also be followed. Visits to military installations and briefings from allied commanders are very valuable, but they should supplement and not replace regular discussion among the members. There is no substitute for the private, frank debate in committee in which members have to defend their own views as well as learn the point of view and problems of their colleagues from other countries.

So far objection to having an official NATO Parliamentary body has come mainly from the United States and Canada, for whom constitutional difficulties are involved. It would be a great pity if these cannot be overcome as a contribution to the greater integration and unity of the alliance. The special characteristics of the United States Congress give its members greater opportunities to obtain information than are available to the defence committees of other nations belonging to NATO and they have the unique privilege of summoning SACEUR to appear before them. The immediate benefits of an official assembly, which would demand far more of its members in terms of time and effort, are not therefore so obvious to the Americans as they are to their European colleagues.

But while European Parliamentarians would gain much from American participation I am sure it would not be wholly a one-way traffic. From my own membership of European assemblies and participation in the economic and defence committees, I can testify to the value of the opportunities they afford for informed discussion as well as for informal contacts. It is just as important for Parliamentarians from different countries to get acquainted with each other as it is for Ministers. It is possible also that a NATO Assembly could promote the greater integration of the alliance in the same way as the Consultative Assembly of the

Council of Europe and the WEU Assembly have blazed the trail for European unity.

A Parliamentary Assembly is, however, only one element in rallying a more informed public opinion behind NATO. Excellent work is done by a number of voluntary bodies on both sides of the Atlantic; but the member Governments must make greater efforts too. It is not that there is a substantial feeling against the alliance. On the contrary, it is widely recognised as the only means of collective defence and in times of tension it receives great attention. The difficulty we are up against is that, quite naturally in a democratic society, there is less interest when there is no imminent crisis. What is not appreciated is that if NATO were working well, the chances of a crisis occurring would be lower and that NATO must have the means at all times of developing its positive function of co-ordinating its members' policies in foreign policy and disarmament as well as its negative function of providing our defence. As it is, NATO, which was founded as a result of Marshal Stalin's intransigent imperialism, seems only to work well in Mr. Khrushchev's truculent periods. What we need is a means to make it function properly in fair weather as well as in foul.

Appendix A

NUCLEAR WEAPONS AND
THEIR EFFECTS[80]

The United States, the United Kingdom and Soviet Russia have in service fusion and fission warheads with an explosive force ranging from 20 kilotons to 20 megatons which can be delivered by strategic bombers or missiles (MRBMS and ICBMS). The United States and Russia have both produced nuclear weapons for tactical use with an explosive force of between one and 20 kilotons.

The power of nuclear weapons

The very heavy bombs dropped by aircraft during the last war were in the one-ton range. The heaviest of them all contained six tons of TNT and was capable of total destruction over an area of approximately 300 sq. yards.

The 'yield' or power of nuclear devices is measured in equivalent tons of conventional explosive (TNT) and is expressed in kilotons (kt.) (thousand tons of TNT), or megatons (mt.) (million tons of TNT) in the case of fusion (thermonuclear) devices. A fission bomb of the Hiroshima type (20 kt.) is thus equivalent in explosive power to 20,000 tons of TNT. It is capable of destroying typical brick houses over an area of three sq. miles (eight sq. km.) and may cause considerable radiation damage over twice that area.

One 10-megaton (10,000 kilotons) fusion bomb is equivalent in energy yield to 500 such fission bombs. Its radius of destruction is eight times greater, covering about 150 sq. miles (400 sq. km.) and may cause damage by radiation over 8,000 sq. miles (20,000 sq. km.). It would therefore be capable of almost completely destroying a built-up area such as one of the main capitals of the world. It has been said that for a country of average size— 200,000–230,000 sq. miles (500,000–600,000 sq. km.) with forty to fifty million inhabitants*—the total destruction of the means of life could be achieved by 6,000 fission bombs or 20-30 fusion bombs if they were well-placed.

Summary of the effects of nuclear weapons

Every nuclear explosion is accompanied by a certain number of phenomena which have effects on persons and matter. These effects fall into three categories: of blast; of thermal radiation; and of nuclear radiation.

The relative importance of these effects depends on the objective, which may be personnel, equipment, buildings or a fleet of ships. The effects of nuclear and thermal radiation are greatest on personnel. Blast and heat together affect equipment, and where a fleet is concerned there is the additional effect of the shock wave in the water.

Airburst explosions: the effects of blast

The physical effects of nuclear explosions in the air are chiefly due to blast from the explosion. The shock wave gives rise to two distinct phenomena:

—an overpressure effect which is the principal cause of damage to buildings, equipment and large ships which are heavy, with solid walls and few apertures;
—a drag effect, depending on the dynamic pressure and the time of application of the drag forces resulting from the shape, apertures, etc., of the object; this effect is the main cause of damage to buildings, equipment and ships with light walls and wide apertures, and structures such as radio towers, metal bridges, etc.

When the shock meets the ground, it is reflected. The incident wave and the reflected wave combine at a certain distance from ground zero† to produce a single third wave, the Mach wave. The overpressure due to the Mach wave is about double that of the incident shock wave.

To describe these phenomena very simply, the blast wave,

---

* France, which has an area, excluding Algeria, of 212,897 sq. miles and a population of 42,731,445 may be cited as an example.
† The point at ground level vertically below the air burst.

moving spherically in a downward direction, crushes the buildings around ground zero, and then to some extent pushes them outwards as one moves away from ground zero; this action continues until the minimum angle is reached at which the Mach wave is produced; this wave, moving parallel to the ground, topples the buildings over.

It can be assumed that an overpressure of 14 lb./sq. inch (1 kg. per cm.²) or more, always entails very heavy damage; that an overpressure in the region of 7 lb./sq. inch (0·5 kg. per cm.²) and above entails very heavy damage to light constructions and moderate damage to more solid constructions; finally, from 1·5 to 7 lb./sq. inch (0·1 to 0·5 kg. per cm.²) the damage is moderate or light.

Damage to light brick houses caused by a nuclear bomb exploding under optimum conditions of effectiveness would be as follows:

	Peak over-pressure p.s.i.	Distances from ground zero	
		Fission Bomb 20 kt.	Fusion Bomb 20 mt.
Total destruction	12	0·8 km.	7 km.
Considerable destruction	6	1·3 km.	10 km.
Heavy damage	1·5	3·4 km.	27 km.
Light damage	0·75	5 km.	42 km.

Blast has relatively little direct effect on the human body. To produce slight injuries—a burst eardrum, for instance—14 lb./sq. inch (1 kg. per cm.²) is necessary; for serious injuries 100 lb./sq. inch (14 kg. per cm.²); and to cause death, over 200 lb./sq. inch (14 kg. per cm.²). In actual fact, a pressure of 200 lb./sq. inch (14 kg./cm.²) with a 20 kiloton bomb is only reached within a radius where thermal effects are predominant and consequently the effects of overpressure are negligible. Injuries due to blast are more often caused by secondary effects: by being thrown to the ground violently, by the movement of various objects, the collapse of houses and shelters, burns from outbreaks of fire, etc.

Airburst explosions: thermal radiation and incendiary effects

At the moment of a nuclear explosion a fireball is formed which, for a 20-kiloton bomb, attains a radius of 15 yards in 1/10,000th of a second and a temperature in the region of 15,000° Centigrade. This temperature decreases rapidly as the radius of the fireball increases. It then rises again to 8,000° Centigrade as the radius of the fireball reaches 180 yards (180 m.) before the final drop in temperature. There are therefore two temperature pulses, or two stages, separated by a minimum temperature. Almost the whole of the thermal energy is released in the three seconds following the explosion.

Radiation causes volatilisation in the neighbourhood of the fireball, fusion, carbonisation or ignition of material within a certain distance, and burns on human beings.

'Flash burns' on personnel are the burns caused by instantaneous thermal radiation, and may arise up to 2½ miles (4 km.) from ground zero for a 20-kilton bomb; they were the cause of 20–30 per cent of the deaths at Hiroshima and Nagasaki. The burns show a distinct boundary between the surfaces exposed to radiation and those which are protected. Although as a general rule only the unprotected parts of the body receive burns, within a short distance burns may be received through several layers of clothing. The seriousness of the burns is often related to the colour of the clothes, white acting as a shield.

For a 20-kiloton bomb, the effects on unprotected personnel in clear weather would be:

—fatal burns up to 1 mile (1·4 km.)
—serious burns up to 2 miles (3 km.)
—slight burns up to 2½ miles (4 km.)

For a 20-megaton bomb the above distances should be multiplied by 20.

Blindness is more often than not only temporary, particularly if the eye does not look directly at the fireball. On the other hand the retina may be irremediably injured up to 45 miles (60 km.) if the image of the fireball is focussed on the retina.

Thermal radiation may cause fires, setting light to dry combustible materials up to some distance from ground zero; but only a few seconds later the strong wind accompanying the blast wave puts most of the fires out. For the 20-kiloton Hiroshima bomb, the area affected by fire was 5 sq. miles (12 km.²). It should be noted that most of the fires are the result not so much of thermal radiation as of damage caused by the blast (short circuits, split gas mains, damaged or overturned apparatus, etc.).

Airburst explosions: the effect of nuclear radiation

With a high airburst, where the fireball does not touch the ground, the radioactive substances from the debris of the bomb itself rise into the atmosphere and as the distance from the earth increases, less and less radiation reaches the ground. It is considered that one minute after an airburst explosion there is no longer any danger and the area affected can be approached, although it may not be fit for military use.

If the fireball touches the surface of the ground or water, the radioactive substances remain on the spot and the area affected is often contaminated for several weeks. Also, by making a crater, the fireball carries up a cloud of highly contaminated radioactive fallout weighing several thousand tons which, once in the air, constitutes a marked danger of immediate fallout of radioactive substances over an area extending over several hundred miles. Possible pollution of the atmosphere and long-term fallout may last for several years.

The effects of nuclear radiation may be divided into three parts:

(i) instantaneous radioactivity, which occurs during the first minute after the explosion of the bomb;

(ii) residual radioactivity and local fallout, whose effects are mainly noticeable in subsequent weeks (this only occurs if the fireball of the bomb has touched the ground);

(iii) global fallout and long-term residual radiation.

(i) *Instantaneous radioactivity*

The dangerous gamma and neutron radiation cannot be detected by the senses and the resulting complications are not immediately apparent except in cases of exposure to a very high dose. The first signs, nausea and vomiting, are followed by other more serious signs only after some lapse of time, the length of which depends upon the time of exposure; laboratory tests enable the characteristic alterations in the blood to be detected very quickly.

In the event of successive exposures, the effects accumulate if the intervals between exposures are short. Thus troops exposed twice in the same day to a dose of 100 roentgens may be considered to be out of action (the effects being equivalent to 200 roentgens received at one time). If the doses are spaced out the body can recuperate to a certain extent between the two exposures and the overall effect is attenuated.

The roentgen is the unit of radioactive dose or exposure.

Immediate sickness effects of whole body
ionising radiation on human beings

Dose in roentgens	Effects
Up to 150	No acute effects but increasingly serious long-term hazard
150–250	Nausea and vomiting within twenty-four hours; some incapacitation after two days
250–350	Nausea and vomiting in under four hours; symptom-free period forty-eight hours to two weeks; some deaths in two to four weeks
350–600	Nausea and vomiting in under two hours; heavy death rate certain in two to four weeks; incapacitation prolonged for survivors
Over 600	Nausea and vomiting almost immediately; death in one week

A dose of about 75 roentgens is considered acceptable in an emergency in war. A dose of 450 roentgens will produce 50 per cent deaths within one month.

If an organism is to be exposed to radiation over a protracted period of time, it is believed that the body as a whole may absorb up to 0·1 roentgen per day without danger for a considerable time.

The overall effects on the human organism are noticeable through the injury caused to four particularly vulnerable organs: the blood-forming organs, the alimentary canal, the skin and the reproductive organs. The overall effects mentioned above are more or less immediate, but there are also other consequences with delayed effect such as cataracts, leukaemia, and delay in the development of unborn children.

The effects on materials are generally negligible, although there may be modifications to the physical characteristics of some. Material damage caused by blast or thermal radiation is generally more serious. Certain materials, particularly steel, concrete, earth and wood, afford some protection for human beings. It should be

noted, however, that a screen between the source of gamma rays
and the person to be protected is not sufficient to stop radiation
because of the diffusion of gamma rays and particularly of neutrons. It is necessary to provide screens which completely sur-
round the person to be protected. Thus a person in an open
trench still receives approximately a tenth of the gamma radiation
dose and a third of the neutron dose he would receive on the
surface in the same place.

(ii) *Residual radioactivity and local fallout*

Residual radioactivity begins one minute after the explosion.
The radioactivity around ground zero comes mainly from fission
products, radioactive isotopes formed when neutrons are cap-
tured by elements of the bomb, and also to some extent from
unfissioned fragments of uranium 235 and plutonium. There is
also neutron-induced activity in bodies not belonging to the
bomb which have become radioactive because they were close
to the explosion.

The neutron-induced activity is important only in cases of low
altitude, underwater or underground explosions and gives rise
mainly to radiosilicon, radiosodium, etc. The total gamma
activity of fission products decreases very quickly. The dose-rate
one hour after the explosion is reduced to a tenth seven hours
later and to one-hundredth after fifty hours.

Local fallout is to be found at a distance of 100 to 300 miles
from ground zero over a width of some 40 miles according to the
yield of the bomb, the direction and speed of the wind and overall
atmospheric conditions. It is formed by the largest radioactive
particles which fall within a few hours under the effects of gravity.
It is possible to sketch approximate areas of fallout; these are
generally elliptical in shape, the major axis being in the direction
of the mean wind. With the wind blowing at ten miles an hour,
the largest particles will reach the ground some $3\frac{1}{2}$ miles from the
explosion.

(iii) *Global fallout and long-term residual radiation*

Even with powerful explosions, the local fallout described
above will never be found at distances greater than a few hundred
miles in the direction of the wind. Likewise, residual radiation,
even if very strong because of contamination of the ground or

water, diminishes very quickly and after a few weeks cannot be considered a serious danger. Global fallout and long-term residual radiation are more dangerous, due *inter alia* to certain radioactive isotopes—caesium 137 and strontium 90.

Global fallout is the result of radioactive products being projected into the upper atmosphere at the time of the explosion. The fallout follows after varying periods of time. For products remaining in the troposphere, i.e. at altitudes of approximately 35,000 feet (10 km.) (as is the case with kiloton nuclear devices), global fallout occurs after a few weeks. It should be noted that fallout tends to move along a parallel of latitude and rarely in a northerly or southerly direction. Rain activates precipitation of fallout.

For products which rise into the stratosphere, from 35,000 to 180,000 feet (10 to 50 km.), as is the case with megaton nuclear devices, fallout may occur over several years over the whole world. Each year 10 per cent of all radioactive debris in the stratosphere reaches the ground.

The most important long-term residual radiation due to radioactive isotopes is that from caesium 137 and strontium 90 because of the relatively long radioactive life of these elements (30 and 28 years respectively). Naturally their effects are to be feared more when the explosion takes place on the surface and when there is local fallout than where global fallout is concerned.

Caesium 137 emits gamma rays. Strontium 90 emits beta particles. If the biological half-life is defined, by analogy with the radioactive half-life, as the time necessary for the isotope dose in the human body to be reduced by natural processes by half, the biological half-life is 140 days for caesium and ten years for strontium. In that it emits gamma rays and has a short biological half-life, caesium 137 is far less dangerous than strontium 90. Strontium follows calcium in its chemical reactions and from contaminated ground it passes into the human skeleton by the intermediary of foodstuffs. A dangerous dose of strontium 90 in the body leads to anaemia, necrosis of the bones, cancer and even leukaemia.

Underwater bursts

If the depth of the explosion is not too great, the fireball remains almost intact until it reaches the surface. The bubble of gas then bursts and the gases spread out, producing a series of complex phenomena. The water is thrown upwards with great force in the form of a hollow cylinder rather like a chimney. A blast shock wave forms in the air at the same instant. The underwater explosion at Bikini in 1946 produced a column of water which probably reached a maximum height of more than 6,000 feet (2,000 m.). A million tons or more of water were thus thrown into the air, mixed with debris torn from the bed of the lagoon and drawn up by the force of the explosion. Ten or twelve seconds after the explosion, the water falling back from the column into the lagoon began to form a cloud of highly radioactive spray which quickly reached a height of more than 900 feet (300 m.) and moved away from the centre of the explosion at a speed of more than sixty miles an hour (1,600 m. per minute). As the speed diminished the cloud began to rise above the surface of the water and gradually mingled with the clouds already in the sky. There was intermittent rain for approximately an hour. The Bikini explosion also caused a series of waves to form which spread over the surface of the lagoon, moving away from the centre of the explosion. Eleven seconds after the explosion, the maximum height of the first wave was some 94 feet at 350 yards (310 m.) from the centre.

If an underwater atomic explosion were to take place at great depth, the bubble of gas might disintegrate into a mass of turbulent water before reaching the surface. In this event there would not be a column of water and foam and consequently no base cloud.

The principal effects on ships are mainly due to the underwater shock wave which acts directly on the hull and indirectly on all interior parts of the ship. The shock wave imparts two distinct movements to the hull: horizontal and vertical. The effect of the first is to distort or break the hull below the water-line. The second causes vibration which produces considerable stresses on the framework of the ship. Inside the ship, the main pipes for fuel, steam, smoke and the boiler furnaces are particularly susceptible to the effects of shock waves. The supports for heavy apparatus such as the engines or boilers may be distorted or collapse because of the inertia of the mass they support. Objects which are not well secured may be thrown about violently, being broken in the process or damaging other objects, and they constitute a grave danger to personnel.

The extent of the damage caused by a 20-kiloton missile exploded at shallow depth is shown in the following table:

Distance from ground zero (metres)	Damage
1,350	light damage to all craft
700	moderate damage to all craft
500	heavy damage to all craft, many sunk

In the event of an explosion of equal yield at great depth, the magnitude of the effects would appear to be increased and similarly the area of destruction would be greater.

Surface bursts

The explosion of a 20-kiloton bomb is said to be at the surface of the ground or water if the height of the explosion is below 45 feet (15 m.) Broadly, the phenomenon is half-way between an air explosion and an underwater or underground explosion; the effects differ in magnitude but have the same characteristics. In particular, as noted above, the effects of nuclear radiation from ground contamination and fallout are much more serious than with an airburst, but the damage caused by blast and thermal radiation is reduced.

The following table gives a few dimensions of craters which have been observed or calculated for surface bursts in dry soil:

Size of bomb	Diameter	Depth
20 kt.	130 m.	20 m.
1 mt.	500 m.	50 m.
5 mt.	700 m.	70 m.

Underground explosions

Official sources give little information concerning explosions whose effects do not reach ground level. During offensive operations in war this type of explosion is unlikely to occur, since no bomb or missile would penetrate sufficiently deeply. Atomic detonators, if they were to demolish anything, would obviously be set off near the surface.

The subject is, however, relevant to the negotiations on the suspension of nuclear tests, since it has been found that explosions sufficiently deep underground cannot be detected by the usual effects—radioactive fallout, acoustic waves, electro-magnetic waves. The seismic waves produced would in some cases be difficult to distinguish from earthquakes.

The United States exploded in Nevada on 19 September 1957 a 1·7 kiloton device 270 metres below the top of a mountain of soft, porous rock. On the top of the mountain slight ridges appeared among the scrub and a little dust was raised, but the explosion left no other trace and there was no escape of radio-activity. It has been estimated[81] that a 20 megaton explosion at 6,000 metres depth would produce equally slight effects at ground level. One estimate[82] of the size of the cavern likely to be produced in hard rock is one cubic metre per ton equivalent—i.e. 20,000 cubic metres for a 20 kiloton explosion; half of the cavern would however fill with molten rock. Further experiments have shown that a 'decoupled explosion'—i.e. a device exploded in the centre of a large cavern so that the surrounding air damped the force of the explosion and reduced the seismic waves produced—might completely escape detection by existing methods.

The following table gives an idea of the effectiveness of tactical weapons used against troops in the field. It shows distances (expressed in metres) from the centre of a ground-level explosion of an atomic warhead within which death will take place immediately, after one hour, and after four hours. This is shown with weapons of varying power, and with men in differing conditions of exposure. For example, referring to the table, a 2 kiloton bomb will kill all men in the open within a radius of 550 metres immediately, within 800 metres after one hour, and within 900 metres within four hours.

Deaths	2 kt. *metres* a) b) c)	5 kt. *metres* a) b) c)	10 kt. *metres* a) b) c)	20 kt. *metres* a) b) c)
In the open	550 800 900	700 900 1,000	800 1,000 1,100	950 1,100 1,300
In trenches	400 550 650	650 700 800	550 750 900	700 900 1,000
In built-up areas	700 750 850	1,100 1,100 1,100	1,200 1,200 1,200	1,500 1,500 1,500
In tanks	450 650 800	550 750 850	650 850 1,000	750 1,000 1,100

a) immediate death   b) death after one hour   c) death after four hours.

The following table summarises the effects of nuclear explosions in terms of the yield of the bomb and the distance, expressed in metres (typical airburst):

Effects of heat		5 kt.	10 kt.	20 kt.	40 kt.
1st degree burns (reddening)		2,300	2,800	4,000	5,600
2nd degree burns (blisters form)		1,500	2,000	2,800	4,000
3rd degree burns (charring)		1,100	1,800	2,200	3,000

Effects of blast	*Peak over-pressure*	5 kt.	10 kt.	20 kt.	40 kt.
Heavy damage to houses	0·21 kg./cm.^{2} (3 p.s.i.)	1,450	1,800	2,300	3,000
Buildings in reinforced concrete or bricks 45 cm. thick completely destroyed	0·7 kg./cm.^{2} (10 p.s.i.)	625	800	1,000	1,200
Total destruction	1·75 kg./cm.^{2} (25 p.s.i)	260	280	350	550

Effects of initial nuclear radiation	5 kt.	10 kt.	20 kt.	40 kt.
50% affected after first day but no immediate deaths, 200 roentgens	1,200	1,300	1,400	1,600
Subsequent death of 50% of personnel and incapacity of most in a few hours, 500 roentgens	1,000	1,100	1,250	1,400
Incapacity of all personnel within one hour, subsequent death of most, 1,000 roentgens	900	1,000	1,100	1,250
Immediate death, 5,000 roentgens	600	800	900	1,000

Appendix B

THE POTENTIAL NUCLEAR WEAPON PRODUCTION CAPABILITIES OF VARIOUS COUNTRIES

Four countries to date—the United States, the United Kingdom, the Soviet Union and France—have successfully exploded nuclear devices of some kind and the former three have developed such weapons and equipped their forces with them. They all have large and costly industrial-scale plants engaged solely on the production of nuclear explosive material, and details of the processes of direct application to weapons production have been kept secret.

However, the basic physical principles of all nuclear weapons have been known since 1939, and much of the necessary physical data has been published. Nuclear physics laboratories with particle accelerators and experimental reactors are becoming common place—sixteen of the OECD* countries, for example, have one or more experimental reactors in operation at the present time and are in a position to determine for themselves any further theoretical data required for weapons production.

The difficulty in the way of any country that wishes to produce nuclear weapons is not lack of basic knowledge, but of finance and of industrial technique for applying laboratory principles on a sufficiently large scale, and finding enough trained scientists and engineers to do it.

To make a nuclear weapon, one of two fissile materials must be produced—either uranium 235 or plutonium 239. The first occurs in natural uranium to the extent of one atom of U235 for every

* The Organisation for European Co-operation and Development is the successor to the Organisation for European Economic Co-operation. OECD came into operation on 1 October 1961 with the same membership as OEEC, except that Canada and the United States are full members instead of associates.

140 atoms of U238, and must be extracted from it by isotope separation in a complex gaseous diffusion plant comprising some thousands of stages and consuming large quantities of electric power. Uranium 235 is, however, a versatile material: it can be used for 'miniature' warheads with yields of less than one kiloton; for warheads of small diameter which can be fired as shells from artillery pieces; and also for setting off fusion (thermonuclear) bombs with yields in the megaton range. At the present time only the United Kingdom, the United States and the Soviet Union have the necessary industrial scale gaseous diffusion plants in operation. France plans to have one running by 1965 or 1966. Plutonium 239 is processed from natural uranium which is used as a fuel in nuclear power reactors. Only the United Kingdom, the United States, France and the Soviet Union as yet have the chemical processing plant needed.

The cheapest and quickest approach for a country wishing to make some sort of a nuclear bang would presumably be to produce plutonium—as France has done. With this material it is possible to construct warheads—albeit rather bulky ones—with yields from some 5 kilotons up to about 100 kilotons. The necessary stages are as follows:

    (i) mining or procurement of uranium ore;
   (ii) milling or refining to produce the metal;
  (iii) construction and operation of a full-scale nuclear power reactor (including the fabrication of the fuel elements from uranium metal);
  (iv) chemical processing of the intensely radioactive fuel elements after removal from the reactor, to extract the plutonium metal;
   (v) fabrication of bomb components and assembly.

Stages (i) and (ii) present no special difficulties. Uranium ore deposits are comparatively widespread, and in any case there is probably surplus uranium production capacity in the world at present. The United States and Canada are prepared to sell natural uranium metal for approved uses, the official United States price being $40 per kg.[83]

Stage (iii), the erection and operation of an industrial-scale nuclear power reactor, requires large numbers of trained technicians. The development and erection of such a reactor from the

Nuclear Power Reactor Projects in countries other than France, the United Kingdom, the United States and the Soviet Union

Country	Name of Reactor	Location	Power (Mega-watts) (thermal)	Status	Date of Comple-tion	Source of infor-mation
Belgium	BR–3	Mol	43	c	1962	1, 2, 3, 4
Canada	NRU	Chalk River	200	o	1957	4
	NPD–2	Des Joachims, Ontario	83	c	1962	1, 4
	CANDU	Douglas Point	698	d	1964	4
Czecho-slovakia	KS–150	Bohunice, Slovakia	590	c	1965	1, 4
Germany (East)	Atomkraft-werk	Neugolbsaw	265	c	1962	4
Germany (Federal Repub.)		Kahl	60	o	1960	1, 2, 3, 4
		Jülich	60	d	1964	2, 4
		Karlsruhe	200	d	1965	4
India	CIR	Trombay	40	o	1960	4
Italy	SIMEA	Latina	710	c	1962	2, 4
	SENN-ENSI	Garigliano (Punta Fiume)	600	c	1963	2, 4
	SELNI	Milan	615	c	1965	2, 3, 4
Japan	BWR	Tokai-Mura	50	c	1962	3, 4, 5
	GCR	Tokai-Mura	600	d	1965	4
Puerto Rico	BONUS	Punta Higuera	50	d	1962	4
Sweden	R 3-Agesta	Stockholm	65	c	1962	1, 2, 4

STATUS: o, operating; c, under construction; d, decided.

SOURCES: 1 *Directory of Nuclear Reactors, Vol. I, Power Reactors*, InternationalAtomic Energy Agency, June 1959. 2 *2nd Report of the European Nuclear Energy Agency*, January 1960. 3 *Annual Report to Congress of the Atomic Energy Commission*, January 1960. 4 *Nuclear Power*, January 1962. 5 *GEC Atomic Energy Review*, September 1959.

N.B. This table lists only reactors of about 50 megawatts thermal power or more (i.e. capable of producing significant quantities of plutonium), the construction of which has been definitely ordered; a few are test or research reactors. There are many more projects for power reactors out to tender, and a list of low-power research reactors would be several times as long and include many more countries. The potential plutonium production capability can be taken to be 2 kg. of plutonium per year per 10 MW gross thermal power.

stage of theoretical knowledge only would take several years in any but the largest and most highly industrialised countries; the capital cost has been tentatively estimated at $20 million,[84] this being the capital cost of a reactor for a weapons project, capable of producing 20 kg. of plutonium a year, inclusive of moderator and fuel element fabrication costs. But here again, the finished product can be purchased. Uranium-consuming power reactors for the production of electricity are on sale; Canada, the United Kingdom, the United States and the Soviet Union are now exporting them, and although the Western countries at least are known to stipulate 'for peaceful purposes only' in the agreements, it is physically possible for the operating country to breed weapons-grade plutonium in such reactors by reducing the time the fuel rods are left in operation. The table on page 259 lists the world's non-military reactors of some 50 megawatt gross thermal power both in existence and planned to be operating by 1963. The rate of plutonium production of a natural uranium reactor is directly linked to its gross thermal power and can be taken to be some 20 kg. of plutonium per year for a 100 megawatt gross heat reactor running at about three-quarter capacity.

Stage (iv), the chemical extraction of the plutonium from the uranium fuel elements after removal from the reactor, is a very difficult technical undertaking, chiefly because it involves handling large amounts of intensely radioactive solids and liquids and the disposal of large quantities of radioactive waste. A suitable plant for this purpose is an essential adjunct to an economically run nuclear power reactor, as it enables the unconsumed uranium to be recovered and re-cycled through the reactor, and because the extracted plutonium is very valuable as a nuclear fuel. The basic principle employed—continuous counter-current columns employing organic solvents for extraction—is a common chemical engineering technique; the novelty is that the plant must be capable of operating almost indefinitely without maintenance behind thick concrete walls. However, the only processing plants in the West are at present government-operated plants in the nuclear-weapon producing countries,* and agreements for the supply of reactors by the United States have always stipulated

* Eurochemic, an international undertaking in the framework of the European Nuclear Energy Agency, plans to have a pilot plant of 350 kg. of uranium per day capacity in operation at Mol, Belgium, by 1963.

that the spent fuel rods should be processed in the United States for an agreed charge.

The United States, in agreement with Canada and the United Kingdom, has, however, released technical details of the recovery of plutonium and the method of producing plutonium metal,[85] so that a country wishing to construct its own processing plant would have a flying start; one tentative estimate of cost, including waste-disposal, is $21 million for development and erection and $3 million per year running costs;[86] it might take two to three years to bring into operation. It is to be expected that such processing plants will be built for peaceful uses in any case during the next decade in countries developing power reactor programmes.

Stage (v), the fabrication and assembly of the bomb components, is a comparatively simple step compared with the preceding one, although fabrication is complicated by the extremely poisonous nature of plutonium. No precise technical data have been released, and an uninitiated country would probably have to carry out some initial research with the first small quantities of plutonium becoming available from its production programme.

Estimates of the critical size of an explosive device range from about 20 cm. to 8 cm diameter; or from some 80 kg. of metal down to 5 kg.[87] for plutonium, so that a programme of 20 kg. of plutonium per year, on the basis of which rough figures of cost were quoted, would provide perhaps one or two bombs per year and would require a reactor of 100 megawatt gross heat. A bigger programme would, of course, reduce the cost per bomb produced.

The conclusion is that any country with a decent-sized reactor running could produce one or two bombs within three years of the decision to do so, at a capital cost for the processing and weapon fabrication plant of about $31 million.[88] The only major industrial plant would be that for plutonium extraction. A team assessed the capabilities of thirty-seven countries and concluded that eleven—Belgium, Canada, China, Czechoslovakia, West Germany, East Germany, India, Italy, Japan, Sweden and Switzerland—could produce nuclear weapons in the near future, and that eight—Australia, Austria, Denmark, Finland, Hungary, the Netherlands, Poland and Yugoslavia—might be able to, although short of scientific manpower.[89]

China, according to intelligence reports,[90] was expected to explode her first atomic device at the end of 1961 or early in 1962. While China's technical capacity has never been in doubt, the rapidity with which she is proceeding from theoretical research to production is very impressive. It would seem that her programme has been speeded up by at least a year. A 10-megawatt thermal experimental nuclear reactor supplied by Russia has been in operation in Peking since June 1958. It has been estimated that China will be in a position to begin making her own nuclear weapons by 1962 or 1963.[91]

Canada, Switzerland and Sweden have all considered the possibility of acquiring nuclear weapons, and while there appears to have been no official discussion in India she will no doubt be greatly influenced by Chinese progress.* Israel is not included in the list and is considered to lack the resources and money necessary to produce an atomic bomb. The reactor built at Rehovoth with the aid of the United States is only of 1,000

---

* *Canada:* On 20 February 1959 Mr. John Diefenbaker, the Prime Minister, stated that negotiations were under way with the United States for nuclear warheads for ground-to-air missiles for the air force and ground-to-ground missiles for the army. Mr. Diefenbaker said that in accordance with her belief that the control of nuclear weapons should remain in the hands of the major Western powers, Canada would not make such weapons herself (*New York Times* 21 February 1959). On 12 September 1961 Mr. Harkness, the Defence Minister, stated that three weapons systems with a nuclear capability were being acquired—the *Honest John* surface-to-surface artillery missile which will be issued to the Canadian infantry brigade in Europe in 1962; the *Bomarc* anti-aircraft projectile, sites for which are being prepared in Canada; and the CF 104 strike-reconnaissance jet aircraft for the Canadian air division in NATO (*The Times* 13 September 1961). According to a Royal Canadian Airforce statement of 13 October 1961, however, no decision has yet been reached concerning the provision of nuclear warheads by the US.

Switzerland: On 11 July 1958 the Swiss Federal Council declared in favour of the principle of acquiring nuclear weapons for the Swiss army and instructed the Federal Military Department to make a study and report in due course. No steps have yet been taken to implement this decision, which would have to be submitted to a national referendum, although in September 1961 the Lower House rejected by a large majority a petition that Switzerland should write into the constitution a renunciation of nuclear warfare (*Daily Telegraph* 28 September 1961).

Sweden: General Svedlund, the Commander-in-Chief, in a report to the Government on 24 October 1957, recommended that the army should be equipped with tactical nuclear weapons. In November 1959 the Government adopted a decision of a socialist party committee headed by Mr. Erlander, the Prime Minister, to postpone any decision until 1965 when Sweden would be producing sufficient plutonium to manufacture its own nuclear weapons (*Sunday Times* 24 November 1957; *Daily Telegraph* 13 November 1959).

India: Mr. Patil, a member of the Indian Government, has expressed the view that India should produce atomic bombs as soon as possible and Dr. Homi Bhabha, the Chairman of the Indian Atomic Energy Commission, has announced that India has all the capabilities for the production of nuclear weapons (*Combat* 3 November 1960; letter to *The Times* 14 September 1961).

kilowatts and is much too small to be of interest for the production of nuclear weapons. Rumours that France was assisting Israel to develop an atomic bomb have been denied and the Israeli Embassy in Paris said in November 1960 that atomic research in Israel 'is devoted exclusively to the needs of industry, agriculture and science.'[92]

Appendix C

COMPARATIVE DEFENCE EFFORT

Country	Defence Expenditure ($ million)		Gross National Product at factor cost ($ million)		Populati (million
	1959	1960[e]	1959	1960[e]	1959
Belgium	374	404	10,520	10,940	9·1
France	3,659[a]	3,872[a]	43,622[a]	45,891[a]	45·1
Germany	2,640	2,836	50,496	54,536	51·7
Italy	1,067	1,100	24,786	26,520	49·1
Luxembourg	8	7	414	429	0·3
Netherlands	396	450	9,328	10,088	11·3
United Kingdom	4,461	4,685	58,458	61,382	52·2
Canada	1,642	1,668	30,340	30,795	17·4
Denmark	143	160	4,864	5,161	4·5
Greece	158	166	2,661	2,799	8·7
Norway	150	155	3,754	3,979	3·6
Portugal	98	99	2,006	2,066	9·1
Turkey	240[a]	270[a]	4,865[ea]	4,960[a]	26·6
United States	46,614	46,194	442,236	453,734	177·1
Total NATO	61,650	62,066	688,363	713,280	465·8

	Defence Expenditure as % of Gross National Product					Defence Expenditure per head of population	
55	1956	1957	1958	1959	1960e	1959	1960e
8	3·5	3·6	3·6	3·6	3·7	41	44
7	9·3	8·8	8·3	8·4	8.4	81[a]	85[a]
8	4·3	4·9	3·5	5·2	5·2	51	54
6	4·6	4·4	4·4	4·3	4·2	22	22
6	2·1	2·2	2·1	1·9	1·5	25	20
2	6·3	5·7	4·9	4·2	4·5	35	39
3	8·8	8·1	7·9	7·6	7·6	86	89
6	7·1	6·6	6·1	5·4	5·4	94	94
6	3·4	3·5	3·2	2·9	3·1	31	35
4	7·3	6·1	5·8	5·9	5·9	18	19
4	4·0	4·1	4·0	4·0	3·9	42	43
6	4·4	4·4	4·5	4·9	4·8	11	11
6	5·2	4·5	4·2	4·9e	5·4	9[a]	10[a]
1	10·8	11·0	11·1	10·5	10.2	263	256
6	9·3	9·3	9·2	9·0	8·7	132	131

Figure affected by devaluation
Estimate

Country	Period of Compulsory Military Service (months)			Total in A Forces (thousand
	1959	1960	1961	1960
Belgium	15	12	12	120
France	......	24 to 27	......	1,026
Germany	12	12	12	260
Italy	18[5]	18[5]	18[5]	400
Luxembourg	12	12	9	3·
Netherlands	18[1]	18[1]	18[1]	135
United Kingdom	24	24[2]	nil[2]	593
Canada	nil	nil	nil	120
Denmark	16	16	16[3]	44
Greece	......	20 to 24[6]	......	158
Norway	16[7]	16[7]	16[7]	40
Portugal	18[8]	18[8]	18[8]	79
Turkey	24[9]	24[9]	24[9]	500
United States	24[4]	24[4]	24[4]	2,489
Total NATO				5,967

[1] Army and Navy.

[2] Call-up in the United Kingdom was suspended from the end of 1960: th already called up complete 24 months service.

[3] May gradually be reduced to 12 months if sufficient regulars can be recruit

[4] Selective—perhaps equivalent to 18 months in 1956 when 70 per cent w called up.

PERSONNEL

Labour Force (millions)	Total in Armed Forces as % of Labour Force
3·6 (1958)	3·4
19·7 (1958)	5·2
25·5 (1958)	1·0
21·5 (1959)	1·9
0·15(1958)	2·1
4·3 (1958)	3·2
24·6 (1958)	2·4
6·2 (1958)	1·9
2·1 (1954)	2·1
4·1 (1955)	3·8
1·5 (1958)	2·7
3·3 (1950)	2·4
12·0 (1955)	4·2
71·9 (1959)	3·4
200·4	3·0

[5] Navy 24 months.
[6] Navy 27–30 months.
[7] Air Force and Navy 18 months.
[8] Navy 48 months; Air Force 36 months.
[9] Navy and Air Force 36 months.

NOTES TO TABLES I AND II

(I) Iceland has no Armed Forces and does not appear in the Tables.

(II) Defence Expenditure and Gross National Product are calculated in national currency and converted to United States dollars at the official rate, which does not always reflect the purchasing power of the currency. The figures shown under these headings are not therefore always comparable between countries, whereas figures of Defence Expenditure as a percentage of Gross National Product do not involve currency conversion.

SOURCES

Gross National Product: OEEC
Defence Expenditure: NATO sources
Labour Force: OEEC
Total in Armed Forces: *The Communist Bloc and the Free World, The Military Balance*, Institute of Strategic Studies, 1960.

NOTES

CHAPTER III

1. Anthony Nutting *Europe will not Wait* (Hollis & Carter, London 1960; Frederick A. Praeger, New York 1960) gives an account of these negotiations.

CHAPTER IV

2. Captain B. H. Liddell Hart *Deterrent or Defence* (Stevens, London 1960; Frederick A. Praeger, New York 1960), p. 3.
3. Alastair Buchan *NATO in the 1960s* (Weidenfeld & Nicholson for the Institute for Strategic Studies, London 1960; Frederick A. Praeger, New York 1960).
4. *Survival* (Institute for Strategic Studies, London) March–April 1961.
5. Cyril E. Black and Frederick J. Yeager *NATO and American Security* ed. Klaus Knorr (Princeton University Press 1959).
6. Major-General N. Talenski in *International Affairs* (Moscow) October 1960, reprinted in *Survival* January-February 1961.
7. Gordon A. Craig 'Germany and Nato' in *NATO and American Security* (op. cit.).
8. *NATO in the 1960s*, op. cit., p. 17.
9. The information in this section is based upon *The Communist Bloc and the Free World: The Military Balance 1961-2* (Institute for Strategic Studies, London 1961).
10. *International Affairs*, November 1960, reprinted in *Survival* March–April, 1961.
11. House of Commons *Official Report* 29 February 1960, col. 863.

CHAPTER V

12. *Saturday Review* (New York) 3 September 1960.
13. *The Times* 29 December 1960.
14. Defence Budget Message to Congress 28 March 1961.
15. House of Commons *Official Report* 19 July 1961, col. 1248.
16. *The Times* 18 August 1960.
17. *The Communist Bloc and the Free World—The Military Balance* op. cit.

18. Defence Budget special message to Congress, 28 March 1961.

19. Mr. Watkinson, House of Commons *Official Report* 14 December 1960, col. 55.

20. House of Commons *Official Report* 1 November 1960, col. 38–39.

21. 'The Polaris Dossier' *The New Scientist* (London) 10 November 1960.

22. House of Commons *Official Report* 13 April 1960, col. 1265.

23. House of Commons *Official Report* 20 July 1960, col. 533.

24. Air Estimates Memorandum 1961–2 Cmd. 1292, HMSO.

25. Speech to the New York Economic Club quoted by Joseph Alsop, *New York Herald Tribune* 26 January 1960.

26. WEU Assembly *Document* 28, J. Fens 'Report on the State of European Security' October 1956.

27. *Deterrent or Defence,* op. cit., p. 74.

28. See Jane's *All the World's Aircraft* (published annually by Sampson Low, London; McGraw Hill, New York).

CHAPTER VI

29. Joint Labour Party-Trades Union Congress statement *Disarmament and Nuclear War: The Next Step* June 1959.

30. *Minutes of Proceedings* 3 December 1959.

31. Communicated to the Assembly on 14 July 1960.

32. Report on Defence, Cmd. 1288, HMSO.

CHAPTER VII

33. Defence Budget special message to Congress 28 March 1961.

34. *The Times* 12 April 1961.

35. Henry A. Kissinger *The Reporter* (New York) 2 February 1961.

36. Speech to NATO Military Committee, Washington, 11 April 1961.

37. WEU Assembly *Document* 119, Addendum of the Fourth *Annual Report* of the Council 19 May 1959, Chapter 1.

38. *The NATO Handbook,* 7th edition 1959, p. 65.

39. *The Necessity for Choice* (Harper & Bros., New York 1961; Chatto & Windus, London 1961).

CHAPTER VIII

40. For a fuller discussion see Roger Hilsman, Chapter 2 of *Nato and American Security,* op. cit.

41. Department of State *Bulletin* XXVI No. 663, March 10 1952, quoted by Roger Hilsman above.

42. *Deterrent or Defence,* op. cit. Chapters 9 and 10.

43. M. R. D. Foot *Men in Uniform* (Weidenfeld & Nicholson for the Institute for Strategic Studies, London 1961; Frederick A. Praeger, New York 1961).

44. *Document* 105 and *Recommendation* 28 of the Western European Union Assembly, December 1958.

45. *The Times* 27 February 1961.

46. House of Commons *Official Report* 8 February 1961.

47. *The Times* 27 June 1961.

48. Defence *White Paper* 1957, Cmd. 124, HMSO.

49. Herr Strauss, speech to WEU Assembly 31 May 1960.

50. *The Times* 27 April 1961.

51. *The Times* 25 January 1961.

52. WEU Assembly *Document* 105, p. 63.

53. *The Times* 17 October 1961.

54. *The Times* military correspondent, 28 January 1961.

CHAPTER IX

55. *Explanatory Statement* on Navy Estimates 1955–6, Cmd. 9390, HMSO.

56. *Explanatory Statement* on Navy Estimates 1956–7, Cmd. 9697, HMSO.

57. Cmd. 124 (1957), HMSO.

58. *Explanatory Statement* on Navy Estimates 1957–8, Cmd. 151, HMSO.

59. *Explanatory Statement* on Navy Estimates 1958–9, Cmd. 371, HMSO.

60. *Explanatory Statement* on Navy Estimates 1961–2, Cmd. 1282, HMSO.

61. *The Times* 17 January 1961.

62. *Algemeen Handelsblad* 16 July 1959 in a comment on my original report to the WEU Assembly.

63. *The Times* 12 and 20 December 1961.

64. WEU Assembly *Document* 128 June 1959.

CHAPTER X

65. House of Commons *Official Report* 12 April 1961, col. 217.

66. 'The Strange Incident of October 5', *Readers Digest* (US edition April 1961; UK edition May 1961).

CHAPTER XI

67. Quoted in *Nato in the 1960s*, op. cit., p. 113.

CHAPTER XII

68. Hedley Bull *Control of the Arms Race* (Weidenfeld & Nicholson for the Institute for Strategic Studies, London 1961; Frederick A. Praeger, New York 1961).

69. Philip Noel-Baker *Disarmament* (Hogarth Press, London 1926) and *The Arms Race* (Stevens, London 1958; Oceana Publications, New York 1958).

70. Evidence given to sub-committees of the Joint Committee on Atomic Energy, United States Congress, 21 April 1960.

71. Hedley Bull op. cit., p. 34.

72. Thomas K. Finletter *Foreign Policy: The Next Phase* (Frederick A. Praeger, New York 1960; Oxford University Press, London 1961).

73. This point is discussed by Fred C. Ikle in 'After Detection—What?' (*Foreign Affairs* January 1961).

74. *New York Herald Tribune* 17–19 April 1961, reprinted in *Survival* July-August 1961.

75. T. C. Schelling 'Reciprocal Measures for Arms Stabilization' *Daedalus* (American Academy of Arts and Sciences, Boston, Mass.) Fall 1960.

CHAPTER XIII

76. Albert Wohlstetter 'Nuclear Sharing: NATO and the N-plus 1 Country' in *Foreign Affairs* (Council on Foreign Relations Inc., New York) April 1961.

CHAPTER XIV

77. *Non-Military Co-operation in NATO*, Report of the Committee of Three, paragraph 42.

78. *The Necessity for Choice* op. cit., p. 331.

79. Max Beloff *New Dimensions in Foreign Policy* (Allen & Unwin, London 1961; Macmillan, New York 1961).

APPENDIX A

80. Information on the effects of nuclear weapons is drawn from: *The Effects of Nuclear Weapons,* United States Atomic Energy Commission, June 1957; *Nuclear Weapons,* HMSO 1959; and other unclassified publications.

81. Camille Rougeron *Forces Aeriennes françaises* May 1958, p. 618.

82. op. cit., p. 621.

APPENDIX B

83. *Studies of the Market for Nuclear Materials,* I. Fuels OEEC May 1959, p. 12.

84. *The Nth Country Problem and Arms Control,* technical report by Davidson, Kalkstein and Hohenemser, National Planning Association, January 1960, p. 22.

85. *Annual Report to Congress* of the Atomic Energy Commission, 1959, p. 133.

86. Davidson, Kalkstein and Hohenemser, op. cit., p. 22.

87. (i) Richtemeyer, Kennard and Lauriston: *Introduction to Modern Physics* 5th edition (McGraw Hill, New York 1955), p. 552; (ii) WEU Agency for the Control of Armaments: *Introduction to Atomics* Part I—General (Paris, 1958), p. 44; (iii) Davidson, Kalkstein and Hohenemser, op. cit., p. 5; (iv) *Nuclear Weapons* HMSO, 2nd edition 1959, p. 65.

88. Davidson, Kalkstein and Hohenemser, op. cit., p. 22, the total for processing, waste disposal and bomb assembly.

89. op. cit., p. 28.

90. *Daily Telegraph* 9 March 1960; *Sunday Times* 20 November 1960; *The Times* 19 June 1961.

91. *Observer* 18 June 1961.

92. *Daily Telegraph* 20 November 1960.

GLOSSARY OF TERMS

ACE	*Allied Command Europe*
Ace High	*The name given to the* NATO *Communications system to be fully operational in 1962*
AFCENT	*Allied Forces Central Europe* ⎫ *Subordinate*
AFMED	„ „ *Mediterranean* ⎬ *European*
AFNORTH	„ „ *Northern Europe* ⎬ *Commands*
AFSOUTH	„ „ *Southern Europe* ⎭
ATAF	*Allied Tactical Air Forces in Europe*
Atlas	*United States first generation* ICBM *(q.v.) now operational*
B 47 (Stratojet) B 52 (Stratofortress) B 58 (Hustler) B 70 (Valkyrie)	*Successive generations of United States heavy bomber aircraft. B 70 is under development but the other three are in service with* SAC *(q.v.)*
Bloodhound	*British Air Force ground-to-air guided missile*
Blue Steel	*British Air Force guided stand-off bomb under development*
Blue Streak	*British* MRBM *programme which was cancelled as a military project in April 1960*
Blue Water	*British Army ground-to-ground missile under development*
BMEWS	*Ballistic Missile Early Warning System for air defence*
Brussels Treaty	*between Britain, France, Belgium, the Netherlands and Luxembourg signed in 1948 and modified in 1954 to include Germany and Italy and to establish Western European Union*
Buccaneer (originally named NA 39)	*British Navy low-level long-range strike aircraft expected in service in 1962 with conventional and nuclear capability*
Channel Committee	NATO *supreme command for the Channel consisting of the Naval Chiefs of Staff of Belgium, France, the Netherlands and the United Kingdom*
Corporal	*United States Army ground-to-ground support missile now in service with* US *and British forces in Germany*

Countercity	Term used to express intention to direct nuclear strategic strike against enemy's civil population as distinct from his military bases
Counterforce	In contrast to countercity, a nuclear strategic strike against the enemy's military bases and especially his retaliatory air and missile forces
Davy Crockett	United States Army small two-man ground-to-ground missile under development
DEWline	Distant Early Warning line of radar stations in North America
Dyna Soar	United States experimental piloted rocket-boosted glider for reconnaissance
EDC	European Defence Community which failed to become effective when France declined to ratify the Treaty in 1954
F 104 (Starfighter)	United States fighter aircraft also adopted by several European countries
Falcon	United States Air Force short-range air-to-air missile
Firestreak	British air-to-air missile for fighter aircraft
First Strike	Surprise all-out nuclear attack
Fission weapon	Atomic weapon in the kiloton range (q.v.)
Fusion weapon	Hydrogen or thermonuclear weapon in the megaton range (q.v.)
G 91	Italian Fiat jet light strike and reconnaissance aircraft adopted as the NATO standard model and under production
Hawk	United States anti-aircraft missile system also in production in Europe
Honest John	United States Army ground-to-ground missile
Hound Dog	United States Air Force stand-off air-to-ground missile
ICBM	Inter-Continental Ballistic Missile, a rocket for delivery of strategic nuclear weapons and with a range of over 2,500 miles
IRBM	Intermediate-Range Ballistic Missile, as ICBM but with a range of less than 2,500 miles. In NATO terminology IRBM has been superseded by MRBM (q.v.) as the term for this type of missile
Infrastructure	The provision of static facilities for forces, e.g. airfields, communication networks, storage installations

Skybolt	*United States air-to-ground ballistic missile under development. It is to be acquired also by the Royal Air Force*
Snark	*The first United States operational missile, declared obsolete in March 1961*
Standing group	*The Military Executive body of* NATO *consisting of representatives of the United States, the United Kingdom and France*
'Sword'	*The strategic nuclear strike forces of the alliance upon which* NATO *strategy depends but which are under national and not allied control*
Thor	*United States* MRBM *operational in the United Kingdom under Anglo-American agreement*
Thunderbird	*British Army ground-to-air missile*
Titan	*United States first generation* ICBM *now operational*
TSR 2	*British supersonic tactical strike and reconnaissance aircraft under development*
V-bombers	*British strategic bomber force of Vickers Valiants, Avro Vulcans and Handley Page Victors*
WEU	*Western European Union, consisting of Belgium, France, Germany, Italy, Luxembourg, the Netherlands and the United Kingdom, established in 1955 under the modified Brussels Treaty (q.v.) of 1954*
X 15	*United States manned hypersonic research aircraft*

INDEX